TITANIC

Victims and Villains

TITANIC

Victims and Villains

SENAN MOLONY

TEMPUS

Ah! What avails the classic bent
And what the cultured word,
Against the undoctored incident
That actually occurred?

Kipling

First published 2008

Tempus Publishing
Cirencester Road, Chalford
Stroud, Gloucestershire, GL6 8PE
www.thehistorypress.co.uk
Tempus Publishing is an imprint of The History Press

British Library Cataloguing in Publication Data.
A catalogue record for this book is available from the British Library.

ISBN 978 0 7524 4570 0

Typesetting and origination by The History Press
Printed and bound in Great Britain by
Ashford Colour Press Ltd, Gosport, Hants.

CONTENTS

TITANIC

CALIFORNIAN

TITANIC

THE EVIL THAT MEN DO

NATURE, NOSTRUMS, AND A MAN-MADE DISASTER

'Down, down, down, on the floor of the sea, two miles under the outlaw bergs, lies the *Titanic*,' opened Herbert Kaufman, editorial director of the *Woman's World* magazine, in a piece for the issue of June 1912. So far, so good. His introductory words are as true today as they were when he first penned them a century ago.

But Kaufman himself went down, down, down, from there, plumbing the depths of bathos and maudlin sentimentality. 'Under the outlaw bergs lies the *Titanic*,' he wrote, 'a splendid mausoleum of steel and brass, in whose shattered hold rests as fair a company of good knights and brave ladies as ever smiled in the face of death'.

Did they indeed, smile in the face of death? Never mind, for Kaufman continues: 'Soldier and sailor and merchant prince – play-actor and journalist – idler and drudge – peasant and nobleman – Saxon and Norman – Latin and Celt – Slav and Jew – strangers in motherhood, wrought into brotherhood, equal at last in the glory of their end.'

Kaufman would have the crippled ship as Camelot, her corridors clanking with errant knights, seeking damsels in distress – within the belly, indeed, of a damsel in distress – the chain-mailed Saxon jousting with narrow-eyed Norman for the right to rescue the nobleman's daughter. And look, forsooth, where yonder peasant's horse hath knocked the basket of apples...

It is easy to scorn. The high-flown (overblown) literary conventions of 1912 are as much a world away from the twenty-first century as everything else belonging to the Edwardian era. But that does not make them, as manifestations of mindset, impenetrable to insight.

Kaufman's microcosm of the *Titanic*'s passenger manifest betrays the hierarchy of the day, the human pyramid of hubris, from the great and the good to the down-

and-out. The irrelevance of social station in the face of extinction is a point that is both old and obvious:

Sceptre and crown must tumble down, and in the earth be equal made
With the poor crooked scythe and spade.

The British dramatist James Shirley (1596–1666) wrote it in the seventeenth century.

But Kaufman goes further, venturing into race. Soldier and sailor and merchant prince are joined by Saxon, Slav, Celt and Jew. Strangers in motherhood, there is no co-sanguinity here. But the equality of death erases the naturally presumed inequality of worth. They are wrought into brotherhood by the glory of their end.

The glory of their end. The idler and the peasant came up to the mark by the mere fact of their yielding mortality, inheriting a crown of martyrdom that could not otherwise be theirs. Their glory was in yelping for life in the bone-cutting cold of Atlantic immersion. And the rich man yelped in the night with the best of them.

An early glorification in the press was entitled *The Deathless Story of the Titanic* – in one sense a denial of corpse-ridden reality. *Author collection.*

O death, where is thy sting? O grave, thy victory? One emigrant ship, among a hundred thousand voyages, has reduced the great 'melting pot' of immigration into a common communion. And out of that melting pot, that sinking barrel, is forged a wholly fictitious folly.

There was no eminence in their end. Individual acts of sacrifice, indeed of an undenied heroism, were matched by panicked wickedness, cowardice, callousness. Selflessness and selfishness marked 'nobleman and peasant' in equal measure, and not necessarily in that order of ascription.

The sinking keg went down, and all were not subsumed in any 'saving grace' of the Unsaved. Humans died as they have always done – in terror, dread and pain, aching anguish that may have eked its way to acceptance, if some were eased this way to eternity. There was no glory here, overarching all, as ten times one hundred died and five times one hundred more. It was wholesale slaughter.

The iceberg glides on. Here is the rock on which they perished, great Nature ever gradual in her grinding indifference. Neither innocent nor enemy, the availing ice easily mastered thin walls of steel and *Titanic* began to succumb.

Kaufman called them 'outlaw bergs', and ten thousand other scribes – it also being the age of execrable odes – reached for their nibs to blame the blameless, many invoking the immovability of Nature's object, as if she had a scheme toward which she inexorably worked.

The Earth goddess yielded in turn to God himself, especially for those to whom the task of consoling the bereaved had fallen. The fathom-falling *Titanic* was all part of His unfathomable plan. And God could not be blamed, even if some of the Babel of dying victims were said to have echoed, in their own tongues, the last cry of Christ on the cross: *'Eloi, Eloi, lama sabachthani?'* – in Aramaic: 'My God, my God, why hast Thou forsaken me?'

The Los Angeles *Evening Herald* printed such an idea, and put it in the mouth of Sir Cosmo Duff Gordon, an aristocratic survivor who escaped with his wife Lucile in a lifeboat of just seven passengers and five crew; a chosen twelve.

The newspaper reported that the Duff Gordon boat (which incidentally refused to accept any additional passengers from another, overcrowded, craft) was close enough to the bobbing detritus after the sinking to hear such supplications as, 'My God, my God'. But Sir Cosmo said at the British Inquiry that there was silence when the ship went down. He heard only a 'confused wailing' afterwards, nothing distinct.

His wife, a high society couturier, was asked about a direct quote from her lips in the same publication: 'I remember the very last cry. It was a man's voice calling loudly, "My God, my God." He cried monotonously, in a dull, hopeless way.' But this Calvary-like final utterance was 'absolutely untrue', Lady Duff Gordon snorted. Hardly gospel, in other words.

Thy Will Be Done

The three authors of the disaster, Rotten Judgement, Glaring Incompetence and Gross Carelessness, conspiring to drag down the *Titanic* in this cartoon by McRitchie for the *Calgary Eye Opener*. What may be significant is the caption, 'Thy Will Be Done', which seems subversive of the general run of maudlin hand-wringing over the whims of Providence. The impulse being indulged was human, the artist contends.

Others, men of the cloth, nevertheless perceived very clear messages, and quickly too. Many cried out from their Sunday pulpits that God was not to be mocked. Their somewhat vengeful Creator appeared to have been almightily angered by advertising claims as to the 'practical unsinkability' of the new White Star liner.

Yet if not suffering from pearly-gate pique at the excesses of the marketing department, the Deity had still delivered deadly consummation for the crime of daring to presume that He would always indulge the caprice of man. Which is akin to having it both ways.

It may have been vanity that impelled the *Titanic* at 22½ knots, or 25 statute miles per hour, in the last stages of her service life. There may have been complacency in the sprint trip of a maiden voyage. And there undoubtedly was utter carelessness about the proximity of ice and the chances of collision.

But the idea of a punishing Providence embodied in ice seems faintly ludicrous today... although in 1912 cartoons of an overtly spiritual dimension were commonplace. One showed the *Titanic* in the crook of a giant submerged palm, fingertips above the surface in imitation of the iceberg. 'In the hollow of His hand', ran the legend.

Which would be all very well, were it not for the fact that the offended Omnipotence did not display any Jovian ire when 'practical unsinkability' was first associated with the *Olympic*, *Titanic's* earlier sister ship, launched in 1910. Nor, indeed, when worse than overconfidence was uttered when the younger vessel foundered.

Yet all the lifeboats prospered on a sea of Galilean calm thereafter, even those shepherded together by the evidently salty-tongued Fifth Officer Harold Lowe.

'He had been so blasphemous during the two hours we were in his boat (No. 14) that the women at my end all thought he was under the influence of liquor', tutted passenger Daisy Minihan, to whom Lowe had allegedly snapped, 'Jump, God damn you, jump!' while attempting to transfer her to another lifeboat.

She probably deserved it, but God just then had 1,500 other things on hand to divert his attention. Another mortal said to have used the D-word (innocuous today, but in 1912 a chilling and dangerous claim that presumed to usurp the Final Judgement) was Quartermaster Robert Hichens in Lifeboat 6. Mrs Lucian Smith commented:

> Our seaman was Hichens, who refused to row, but sat in the end of the boat wrapped in a blanket that one of the women had given him. I am not of the opinion that he was intoxicated, but a lazy, uncouth man, who had no respect for the ladies, and who was a thorough coward.

Odd, this. The idler and the drudge were supposed to have gone down – not to have been wrought into brotherhood with their betters, equal at last in the glory of their survival. No, it shouldn't quite work this way.

We look back through rose-tinted glasses, as if the modern myth of the *Titanic* has elevated all aboard her into a pantheon of universal nobility. Yet she was an emigrant ship, carrying the poor, the huddled masses, and the venal. Swedish passenger Gunnar Tenglin told the *Burlington Daily Gazette* on 25 April: 'I lost everything I had.' But then he added, revealingly: 'I had about $30 in a suitcase, concealed well, as there had been several robberies among passengers the day before the accident.'

Six days earlier the *Waterford News* had claimed that among the *Titanic's* third class passengers was 'one of the men connected with the alleged pilfering at Bonmahon mines.' There was only one man from that locality aboard, sixty-seven-year-old Frank Dwan, and his drowning may have prevented a costly libel case.

But even if steerage was not a nest of thieves, there is no reason to believe its composition differed from any general grouping of today. The passengers aboard the RMS *Titanic*, whether in first, second, or third class, were not an assembled array of saints, and neither were the crew.

Fireman Joe Mulholland, a stoker on the delivery trip from Belfast to Southampton, knew Thomas Andrews, the managing director of Harland & Wolff, who was lost in the disaster. He recalled half a century later that during that positioning voyage:

> He [Andrews] came down to me and pointed to some of the insulting slogans about the Pope which had been chalked up on the smoke-box. Some of them were filthy and I had already heard about similar slogans, which had been painted on the hull before the *Titanic* was launched.
>
> Mr Andrews said, 'Do you know anything about these slogans?'
>
> I did not, so he said 'They are disgusting' and went off and returned with some sailors and had them removed.

(After the sinking had come rumours, wholly unsubstantiated, that the *Titanic*'s official registration number had been devilishly arranged to be 3909-04, in order to approximate 'No Pope' when held up to a mirror. Her actual number was 131428.)

The reality is that coarseness and cheating were widely evident before the accident, (so much so that the White Star Line routinely warned about card sharps in onboard publications) – just as opposite values prevailed, then and afterwards, as in the case of a gentleman that scullion John Collins testified about.

This was the fellow who came up to a crowded overturned collapsible on which scores of *Titanic* survivors were clinging for dear life. 'We were all telling him not to get on. He said, 'That is all right, boys, keep cool. God bless you.' And the man swam on alone until seen no more.

Fireman Joe Mulholland cradling a cat in 1962. A stoker on the delivery trip from Belfast to Southampton, he told of 'disgusting' anti-Catholic slogans being chalked up in the *Titanic* stokehold – which Mr Andrews ordered to be removed. *Sunday Independent.*

God indeed works in mysterious ways, so that any catastrophe can be interpreted as being ultimately for purposes of goodness, since He allowed it to happen. And it need not be punishment – despite the early and altogether predictable appearance of a book by one Alma White who saw the *Titanic* tragedy as 'God speaking to the nations'.

In her terms, He was lecturing in somewhat forbidding tones, as if the sunken White Star vessel had been a kind of ocean-going Gomorrah in which every on-board indulgence – particularly in first class – mocked the Creator. He had therefore, in His own unmockability, promptly consigned this floating false idol to an appropriate abyss.

Ironically, the 1953 film *Titanic*, starring Clifford Webb and Barbara Stanwyck, had featured the entire ship's complement (that is, those remaining on board the great vessel after all the lifeboats had left) joining together at the rails to sing *Nearer, My God, to Thee*, as if they uniformly recognised the higher purpose to which they were all to be forfeit.

The actual occupants didn't. It is a striking feature of the *Titanic* shipwreck that although that hymn has become forever bound up with the disaster, not a single person referred to it, either by name or obliquely, at either the British or American Inquiries. Extolling their nearness to God, whatever the newspapers thought, seems to have been the furthest thing from their minds.

In an article entitled 'The *Titanic* – and God', carried in the June 1912 issue of the humanist and 'rationalist' *Literary Guide*, the early dissenter Joseph McCabe wrote:

It is a noble picture, this of six poor devils nervously fiddling a hymn as they slowly sank into the grave; though it is a pity they did not choose a less ghastly hymn, since the deepest hope and frantic endeavour of every man on board were to keep away from God, to avoid death. Nor does a single man or woman of the millions who are singing *Nearer, my God, to Thee* throughout England and the United States not shrink from its implication.

Yet from end to end of Britain, religious people are talking with weird or flippant confidence about the loss of the *Titanic*: the churches ring with a hymn that recalls to crowds of worshippers the last appalling moment when the great ship reared on her bows, and, with a shriek and moan that shook the night, a thousand men slid into the arms of death.

[Elsewhere he writes: 'No one, apparently, has proposed to set all the churches singing *Eternal Father, strong to save…*']

The Press, fancying that it knows the mind of the community, hesitates not to raise above the horrible ruin it describes the dim outline of the Christian God; and bolder spirits even snap up stories of heroism as texts for resonant discourses on the immortal spirit of man and the efficacy of the Christian religion in training it. In one hundred years literary antiquarians will read these things with amazement.

It is useful to challenge convention in this way, a century after McCabe, to see if there are routes to clearer thinking on what happened that night, and not just on the ever-tangled question of the Deity.

It was natural for newspapers, starved of actual news as the silent *Carpathia* brought survivors to New York and eschewed all wireless contact, to have filled up the news space with what they thought *ought* to have happened, or what would most thrill the hearts of their readers. The fact that most of the supposition was entirely off-target did not prevent some of the early speculation from taking root as perceived fact.

God would not appear to have authorised the disaster, nor was he recognised as its author by those actually present on the deep that night – although naturally, many will have prayed with a heart and a half as the dreadful situation developed. To latterly ascribe all that happened to an impenetrable mystery of God's power, let alone revenge, seems facile and rather to miss the point. Something undoubtedly caused the *Titanic* disaster, but it was not the Divinity – at least, not unless heavily abetted by an array of infinitely lesser beings.

Second class passenger Lawrence Beesley, in a book about his experiences, wrote of his fellow survivors:

> I heard no one attribute all this to a Divine Power who ordains and arranges the lives of men, and as part of a definite scheme sends such calamity and misery in order to purify, to teach, to spiritualise. I do not say there were not people who thought and said they saw Divine Wisdom in it all – so inscrutable that we in our ignorance saw it not; but I did not hear it expressed.

He also opined: 'It should undoubtedly appeal more to our sense of justice to attribute these things to our own lack of consideration for others than to shift the responsibility onto a Power whom we first postulate as being all-wise and all-loving.'

And so the conceptualisation of monumental human extinction shrinks from an awestruck contemplation of eternity and all that lies beyond, to a narrower focus within the species. *There is nothing either good or bad, but thinking makes it so,* observes Hamlet in Act 2, Scene 2.

Shakespeare offers a further distillation in Julius Caesar: *The evil that men do lives after them; the good is oft interred with their bones.* If the poetic vision of the disaster would have us believe in bad men achieving goodness through the accident of dying alongside those of greater moral worth than themselves, then there was little immediate recognition of the sanctifying nature of escape.

Instead, perceptions would quickly turn the other way, as if, by some immutable natural law, it having first been ordained noble to die, it thereby became ignoble to endure. Good men may have achieved badness by the reverse yardstick...

The Caesar against whom this principle, or rather instinct of human nature, was first tested was J. Bruce Ismay, the chairman and managing director of the White Star Line, whose vessel had broken its contract with its passengers for the Atlantic crossing by journeying instead to the bottom of that ocean.

Ismay clambered into a collapsible lifeboat, the one designated as C from the four listed as A, B, C and D on the ship's plans. He appears to have saved himself forty minutes before the ship went down.

It further appears that he was invited to get into the boat by a ship's officer after a spell when no further women and children were forthcoming. The boat was located at the extreme forward end of the Boat Deck on the starboard side, whereas the mass of Ismay's paying passengers were by then bunched astern.

Joseph Bruce Ismay, chairman and managing director of the White Star Line. *Author collection.*

If Ismay was to be preserved as a 'vital witness' for a future Inquiry, it would seem both remarkably prescient yet also obtuse, in that he was not sent away with the ship's log, a hugely important document, which would instead sink 2 miles deep.

Perhaps the motivation of the officer in suggesting he get in lay instead with usual notions of deference and the prestige of Ismay's person. It was surely no accident, after all, that the lifeboats were located on the deck used exclusively by saloon passengers, with none available where the steerage stood. Rank has always had its advantages.

An interesting parallel, to digress for a moment, occurred four years earlier, when the steam yacht *Argonaut*, of 3,274 tons (Captain C.W. Redman), collided with the steamer *Kingswell* off Dover. It happened at 8.35 a.m. on 29 September, 1908.

A director of the Co-operative Cruising Company, which owned the vessel, was aboard. He was Edward Lunn, travelling in charge of a cruising party bound for Lisbon. The director wrote in May 1912 of his 'Experience of Shipwreck' as it touched on the case on Ismay:

> The fortunate facts of our case were as follows – The captain, chief officer, purser, many of the crew and stewards, and myself, had been connected with the ship for years. Many of the passengers had been frequently on board for cruises, and were thoroughly at home with the officers, crew and stewards. The passengers knew and had confidence in the ship's discipline.
>
> The ship had an excess of lifeboat accommodation, apart from a launch capable of holding forty or fifty, and a raft, neither of which latter were used.
>
> The ship was lost in broad daylight. Practically all the passengers were in the saloon, breakfasting together when they received the first intimation. These facts, taken together, struck from the first a note of calm preparation for our tense ordeal of six hours' instant fear of death.
>
> We had further no false security based on any theory that our ship was unsinkable. Immediately after the collision, the alarm was given and the crew took boat stations as a preparation for eventualities.
>
> As a result of these favourable conditions – all absent in the case of the *Titanic* – the entire ship's company of passengers, captain, officers, crew and stewards were saved – in all 230 souls. Yet we had a much shorter warning than the *Titanic*, as our captain – the last to leave the ship – left within nineteen minutes of the collision. When I left the ship's name was already awash – 'going down by her head'.
>
> My position, as the only director on board of the company owning the *Argonaut*, was somewhat similar to Mr Bruce Ismay's, but different from his in that I was in an official capacity, representing the owners, as 'director in charge' of the cruise.
>
> After our captain's precaution of calling the crew to boat stations and his examination of the ship's side followed by the report of: 'No serious damage above the

water-line', I accompanied him back to the bridge deck, where he awaited the report of the ship's carpenter. On receiving it as, 'Six foot six in No. 2 hold, Sir,' the captain gave the order: 'Lower away all the boats immediately.'

I then asked the captain, 'May I stay with you, Sir?' to which he replied, 'No, Mr Lunn. Your duty is with the passengers. Mine is with the ship as long as there is a soul on board.' The important point to bear in mind is that the captain of any ship – whilst under orders from his owners in everything else – is supreme in regard to navigation and the lives of those on board.

This tradition of the sea may demand heroic sacrifice, as it did with Captain Smith. But the duty of a director is quite different. He has no direct responsibility for the lives of those on board, but his indirect responsibility is the gravest, and it is his duty to be saved!

It may involve odium and ignominious accusations of cowardice as the alternative to heroic sacrifice. That is the bitter cost. But his duty is to live to facilitate in every possible way the most searching official inquiry into the loss and the blame, and later, by the knowledge gained through such painful experience, to assist in establishing every possible safeguard for the future.

If that is the general duty of a 'director in charge', how much more does it become the duty of a chairman travelling as a passenger, to whom is laid the stern and sacred charge of drastic initiative, to prevent for all future time not only needless sacrifice, but needless risk of human life on board his company's ships. In the supreme moments – worth dying for or living through – death holds no fear for men. They act on duty's call.

I would willingly have gone down with my captain had duty called, as I am sure Mr Ismay would with his, but whilst the captain's duty was by the ship, his (Mr Ismay's) was to take the reasonable chance of safety after giving preference and precedence to all others within sight or call in such a dire and frantic emergency.

I am, Sir, your obedient servant,
Etc.

In the more egalitarian United States, such class-ridden concepts as saving the better type of people, whether or not by design in providing boats only on the saloon decks, were promptly and publicly derided. The newspapers owned by William Randolph Hearst, himself no stranger to power and its misuse, rounded on Ismay in the safe knowledge that their stance on his 'disgrace' would be both populist and penny-spinning. One man's misery is another's delight.

Consider this contemporary diatribe against the White Star Line figurehead, its exceptionally harsh assessment cloaked in gentle ebb and flow of verse:

God and yourself alone can judge your case;
You were the captain of the fleets – the Master, you;
Every tradition of the British race,
Your creed, your caste, your office, well you knew.

The honour of the sea, the code that cries
That women first and children shall be spared,
Commanded that you make the sacrifice
And fare no better than your sailors fared.

Yours was the ship, and on the bridge your place;
You might have won the crown that Fame designed
Immortal honour stared you in the face
Fame waited at your side; but you were blind.

Where is the pride of which you were so proud?
Where are the friends who once sat at your board?
To them you're now a stranger in the crowd,
And to the crowd you are a thing abhorred.

You chose to rescue self, while honour drowned.
Too late, too late! The ocean holds its prey;
'Twere better far that Honour stood a-ground
And down in the *Titanic* slept Ismay.

Such was the hostility whipped up against him that the White Star Line had to provide its managing director – a quiet, even meek, individual – with a pair of bodyguards in the shape of armed private detectives on landfall. By that stage, survivors' accounts of Ismay's shattered seclusion on the *Carpathia* were being portrayed in the American public prints as a selfish disregard for the others spared, they being merely passengers or incidental crew.

Ismay bleated once or twice about the unfairness of his treatment by the US press, but it was left to the great thundering organs of his home country to take up the perceived slight. And thus complicating factors of loyalty, nationalism, my-country-right-or-wrong, and sheer Transatlantic rivalry came into play.

One man became a pawn in a power play. Mudslinging references were highlighted and thrown right back by the London press. If it was seen in Britain as crass and shocking for feral newspapers to tear down a public man, still they could not restrain themselves from sneering in their own turn – at the Chairman of the

American Inquiry into the loss of the *Titanic*, the most un-nautical Senator from Michigan, William Alden Smith.

This tit-for-tat sniping is illustrative of how the sinking became a battleground for all kinds of interests. The question of an objective allocation of responsibility, even blame, was trampled underfoot in the rush for point-scoring, much of it political, or arising from an international contest of *amour propre*.

It is therefore again instructive to learn that William Carter, a Pennsylvania businessman, happened to back up the 'foreigner' Ismay's account of how he left the ship:

> Mr Ismay and myself and several of the officers walked up and down the deck crying, 'Are there any more women here?' We called for several minutes and got no answer. One of the officers then declared that, if we wanted to, we could get into the boat if we took the place of seamen. He gave us this preference because we were among the first-class passengers.
>
> Mr Ismay called again, and receiving no reply, we got into the lifeboat. We took the oars and rowed with the two seamen.

Carter's account has a ring of truth, with the failure of more women and children to present themselves backed up in testimony by many occupants of Collapsible C, and even more credibly supported by some crewmen who were left behind as the craft departed and later gave their descriptions of the scene.

If there was no idea of saving Ismay as a person of great worth, corporately or evidentially, there also seems to have been – in the midst of coping with the crisis – no sense on his part of a duty not to be saved, but to drown. As Carter tells it, we can picture a harassed officer needing to get this boat away but also needing to retain crewmen about him to launch others.

The officer asks Ismay and Carter to further do their duty by helping to man the oars… the two men obeyed, and indeed Ismay was by common consent to be seen strenuously rowing thereafter. If he 'shuttered himself up' on the *Carpathia*, he unquestionably did not shirk lending his arms to the oar in the lifeboat. And if self-preservation was involved, at least he was simultaneously saving many others.

Carter's account appears to be guile-free. It rather defeats his purpose to admit that the officer, identified in testimony as Chief Officer Henry Wilde, 'gave us this preference because we were among the first-class passengers'. There it is – preferential treatment, and the press are right to scream.

But are they? The officer made an operational decision, and the passengers, like good passengers should, complied with it. It seems rather foolish to imagine that Ismay could have objected to getting in the boat on the principle that Honour must stand a-ground and that, notwithstanding these on-the-spot instructions, he was 'commanded' instead by higher consideration of the immortal fame that must attend his self-sacrifice.

One can imagine the officer's reaction. It might have been similar to that a few years later of the Irish patriot and socialist organiser James Connolly, reacting to a fellow Nationalist's ridiculously cloying welcome for the First World War as a source of sanguine renewal: 'No, we do not think that the old heart of the Earth needs to be warmed by the red wine of millions of lives. We think anyone who does is a blithering idiot.'

That observation, in December 1915, must surely hold good when scaled down from Patrick Pearse's 'red wine of the battlefield' to the case of a single individual. Indeed, as the British Inquiry observed with a clear eye in its final report of July 1912: 'Had he not jumped in he would merely have added one more life, namely his own, to the number of those lost.'

This prosaic evaluation does not appear to appreciate the value of the martyr's crown that Ismay, in earlier estimations, had foolishly foregone. On the contrary, it may indicate that the fame to be won by the simple act of expiry was not immortal, but might not have lasted even a few months.

Ismay always said he was a passenger. Critics imagine that passenger or not, he cannot be separated from his august position within the shipping line, and that therefore no officer would choose to regard him as simply a useful pair of hands on deck, and later for rowing.

But officers that night were not overly deferential to Ismay. Third Officer Herbert Pitman did not even know who he was while they were working together at No. 5. 'He remarked to me as we were uncovering the boat, "There is no time to lose". Of course I did not know who he was then, and therefore did not take any notice.'

The boat was lowered and brought level with the Boat Deck. 'Mr Ismay remarked to me to get it filled with women and children, to which I replied, "I will await the Commander's orders"'. The rebuke put Ismay firmly in his place. Pitman then went to the bridge to see Captain Smith, and someone seems to have told him he had just snarled at the managing director. Returning, Pitman and Ismay both helped to fill the boat, saying, 'Come along, ladies'.

Incidentally, the flow of women and children ended quickly at this boat too when no more were forthcoming. But while the sudden lack of occupants for the boat that Ismay eventually occupied is looked upon with suspicion, similar problems in channelling people to other boats have not been widely commented on. And yet the *Titanic's* boats were on average only two-thirds full, despite the luxurious two-and-a-half hours which there were to fill them. It is statistically apparent, therefore, that there were major shortcomings in organising the exodus.

Back to Ismay, who was rubbing shoulders with the crew in his efforts to help – but nonetheless rubbing some of them up the wrong way. Also here at the starboard side was the caustic officer Lowe, cited earlier for 'blasphemously' telling Daisy Minihan to jump.

Lowe was told by a steward on board the *Carpathia* that he had used very strong language with Ismay on the Boat Deck. 'Did I?' asked Lowe, not realising who Ismay had been. Told the identity of the man attacked, Lowe soon retailed the story to the American Inquiry. Mr Ismay was 'over-anxious and getting a trifle excited,' he related. 'He said, "Lower away! Lower away! Lower away! Lower away!"'

At this point Lowe was unsure whether to say what rejoinder he had thrown in Ismay's face, but remarkably, Ismay, who was then present in the committee room as Lowe was examined, contributed from the floor: 'Give us what you said.'

It seems Ismay was trying to be helpful, and at his own expense, lest Lowe should feel restrained from plain speaking by the potential embarrassment to his supreme employer. But, incredibly, Lowe regarded it as more insufferable interference. He snapped back at Ismay: 'The chairman is examining me.'

He had now demeaned his managing director not once, but twice. This latest, more public put-down, is rather at odds with claims that Ismay was saved because forelock-tugging underlings were enslaved to his towering importance.

Taking cover: White Star manager Philip Franklin provides shelter for Ismay as they leave the Senate inquiry in Washington DC. White Star Line attorney Charles Burlingham follows. At least one of the men in the background, atop steps, is a private detective hired for the managing director's protection. Ismay's own umbrella remains furled. *Illustrated London News*.

Lowe was eventually allowed to proceed, and explained how he had blasted Ismay in the heat of the moment:

> ...because he was, in a way, interfering with my duties, and also, of course, he only did this because he was anxious to get the people away – and also to help me. I told him: 'If you will get to hell out of that, I shall be able to do something.'

Ismay shrank back at this, making no reply, and Lowe gave free rein to his fit of temper: 'I said "Do you want me to lower away quickly? – You will have me drown the whole lot of them!"' Chastened, Ismay slunk away to the next boat forward. Lowe could see that the managing director was not standing on his dignity or sulking there, much less complaining to the captain, because he was making himself useful at that boat also.

And if Lowe did not think him useful, at least Ismay's intentions were honourable. Lowe said he could see the managing director at this next boat, 'getting things ready there', adding immediately and somewhat sourly: 'To the best of his ability.'

So here we are. Two officers, Pitman and Lowe, effectively gave coarse orders to Ismay. He complied with both of them. Carter suggests he also obeyed another order, this time from Chief Officer Wilde – an order which clearly seemed to value Ismay, not insult him, and to offer him an opportunity to be both appreciated and of assistance. He was invited to enter Collapsible C as an extra pair of arms, and, as we know, he did so.

Was Ismay a good or a bad man? The officers seem to have regarded him as a typical meddling passenger during the emergency. Yet Ismay's insistence that he was non-meddling in navigational matters seems always to be looked at askance by modern judges, as if meddling after the accident should equate to officious interference beforehand.

It is as if a presumption of *mala fides*, stemming from his eventual safe deposit on dry land, should extend back from his entry into a lifeboat, to his conduct on the Boat Deck, and even to the operation of the ship itself prior to her calamitous charge into an iceberg.

It is as if Ismay personally inspired the disaster by encouraging his captain to attempt a record, or at least a top speed, crossing. This analysis presents to us the assumption that the commander of a single ship would naturally do the bidding of the owner of the fleet.

Ismay was plainly aggrieved at claims that he had anything to do with the navigation of the vessel. He declared emphatically that he did not consult with her captain regarding the *Titanic's* conduct at sea, nor make any suggestion as to her course or other nautical matters.

He exercised no privilege that did not belong to any other first cabin passengers, he declared, did not sit at the captain's table, was not dining with him at the time of the accident, and was in fact abed when the collision occurred. 'When I went on board the *Titanic* at Southampton on 10 April, it was my intention to return by her. I went merely to observe the new vessel, as I had done in the case of other vessels of our Line,' Ismay said in a statement issued on his return to Europe:

> During the voyage I was a passenger and exercised no greater rights or privileges than any other passenger. I was not consulted by the commander about the ship, her course, speed, navigation, or conduct at sea. All these matters were under the exclusive control of the captain.
>
> I saw Captain Smith only casually, as other passengers did; I was never in his room; I was never on the bridge until after the accident; I did not sit at his table in the saloon; I had not visited the engine-room, or gone through the ship, and did not go, or attempt to go, to any part of the ship to which any other first cabin passenger did not have access.

But there were rumours, 'absolutely and unqualifiedly false', that he had said that he wished the *Titanic* should make a speed record, or increase her daily runs. In fact the vessel was going at her fastest rate of the voyage when the collision occurred, even if, being built for luxury, she could not have seized the Blue Riband from other ocean greyhounds.

Ismay's ordinariness while at sea was borne out in a letter to *The Times*, published somewhat belatedly on page eight of its 8 June, 1912, edition:

A DEFENCE OF MR ISMAY
To the Editor of *The Times*

Sir – In view of the efforts made by the Attorney General to force the conclusion that the loss of the *Titanic* was more or less due to 'interference' on the part of Mr Bruce Ismay, a conversation I had a few days ago while a passenger on the *Olympic* with one of the stewards may be of interest. This man, who was head steward in the reception room of the *Olympic*, mentioned that he had been steward to Mr Ismay himself on the maiden trip of the *Olympic* [June 1911], as well as on another crossing. He informed me that it was a common by-word among the stewards that 'if they wanted to keep out of Mr Ismay's bad books' they must be sure to 'treat him exactly as they would an ordinary passenger', as Mr Ismay seriously resented even so much as the placing of anything 'extra' on his table. He went on to say that Mr Ismay religiously observed the rules that passengers are expected to adhere to, that he was never known to go on the bridge, the compass platform, or any other parts of the ship to which first class passengers are forbidden access, and he had consistently refused to dine or mingle with the captain or other officers, with the exception of the doctor (who is the ship's social representative, as it were). I might add that these statements are borne out by similar things I have heard about Mr Ismay – long before the *Titanic* disaster – and that I myself have crossed with other high officials of the line who personally informed me that they were not allowed to interfere in any manner with the ship's employees, and that they could only make 'recommendations' upon their return home.

As one who has been an Atlantic passenger for nearly twenty years, having at one time and another crossed on nearly all the big liners, I feel that the attempts to discredit Mr Ismay and the White Star Line are wholly unjust. Let me add that I have no interest in the White Star Line and am not even acquainted with Mr Ismay. I am simply a businessman who crosses several times a year on business.

Notwithstanding the loss of the *Titanic*, I still believe that the White Star and Cunard lines in an equal degree are the safest ships afloat, well managed and cautiously navigated, and that the only charge that can be brought against White Star officials was misplaced confidence (shared hitherto by all steamship men alike) in the unsinkability of modern ships.

Charles H. Fryer
12 Charing Cross Chambers, Duke St, WC.

Yet there was one unusual aspect to the whole Ismay affair. *Titanic* Captain E. J. Smith, on the afternoon of the day of impact, a Sunday, handed to the company chief a wireless message received from the White Star liner's fleet mate, the *Baltic*.

Smith did it 'without any remark', as he was passing Ismay on the promenade deck, just before lunch. It was a message about the sighting of ice, sent to the *Titanic* at 11.52 a.m.:

Have had moderate, variable winds and clear, fine weather since leaving. Greek steamer *Athenai* reports passing icebergs and large quantity of field ice today in Latitude 41° 51' N, Longitude 49° 52' W.

'If the information I had received had aroused any apprehension in my mind – which it did not – I should not have ventured to make any suggestion to a commander of Captain Smith's experience,' Ismay insisted, adding accurately, if deflectively: 'The responsibility for the navigation of the ship resided solely with him.'

A Mrs Mahala Douglas, whose husband was drowned, told the American Inquiry of stories she had heard among the rescued on board the *Carpathia*. One told in company by Emily Borie Ryerson was as follows:

> On Sunday afternoon, Mr Ismay, whom I know very slightly, passed me on the deck. He showed me, in his brusque manner, a Marconigram, saying, 'We have just had news that we are in the icebergs'. 'Of course, you will slow down,' I said. 'Oh, no,' he replied, 'we will put on more boilers and get out of it.'

Ismay vehemently rejected this damaging assertion. 'I deny absolutely having said to any person that we would increase our speed in order to get out of the ice zone, or any words to that effect', he complained.

Interestingly, Mrs Ryerson, who lived in Chicago, submitted her own detailed affidavit to the American Inquiry and signally failed to tell anything about any alleged Ismay encounter. Nonetheless the story has an interesting plausibility. Smith did give Ismay a useful theatrical prop on deck, and it seems quite likely that the latter may have brandished it. But a bit of bravado with a passenger does not a Svengali make.

If it was a coincidental and harmless episode, Mrs Ryerson's silence on it suggests she may have embellished its importance – and what was said during it – once aboard the *Carpathia*. It would be a case of what subsequently transpired lending the incident a sinister character only in retrospect.

The cheeriness relayed in hearsay by Mrs Douglas would not ordinarily suggest that White Star Line executives were in the habit of telling their customers that they intended to hurl their vessel, and all lives aboard, into harm's way.

At the end of the day it is an unsupported tale, while one can imagine that it is not uncommon for directors to make grand pronouncements when they actually have absolutely no idea of what their managers, or in this case the captain, might really have in mind.

Ismay said Smith passed on the *Baltic* message wordlessly – it not being a matter for conversation or consultation, but merely for information. It could conceivably be a case of the captain preparing the owner for a poorer day's mileage on the morrow, for operational reasons. This is an interpretation that would go to caution, not to carelessness.

Nothing is proven by the *Baltic* message, which nonetheless becomes a stick with which to beat Ismay. And why? Well, because he is a natural focus for blame. Fifteen hundred died, but the head of the Line was saved. All interpretation of the facts must be directed, harnessed, *bent*, to the desired confirmation of an outcome – which stems from the simple equation of two facts, and works backwards.

On the other hand, the obvious empirical deduction from the known circumstances are that the *Titanic* sinking was not ordained by God, nor imposed by Nature. It was a man-made disaster, or more accurately, a men-made disaster. Many human factors influenced the outcome.

It has long been said that success has many fathers, but failure is an orphan. This is but one aspect of a syndrome known throughout the generations, whereby there is a need to leave one person holding the baby – even if that baby should be a tiny corpse, a blue-frozen mite plucked from an icy Atlantic that teems with many more besides.

The orphans of the *Titanic*, even at this remove, may be owed something of a more educated and more adult response than that.

COMPARISONS ARE ODIOUS

TWO MANAGING DIRECTORS, MAJORS, MARGARETS

The Ismay business shows how society likes to have a totem of condemnation. The large and complex meets the human desire for reductionism. Is it any wonder that the 'iceberg of impression' – elemental, uncomplicated, surface-based – always seems to win out over layer upon layer of illumination?

Simplicities may not tell the whole truth, and may even be its complete negation, but they are at least comfortingly plain, offering instant understanding and the chance to move on. At its most basic, the fact is that an iceberg accounted for the *Titanic*. Yet this is a simplicity too far – there must always be someone to blame.

If Ismay had not taken the maiden trip it is probable that all vituperation would have centred on the captain for his navigational recklessness, since there was no-one to butter-up but the passengers and the branch managers, and possibly the press, on posting an early arrival in New York.

And if Ismay had died aboard, instead of living, he would most likely have been free from whatever odium was to be dispensed as the blood-price of so many deaths. It is interesting, in this context, to note that another managing director intimately involved with the *Titanic*, one Thomas Andrews Jr, lost his life and 'enjoyed' such an absolution.

Indeed it almost became a canonisation. Ismay was managing director of the owners, whereas Andrews held that post with the builders, Harland & Wolff. And arguably, in a reductionist fashion, the famous Belfast shipyard and the White Star Line shared equal responsibility for the fact that the vessel went to sea with far too few lifeboats for those aboard.

Another portion of guilt for this fact certainly resides in the prolonged failure of the British Board of Trade to update regulations relating to the safety of life at sea, in particular lifeboat provision, which had not been amended since 1894 – fully eighteen years before the disaster.

But the Board of Trade is a hydra-headed beast, and thus hard to embody as an identifiable target. Indeed there was a popular civil service joke about the Board at this time, referred to at the British Inquiry, that it had plenty of eyes and ears – but not enough brains.

Harland & Wolff had anticipated coming changes in the regulations. Their chief designer, Alexander Carlisle, actually envisaged the provision of sixty-four lifeboats on the *Titanic*, far more than the sixteen standard lifeboats and four collapsibles she eventually sailed with. But the builders did not press their case when met by strong White Star objections that too many boats would clutter the promenade deck and hamper the view of passengers taking the air.

Andrews, Harland & Wolff's managing director, was aboard the *Titanic* as the head of a 'Guarantee Group' to hunt out snags for future remedy. The ship did have an inner hull, but it did not extend far enough and was hardly worth the name of 'double skin', while her bulkheads were not extensive enough to cope with widespread flooding. Andrews had been in personal correspondence with the Board of Trade, which wanted improvements to the latter – only to be ultimately frustrated by Harland & Wolff saying they had already built to the original plan. Yet Andrews escaped any 'personalised' censure by dint of his death.

Thomas Andrews, managing director of *Titanic* builders Harland & Wolff. He was also principal designer of the largest moving object ever constructed, which failed to withstand being grazed by an iceberg. *Maunsell*.

Imagine if the roles had been reversed. If Ismay had helped to load lifeboats and gone down with the ship, a mighty vessel left subtly vulnerable by the builders without his knowledge. And now here was Andrews, stepping lively from the *Carpathia* gangplank, saved from the leviathan he had built, but which had cost the lives of two-thirds of its complement.

It is hard not to see Thomas Andrews inheriting the criticism that was to be Ismay's, nor to see him vigorously protesting his innocence and decrying the castigation. Similarly, he would have been assured of pained and vigorous defence in his home country.

As it was, the Belfast newspapers reported in September 1912 that:

…the Belfast *Titanic* Memorial Fund has now reached the handsome sum of £2,500, and the Lady Mayoress and the other members of the General Committee are to be congratulated on the success of their efforts.

It is only fitting that Belfast, which was so intimately connected with the construction of the *Titanic*, and on board of which at the time of the disaster were so many Belfastmen, should be in possession of a memorial to commemorate the heroism of those, like Mr Andrews, who willingly sacrificed their lives to save the women and children.

In point of fact, and not to deny or denigrate Andrews' efforts, there is no evidence of his saving women and children in the way that there is of Ismay. Andrews did not notably work at filling the boats, and there are no testified sightings of him on the boat deck, certainly not by Ismay, who was asked.

But this has not stopped Andrews from being the focus of romantic gallantry – the 1958 movie *A Night to Remember* has him chiding a young couple to save themselves, then standing staring into the painting above the fireplace in the *Titanic*'s first class smoking room, a picture himself of grim determination and striking fortitude.

It is plain that Andrews was involved in early efforts to assess the ship's damage and how long she could endure. He also briefed stewards to make sure the passengers opened their doors, and to tell them that lifebelts were on top of their wardrobes. He personally encouraged passengers to go to the boat deck.

First class stewardess Annie Robinson, later a tragic suicide at sea, told how:

We had already got the blankets and the lifebelts out of the rooms which were unoccupied at the foot of the staircase. Mr Andrews said to me, 'put your lifebelt on, and walk about, and let the passengers see you'. I said to him, 'It looks rather mean', and he said, 'No, put it on', and then after that he said to me, 'Well, if you value your life, put your belt on.'

There were differences in the evacuation on the port and starboard sides. To starboard, Officer Murdoch – helped in part by Bruce Ismay – loaded women into boats, but then encouraged male passengers to fill empty places. To port, Officer Lightoller practised *women and children only* – and told the American Inquiry that he even refused entry to stewardesses because they were 'employees'. *The Graphic.*

This is curiously similar to a tale of the Boat Deck involving Andrews' fellow managing director, J. Bruce Ismay. Bedroom steward Harold Etches told the American Inquiry that Ismay had called out twice in a loud voice 'Are there any more women before this boat goes?' It was Lifeboat 5, and there was no answer.

The first officer, Mr Murdoch, similarly called out, 'and at that moment a female came up whom I did not recognise. Mr Ismay said: "Come along; jump in." She said: "I am only a stewardess." He said: "Never mind, you are a woman, take your place."'

But Ismay does not get the chivalrous conduct medal in the way that Andrews does, the latter being ever depicted in celluloid treatments of the *Titanic* disaster as solicitous and sympathetic of the stewardesses, when he likely had as much or as little to do with them as Ismay – who happened to be their employer. Indeed, such is the shaping of material into expected patterns of recognition that Ismay's insistence that the stewardess take her place by virtue of her sex is sometimes ascribed to Andrews.

Here it meets and fuses with a story told subsequently, and not in evidence, by surviving Belfast stewardess Mary Sloan, who has been 'placed' by researchers in

Lifeboat 16, whether accurately or not. She claimed Andrews was at the boat and invited her to get in. She said she would feel rather mean to do so, since many of her friends were staying. Andrews apocryphally responded that it would be mean not to go when there was a place a-begging.

Ismay had known and respected Andrews for many years, and it is likely that the admiration was mutual. Yet while both appeared to have acted broadly similarly during the sinking, their names diverged thereafter when it came to the bestowal of the mantle of heroism and the shaming cloak of cowardice.

Andrews would be the subject of a book, a paean of praise to his character entitled, *Thomas Andrews, Shipbuilder*. Composed of a series of anecdotes and testimonials, it was printed and reprinted in 1912, and is now one of the scarcest and therefore most avidly hunted of *Titanic* first editions.

The firsthand accounts therein of Andrews' dedication, kindness and consideration for others during his short life – he was thirty-nine, although Ismay thought him forty-two or forty-three – remain a glowing tribute to his memory and devotedness.

One of the many letters of condolence that Helen Andrews received about the loss of her husband contained this extract:

No-one who had the pleasure of knowing him could fail to realise and appreciate his numerous good qualities, and he will be sorely missed in his profession. Nobody did more for the White Star Line or was more loyal to its interests than your good husband, and I always placed the utmost reliance on his judgement.

The letter, dated 31 May, 1912, was from J. Bruce Ismay, the man vilified in the American press as 'J. Brute Ismay' among other sobriquets. Clearly he was not an unfeeling man, however, and the similarities and solidarity of the partnership between himself and Andrews, Harland & Wolff and White Star, suggest that had the roles been reversed, Thomas Andrews could – and would – have penned the same sentiments about the late J. Bruce Ismay.

But Ismay, this 'thing abhorred', would stay stubbornly alive until October 1937, a quarter of a century later. His *Times* obituary omitted all mention of the *Titanic*, observing only that:

In business Mr Ismay was accounted an austere man. He was certainly taciturn by nature, but could be a charming host. He had an extraordinary memory; his success was due to his industry, integrity and acumen, qualities which he inherited from his father. Last year Mr Ismay suffered from a serious illness and decided to withdraw from most of his business activities. A few days ago he was again taken ill, and the end came quickly.

He was 74. Ismay was cremated, and some of his ashes scattered on the prime fishing estate he had bought on the west coast of Ireland in January 1913. Costelloe Lodge at Casla, Co. Galway, is lapped by the same Atlantic that had proved his undoing.

Shortly thereafter his wife Florence, who had taken a steamer to Queenstown to meet him when he returned from the United States aboard the *Adriatic* in 1912, had a stone inscribed on the estate. It reads: 'In memory of Bruce Ismay, who spent many happy hours here 1913-37. He loved all wild and lonely places, believing that what we see is boundless as we wish our souls to be.'

De mortuis nil nisi bonum. Speaking nothing but good of the dead, or at least those notables who died, is a recurrent aspect of the disaster. Prominent figures, such as President William Howard Taft's aide-de-camp, Major Archie Butt, were claimed to have 'played the part of a hero', even though there was no information whatever about their actions.

Many American newspapers assumed Butt had proven a bulwark of military discipline against panic. They claimed he had shot down a succession of 'dagoes' or lily-livered 'Latins' (meaning those from Southern Europe) and some even printed line-drawings or artistic impressions of him emptying his revolver into such wretches as they attempted to seize places in the boats.

But in fact Butt was last seen in the gentlemen's smoking room at 1 a.m., may not have been armed at all, and could have reasonably concluded that the most appropriate course of action was to step back and not to interfere in any way with the organisation of the ship's evacuation, even if that must necessarily be only a partial evacuation.

If he sat in an armchair throughout, calmly smoking, would it have been any less noble an action than Thomas Andrews' prolonged cultivation of art appreciation in the same venue? As an army officer, Butt may have had the very practical realisation – stemming from his understanding of naval ways – that his best contribution was to stay out of the seamen's road. But he would not be allowed that self-effacing sacrifice by the newspapers.

There was a Canadian army officer, on the other hand, who did do something dramatic. And he was another Major – Arthur Peuchen of the Queen's Own Rifles in Toronto. When Lifeboat 6, having been already lowered, cried out that it was short of sailors, Second Officer Lightoller appealed for anyone so qualified that might be standing nearby on the deck.

Lightoller testified:

The boat was halfway down when the women called out and said that there was only one man in the boat. I had only two seamen and could not part with them, and was in rather a fix to know what to do, when a passenger called out and said, 'If you like, I will go'.

Is the officer's dilemma not similar to that of Chief Officer Wilde in the Ismay case, as related by passenger Carter? Two sailors, being the term for able seamen, were officially recommended to go into each of the twenty boats, but the *Titanic* only had thirty-two ABs aboard, of whom only twenty were saved. They were also needed for lowering the boats, a particular responsibility of these skilled crewmen.

Peuchen stepped forward, and Officer Lightoller continues:

> I said, 'Are you a seaman?' and he said, 'I am a yachtsman'. I said, 'If you are sailor enough to get out on that fall' [the dangling lifeboat rope] — that is a difficult thing to get to, over the ship's side, 8ft away, and means a long swing on a dark night — 'if you are sailor enough to get out there you can go down'. And he proved he was, by going down. And he afterwards proved himself a brave man, too.

Major Peuchen thus did Lightoller a favour, while displaying personal courage. Lightoller, who was miraculously also saved after the ship went down, later testified to expressly seeking out the Major aboard the rescue ship *Carpathia*. At this meeting, Peuchen asked for and received a letter from the officer stating that he had entered the boat under orders.

It seems Peuchen was already realising the likelihood of a whispering campaign against any soldier who quitted the field, as it were, while women and children were left behind to die by the hundred. Even if Peuchen helped to save the small cockleshell of women and children he became responsible for, it would weigh little in the balance against the myriad others.

What was Peuchen supposed to do? Ignore the plight of the weak? Ease himself into upholstery and an honoured ending like his American equivalent, Major Butt? He was following orders and saving lives, but in the course of doing so, inescapably saving his own. Unintended consequence or source of shame? Having acted bravely, in the words of the officer watching him, was he to hide behind his 'letter of comfort' for the rest of his life? A poor weapon for a military man.

Shortly after coming home safe, Peuchen found himself subjected to the sniping slurs and calumnies he had feared. Even the *Toronto Mail* sniffed: 'He put himself in the position of a man who had to defend himself before the necessity for the defence was apparent.' One could imagine a furious Peuchen, perfectly understandably, wanting to box the ears of a commentator who would dignify the gossips with such throwaway disdain.

Meanwhile *Harper's Weekly*, in its edition of 4 May, was extolling Butt:

> He saved the weak, beat back the craven; gentle and heroic, smiling and steadfast, he died the death of a soldier, the death of a gentleman. Not a nation merely, but a race, a civilization, finds its consolation in that sole word. It embodies our supreme tradition, breathes our uttermost ideal.
>
> The fact is all. Our dead young soldier was but a simple American citizen, yet he has won for us all the pride in grief, the triumph in agony, that swells forever in Horatio's long farewell to Hamlet:

> *Now cracks a noble heart! Goodnight, sweet prince.*
> *And flights of angels sing thee to thy rest.*

What about Hamlet's own quandary: *O, that the Almighty had not fixed his canon 'gainst self slaughter!* Peuchen, as a Canadian, would hardly have merited a single line in an American magazine if he had died. But if the Majors had been swapped, it is probable that Butt's dangle over the jaws of death would have been extolled as one of the extraordinary American ornaments on a night of crisis.

'Our poor finite imagination demands a single figure, not a mass of sacrifice,' wrote *Harper's Weekly* in its long eulogy that began with the words, 'Thank God for Archie Butt!' If it was an excuse for a bout of tub-thumping, it was nonetheless true of the search for a redeeming feature in the desperate drowning of a small town's population under jewelled skies.

The same is true in reverse, through the singling-out for criticism. Praise and blame were allocated to individuals with the sole equality being their unfair and undeserved nature. In all probability, Major Butt and Major Peuchen behaved equally well, one living and one dying by the aimless unscrolling of fate. But the better one, by the reckoning of the day, was Archie, not Arthur.

Neither, of course, had anything to do with the sinking of the ship. They were passengers, uninvolved with the navigation of the vessel, and therefore not targets in the way that the shipowner or the shipbuilder might be. The approval and scorn apportioned to them were by-products of how an event fractured into shards of right and wrong.

If some were to be celebrated in death as part of a process of mythmaking, the corollary character assassination of men like Peuchen for the offence of overcoming the emergency may have been inevitable. Indeed, such was the scale of the panegyrics to 'the lost' that what befell the Canadian and others may have represented not so much the reverse side of the coin, as a deeply subconscious and shared subverting of myth.

To explain – the public instinctively knew that those among them were creatures of flesh and blood, prey to all the usual shortcomings of our state. It is bad enough to be expected to venerate the dead for the unknowable manner of their passing, but to be asked to honour the 'ordinary' escapees may have proved a little too much. If the living and the dead should both belong to our level, then at least the living may be dragged back down to it.

Gossip has always thrived on jealousy, even if it is so deep-seated and alloyed with suspicion of the mediated story, not to mention the motiveless spur of wanton spite, that the true reasons for stories about men escaping 'dressed as women' may never be known – for all the actual damage that such claims inflicted.

Only women did not have this form of survivor guilt thrust upon them. Both the women who survived, and those who died, were together beyond reproach. In the chivalrous construct of 'Women and children first!' the females in every boat were seen as living proof of the honour of the men who had died – and must therefore have been angels themselves.

The emerging yardstick of Saved-Man-Bad/Drowned-Man-Righteous presumed the righteousness of all women, whether saved or lost. There are no wicked stepmothers in the *Titanic* morality play. All are seen as inherently honest, creatures of pedestal.

On the other hand, a saved man could be perceived as a bad man precisely because he occupied a place in a boat that could have been taken by a woman, or indeed a child, the latter consideration an additional source of shame.

In certain ways crewmen survivors were immune to this irrational 'reasoning', being understood to be a kind of necessary evil in every lifeboat. Male *passengers*, however, were in a much more vulnerable category, even if lifeboats could not practically live without such muscular makeweights. The agreed societal code of conduct undermined these men, even if it did not directly take their lives – as it did those of their brothers who felt bound to stay on deck.

Thus, as soon as the lifeboats cast off, the stronger sex became weak indeed under the terms of that honour system. And, in see-saw counterbalance, some of the weaker sex assumed positions of decided advantage.

Society expected the women to be saved, and it swiftly celebrated the 'strong' woman believed to have emerged from the *Titanic* tragedy, as if to further justify or drive home its countervailing low opinion of surviving males, which was hardly logically grounded.

Women who survived were lauded for such apparently insignificant acts as taking a hand to the tiller, as in the case of the Countess of Rothes (which rather risked sullying her gloves), or keeping a sharp lookout, or even for encouraging men at the oars. This was the damsel-in-distress for the Suffragette age – and it is possible that behind the applauding of faintly worthwhile acts lay an ulterior motive.

None was portrayed as stronger than the 'Unsinkable Molly Brown', one of the most lionised characters of all those aboard the doomed vessel. Margaret Tobin Brown was aged forty-four, of Irish extraction, and had been assisted into Lifeboat 6 at the Boat Deck – the same lifeboat Major Peuchen would later join through his Indian rope trick.

Margaret was never called Molly (a later Hollywood affectation) but she was quickly dubbed a 'Heroine of the *Titanic*'. This seems to have stemmed in large part from her industry on the *Carpathia* in drawing up a programme of necessary good works for the benefit of the less fortunate saved, while also appointing herself as a leading light of the Survivors' Committee soon formed aboard.

A wealthy first class passenger, these efforts may have amounted to little more than a sense of *noblesse oblige*, but what made her more unusual was that she happened to be travelling alone, without the benefit of male escort. Nor did its absence seem to bother her one whit.

Brown also made her name through apparently 'speaking up' – the temerity of it – in Lifeboat 6. Although she never gave formal evidence, she was made the subject of a front-page story in her home town newspaper, the *Denver Post*, as soon as the rescue ship docked.

Headlined: 'Mrs J.J. Brown of Denver is Heroine of the *Titanic*', the article spoke of her nursing women and children as the Cunard steamer that plucked them all from lifeboats headed back to New York. She then told her story (while still aboard *Carpathia*) of how she had been saved, 'between sobs and cries, which necessitated the presence of the ship's assistant surgeon.'

The interview seems heavily fictitious, with Mrs Brown being 'literally thrown into a boat' and claiming to have 'rowed with all my might for seven and a half hours.' She added: 'I rowed until my head was sick, until I thought I was dead. I owe my life to my exercise. Two women died at my side through exposure, while my blood was at boiling point.'

In fact women rowed in many of the lifeboats, while no woman died aboard any launched lifeboat. At the same time, however, Brown seems to have later become the embodiment of a 'blood boiling' row between the occupants of Lifeboat 6, predominantly female, and the sailor in charge, Quartermaster Robert Hichens, who had actually been at the ship's wheel when the *Titanic* struck her iceberg. Major Peuchen told how:

Margaret Tobin Brown somehow achieved legendary status as a kind of lioness of the sinking, although she seems in retrospect more of a Good Samaritan, with a kindness that in later years extended to decorating every *Titanic* grave with flowers while on a visit to Halifax, Nova Scotia.

Hichens was at the tiller all the time, with the exception probably of a couple of minutes. I know he asked one of the ladies for some brandy, and he also asked for one of her wraps, which he got. We got a couple of women rowing aft, on the starboard side of our boat, and I got two women to assist on our side; but of course the woman with me got sick with the heavy work, and she had to give it up. But I believe the others kept on rowing quite pluckily for a considerable time.

Some of the women urged Hichens to return to the scene of the wreck to pick up more people, and Peuchen was moved to advise them: 'It is no use you arguing with that man, at all. It is best not to discuss matters with him.' Hichens allegedly said it was, 'no use going back there, there was only a lot of stiffs there', which Peuchen found very unkind. 'The women resented it very much.'

Hichens maintained, 'No, we are not going back to the boat. It is our lives now, not theirs', insisting upon rowing farther away. But there was a 'rebellion' made by 'some of the married women that were leaving their husbands,' Peuchen declared. Margaret Brown, travelling solo, was not in this category.

Peuchen did not join the protests:

I knew I was perfectly powerless. He was at the rudder. He was a very talkative man, had been swearing a great deal, and was very disagreeable.

I had had one row with him. I asked him to come and row, to assist us in rowing, and let some woman steer the boat, as it was a perfectly calm night. It did not require any skill for steering. The stars were out. He refused to do it, and he told me he was in command of that boat, and I was to row.

Other female passengers, including Mahala Douglas and Eloise Smith, gave affidavits speaking of Hichens' 'brutality' and 'lazy, uncouth' nature. The quartermaster himself conceded that one lady had been 'rather vexed with me in the boat' – but identified her as Mrs (Leila) Meyer, a New Yorker.

Hichens admitted:

I spoke rather straight to her, and she accused me of wrapping myself up in the blankets in the boat, using bad language, and drinking all the whisky, which I deny, sir. I was standing to attention, exposed, steering the boat all night, which is a very cold billet. I would rather be pulling the boat than steering.

Mrs Brown later gave various versions of the dispute, in which she portrayed herself as threatening to throw Hichens overboard and eventually taking effective control of Lifeboat 6 – but only when the night had passed. Photographs of the craft approaching the *Carpathia* paint a different story – with Hichens still firmly standing at the tiller, while Peuchen and a *Titanic* lookout named Fred Fleet are prominent in the bow.

In a letter to fellow survivor Colonel Archibald Gracie, who published her account in his 1913 book *The Truth About the* Titanic, Mrs Brown told how the quartermaster had hailed another lifeboat (No. 16) after dawn and made both craft lash together. Thereafter they drifted – but a breeze sprang up. Gracie turned it into a form of reportage:

> Mrs Brown and her companions at the oars, after their exercise, felt the blasts from the ice-fields and demanded that they should be allowed to keep warm. Over into their boat jumped a half-frozen stoker, black and covered with dust. As he was dressed in thin jumpers, she picked up a large sable stole which she had dropped into the boat and wrapped it around his limbs from his waist down and tied the tails around his ankles.
>
> She handed him an oar and told the pyjama man to cut loose. A howl arose from the quartermaster in charge. He moved to prevent it, and Mrs Brown told him if he did he would be thrown overboard. Someone laid a hand on her shoulder to stay her threats, but she knew it would not be necessary to push him over, for had she only moved in the quartermaster's direction, he would have tumbled into the sea, so paralysed was he with fright.
>
> By this time he had worked himself up to a pitch of sheer despair, fearing that a scramble of any kind would remove the plug from the bottom of the boat. He then became very impertinent, and our fur-enveloped stoker in as broad a cockney as one hears in the Haymarket shouted: 'Oi sy, don't you know you are talkin' to a lidy?' For the time being the seaman was silenced and we resumed our task at the oars.

In short, Margaret Brown does not appear to have been especially involved in the low-level grumbling rebellion in Lifeboat 6 about returning to the wreck site, and if she did later assume a confrontational stance it was only after daylight had begun to creep over the scene – and while another lifeboat, notably containing the master-at-arms, was immediately alongside.

Gracie's book was for decades the standard American text on the *Titanic*, helping to elevate Margaret Brown into an audacious figure, even an Amazon, when she had done little more than engage in some backchat. Yet there is no doubt that her name has enjoyed a 'cult of personality' in book, stage and movie portrayals since the Second World War. Even if in 1912, in the immediate aftermath, she was acclaimed a heroine only in the Florence Nightingale tradition.

Incidentally, of all the righteous women saved, some were very self-righteous indeed. A number seemed to hold the crew in their lifeboats in common contempt, especially once they gained the secure foothold of the deck of another steamer.

Colonel Archibald Gracie, a veteran of the Civil War, was highly solicitous towards many of the womenfolk aboard the *Titanic* and escorted several to lifeboats. He published a 'delightful, graphic' account by Margaret Brown in his 1913 book on the shipwreck, *The Truth about the* Titanic.

Mrs Ella White was typical of complaints about smoking. 'Imagine getting right out there and taking out a pipe and filling it and standing there smoking, with the women rowing, which was most dangerous – we had woollen rugs all around us.'

The crew may have been phlegmatic, in more ways than one. Jocose remarks of apparent unconcern from one hand to another horrified the female passengers who overheard them. Similarly, crewmen pulled from the water who lay in the bottom of boats moaning and raving in slurred tones – a common effect of hypothermia – were deemed to be disgracefully drunk.

Some of the disapproval of rough-hewn crewmen, with widespread criticism of their boat-handling skills, may have been a manifestation of, or heightened by, the realisation that society women had left their husbands behind to die.

'I never saw a finer body of men in my life than the men passengers on this trip – athletes and men of sense,' said Mrs White:

> If they had been permitted to enter these lifeboats with their families the boats would have been appropriately manned and many more lives saved, instead of allowing the stewards to get in the boats and save their lives, under the pretence that they could row, when they knew nothing whatever about it.

Margaret Rice surrounded by her five sons; Albert, George, Eric, Arthur and baby Eugene Francis. A widow travelling in steerage who had to cope alone with her clutch of offspring, she had little chance of reaching a lifeboat. All were lost.
Author collection.

Yet these saved females were *all* good women – even if some would also allow themselves the doublethink of having their husbands saved too, when the price of that might be to make others of their sisterhood, doubtless good women also, entirely expendable.

Over a hundred women were left behind when the *Titanic* broke up and sank. One of them was Margaret Rice, a thirty-nine-year-old frontierswoman, similar in many ways to Margaret 'Molly' Brown. Rice was Irish too, and like Brown was travelling without the accompaniment of any adult male.

But while Brown was unencumbered by that fact, Rice was heavily burdened. She alone had to care for her five young sons aboard – Albert, ten; George, eight; Eric, six; Arthur, five, and the two-year-old, baptised Eugene, whom she called Frank. All would die.

Margaret had been widowed two years earlier when her railway-worker husband William was crushed to death by a locomotive in Spokane, Washington. She had earlier lost an infant through a tragic choking on a dislodged pacifier teat.

'There are many pathetic incidents connected with those Irish passengers,' opined the *Cork Examiner* on 19 April, 1912:

We have turned in vain to every list for some trace of Mrs Rice and her fine young family of five children, with whom she had been in Athlone on a brief holiday, or what was more a rest after a great affliction, she having lost her husband recently. Mrs Rice's fine handsome children evoked all-round admiration. Two were quite young ones in arms and all seem to have perished.

The family was travelling in steerage – which would turn them into the very highly sinkable Margaret Rice and sons. Nellie O'Dwyer, another Irish third class passenger, may have witnessed the last moments of mother and offspring:

> The cries that came from that ship I'll never forget. I could see just before the explosion, just dimly, the face of a woman who had six children with her on board. I think none of the little ones got up soon enough to be saved. The poor mother never left the ship.

Nellie also spoke of previously seeing 'a sweet little boy' and of hearing, 'the grandest prayers that one could hear from a child'. There was no trace of any of them the next morning in any of the lifeboats.

Another steerage woman, Bertha Mulvihill, was from the same Irish town as Margaret Rice. She claimed to have seen Margaret on the port side of the *Titanic* Boat Deck, holding one child in her arms, with the others clutching at her skirts. It was just before the end.

Speaking on the forty-fourth anniversary of the sinking in 1956, Bertha declared fiercely:

> I don't know where they get all that 'Women and Children First!' business. I never saw it. I'll tell you what I saw. I saw a mother and her five children standing there on the ship. When the ship split in half, I saw the mother and five children drown.

This is the dichotomy, between not just the two Margarets, but in the exaltation of some women who escaped – preferably blue-bloods or sparky characters – and the virtual denial, or at least downplaying, of the fact that women had actually been lost. And not just women, but very many children too.

The mythmaking has suggested that almost everything about the *Titanic* was heroic, representing a splendid surmounting of bitter fate. But this would mean overlooking the fact that every ship's lifeboat was, on average, one-third empty.

The popular impression of women and children first, in addition, suggests at least that these were saved. In fact a quarter of all women aboard drowned, and the odds were heavily stacked against the steerage. Not for them the luxury of complaining about crewmen smoking or swearing in the boats.

Titanic survivors arriving at the *Carpathia* in lifeboat Collapsible D, with Quartermaster Arthur Bright at the tiller. Marked with an X at an oar is Swedish passenger Håkan Björnström-Steffansson. Between his head and that of another man is arrowed the profile of one of the Navratil boys, the 'Titanic waifs', put in this boat by their father, who was travelling incognito and abducting them from their mother in Nice.

Half of all children aboard the *Titanic* were drowned, despite the shibboleth of *women and children first*. Just over thirty people are visible in this boat, although the British Inquiry said it carried forty-four. A woman in a straw hat is at one oar, and the man behind her in dark clothing, without a lifejacket, is thought to be Frederick Hoyt, a swimmer picked up from the sea.

The chances were even worse for children. A child's prospect of surviving the sinking was barely 50/50. This is not 'women and children first,' but saloon women first (first and second class passengers), and only then the humblest little ones.

The statistics are damning. There were thirty-one children booked aboard in the saloon classes. All but one were saved, the mysterious death of little Lorraine Allison possibly explained by the fact that her mother, not knowing the nurse had taken the other child into a lifeboat, held on, searching, until it was too late.

One first class child died, and none at all in second class – yet fifty-four third class children went to their icy end. Of the 109 children aboard, almost exactly half the total was therefore wiped out. Yet not one of them should have lost their short lives if the principle of 'women and children first' had been a reality and not a fantasy.

The ship struck at 11.40 p.m. and sank at 2.20 a.m. The *Titanic* command had over two hours to save the women and children, and what woman would not have put her offspring first, passing up the youngsters over the heads of adults if necessary?

Far left: Grave of the Unknown Child, Fairview Lawn Cemetery, Halifax, Nova Scotia. Finally identified by genetic dental analysis in 2007 as English toddler Sidney Goodwin, this marker has always symbolised the fifty-five children lost in the sinking – proof of the deceptive myth of *women and children first!*

Above left: Sidney Leslie Goodwin, one of a family of eight, all lost in the disaster. *Daily Mirror.*

Below left: Captain Frederick Larnder, of the main search vessel *MacKay-Bennett,* who described the panorama of victims as akin to 'flocks of swimmers asleep'. *Author collection.*

Those who want to see evidence of steerage maltreatment need not look for guns or locked barriers. They need only look here. Only twenty-seven steerage children lived, out of 79 aboard. That's barely one in three (34 per cent). *Emigrant children last!*

The five beautiful sons of Margaret Rice never had a chance. She had to organise them all on her own. It was the same with the Sages, a family of eleven, and with Frederick and Augusta Goodwin and their six children. All steerage families, and all lost in their entirety.

But instead of being given a chance, they ought to have been prioritised – if the old catch-cry about the weak and defenceless was to have any credibility. If the *Titanic* high command had invited the steerage to send up their young, as they certainly should have done if the evacuation were to be humanely managed, these children would all have been saved. The average of twenty-three empty spaces *per lifeboat* – more than 460 vacancies in total among the escape craft – would have been greatly lessened.

The recovery vessel *MacKay-Bennett,* chartered by the White Star Line and despatched from Halifax, began picking up bodies on Sunday 21 April, 1912, a week after the fateful Sunday when the *Titanic* collided. The fourth body picked up was the Unknown Child – Sidney Goodwin, as it turns out. The twelfth corpse plucked from the sea that Sabbath was Margaret Rice – but of her five sons there would never be the slightest trace.

Identified by a box of pills on her person that she had bought from a chemist in Ireland – who confirmed the dispensation number and customer – Margaret was found to be wearing a protective 'miraculous medal' honouring the Blessed Virgin Mary. A common amulet among Irish Catholics attempting the Atlantic, it is likely her sons had been wearing them too.

Margaret was buried in Mount Olivet cemetery in Halifax, Nova Scotia, thousands of miles from her ancestral home in Ireland and a similar distance from her husband's grave in Spokane.

The other Margaret, Unsinkable Mrs Brown, in the same month presented Captain Arthur Henry Rostron of the rescue steamer *Carpathia* with a silver loving cup to mark his gallantry and that of his crew. It all made for further purple passages about heroism, with the grimy faces of firemen 'shining like suns' as they queued up to collect medals handed out to honour their efforts in the stokehold.

This recognition was appropriate, if a little over-publicised, with press photographs dominated by the imposingly large trophy and by Mrs Brown's enormous hat, which somewhat resembled a headless ostrich of lustrous plumage.

But while Captain Rostron warranted his laurels and accolades, there was no equivalent recognition of the villainy that had ordained 1,500 deaths in the perishing cold of an April night. There were no public manifestations, no demonstrations with mock coffins, and no-one called for a boycott of the White Star Line.

It was as if there was unquestioning acceptance of the fact that 'ships return, and some go down' – even though it had been years since there was any serious loss of life on the North Atlantic route, and never anything as staggering as this.

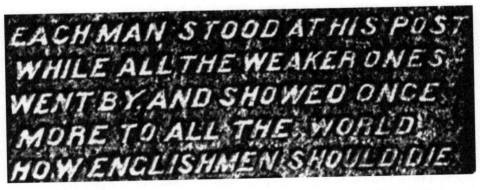

Verse at the base of the headstone of Everett Edward Elliott, 'of the heroic crew, SS *Titanic*. Died on duty.' A trimmer, or coal shifter, twenty-four-year-old Elliott became body number 317, buried in Halifax. The verse is part of a poem composed in tribute by his grieving father, J. Arthur Elliott. It ends: 'The hour had come when science failed and fate its might defied; The vessel sank and that is how some Englishmen have died.' *Author collection.*

The *Titanic* was only 63 per cent full on her maiden voyage, having a certificate to carry 3,500 passengers and crew. She complied with the law in having lifeboat spaces for 1,178 – but only 712 of those spaces would actually be occupied. A huge crowd was nonetheless left behind on the vessel, despite the fact that this was the most leisurely and even-keel sinking, on a calm and clear night, that any mariner or lay person had ever heard about.

A gigantic steamer with a heavy insufficiency of lifeboats was impelled into an icefield at such a rate that she was unable to avoid collision with an iceberg when one was seen ahead. No amount of courage and steadfastness, chivalry and honour, newspaper tripe and arrant nonsense, can disguise that unalterable fact. Nor can it obviate the serious, if not criminal, deficiencies that came together after the collision to kill masses of men, women and children.

In the final analysis, stripping away the offered frippery of saints, Sir Galahads and silver trophies, responsibility for the grimmest of disasters must return to the ship.

CONSCIENCE AND THE CAPTAIN

—— ⋅◆⋅ ——

RESPONSIBILITY RETURNS TO THE SHIP

There has always been, mysteriously, an honoured place allotted to Captain Edward John Smith of the RMS *Titanic*. His bronze statue in Beacon Park, Lichfield, close to his home town of Hanley, declares that he: 'bequeathed to his countrymen the memory and example of a great heart, a brave life and an heroic death'. It then adds his supposed last words: 'Be British!'

It is tempting to observe that if Captain Smith's watchword had rather been 'Be Cautious', there would be no statue in the park and no need to honour his 'heroic death'. The new vessel would have made a perfectly pleasant landfall in New York, and the good captain could have eventually breathed his last over the coverlet of his bed at home.

The homage paid to the captain, even if he was a gentle soul, has been quite extraordinary in light of what befell his ship. Margaret Brown, who presented that trophy to Captain Rostron, was evidently charmed by gold braid and gave a further swooning tribute to Smith, here mediated through the memoir of her fellow-passenger Archibald Gracie:

> When the sea was reached, smooth as glass, she [Brown] looked up and saw the benign, resigned countenance, the venerable white hair and the Chesterfieldian bearing of the beloved Captain Smith, with whom she had crossed twice before, and only three months previously on the *Olympic*.
>
> He peered down upon those in the boat, like a solicitous father, and directed them to row to the light in the distance…

This Father Abraham ideal of Smith assures us repeatedly of his nobility, even if it must at first appear foolish, and not noticeably fatherly, to allow one's brand new ship to be wrecked on a spur of ice in the middle of both night and Atlantic.

But Captain Smith would have his redemption. He went down with his ship in the expected manner – although nobody may be quite sure why such a thing was required. In fulfilling this allegedly ancient ordinance of the sea (no doubt bound up in the same canon as 'women and children first'), he thereby threw a lifeline to his posthumous reputation, and, incidentally, cast Ismay somewhat adrift.

That is how the newspapers saw it. Smith, the millionaires' captain, was faithful unto death. The *Sphere* printed an iconic image of the bearded Master, arms firmly folded, and added a quote from John Milton:

Nothing is here for tears, nothing to wail,
Or knock the breast, no weakness, no contempt,
Dispraise, or blame; nothing but well and fair,
And what may quiet us in a death so noble.

There was more than a hint that the captain was now beyond dispraise or blame through the expedient of being below the waves. And so he remained the unassailable figurehead of the greatest ship in what was literally a flagship industry – Britannia ruled the waves, whether by warship or prestige merchantman.

There had been huge shock when it was first reported that the captain had committed suicide. A Reuters news wire from New York read: '*Titanic* survivors state that the captain of the *Titanic* shot himself on the bridge.'

It was merely a rumour, quickly contradicted by other alleged witnesses, and the British press soon had some catching up to do. One apology ran:

In a portion of yesterday's issue, the *Daily Mirror*, in common with many other newspapers, published a Reuter telegram stating that, according to the survivors of the *Titanic*, Captain Smith had shot himself on the bridge of his vessel before it went down.

Some time later a contradiction came in, but by this time it was too late for the *Daily Mirror* to delete the original statement from its columns. Asked to explain their unfortunate blunder yesterday, Reuter's Agency stated that their messages to the effect that Captain Smith had committed suicide were afterwards denied; that the tragedy was reported by some of the passengers on the *Carpathia* during the confusion of the landing of the *Titanic* survivors, and that afterwards, in the hurry of sending out messages to the various newspapers, two telegrams were confused.

The *Daily Sketch*, which had either missed the 3.11 a.m. despatch from New York or chosen not to gamble on it, crowed at its rivals' misfortune on the next day, 20 April. It printed a huge front page photograph of Smith on the

Titanic's bridge, taken the day before she sailed from Southampton, with the good captain resplendent in a uniform graced by the Royal Decoration and Royal Navy Reserve medals. Above the image was emblazoned the headline: 'Where the British Captain Stood Till Death', immediately equating his resolution and fortitude with his Britishness. Another headline inside proclaimed: 'Captain Smith Dies Like a British Sailor'.

In its front-page caption, the paper snorted; 'It is evident that the disgraceful story circulated in some newspapers yesterday that Captain Smith shot himself are hysterical inventions.' It then reproduced three brief statements allegedly made by surviving passengers:

The captain stood on the bridge and continued directing his men right up to the moment when the bridge on which he stood became level with the water. He then calmly climbed over the rail and dropped into the sea

Mr Laurence Beesley, of London.

Captain Smith was the biggest hero I ever saw. He stood on the bridge, shouting through the megaphone, trying to make himself heard.

Mr Robert Daniel, of Philadelphia.

I saw Captain Smith while I was in the water. He was standing on the deck all alone. Once he was swept down by a wave, but managed to get to his feet again. Then, as the boat sank, he was again knocked down by a wave and the disappeared from view.

Mr G.A. Braden, of the Union Trust Building, Los Angeles.

Unfortunately, the *Sketch* was still basing its conclusions on 'sketchy' information. Braden was actually Brereton, a card sharp who had signed aboard under the name of 'Brayton' with the object of bilking his fellow first class passengers.

His account clashes with that of Beesley – but then Beesley himself would clash with Beesley when he finally got to give his own unfiltered account. That came in a book entitled *The Loss of the SS* Titanic, *Its Story and its Lessons*, in which he denounced, 'false reports… of Captain Smith shouting 'Be British' through a megaphone or committing suicide'.

Lawrence (not Laurence) Beesley made it clear that his Lifeboat 13 had been 'a mile to 2 miles away' shortly before the *Titanic* sank, and thus he made no claim to see anything of Captain Smith's last moments.

The suicide claim about Smith was not an isolated one – it quickly became more focused on First Officer William McMaster Murdoch, the officer of the watch at the time of the collision. Beesley was dismissive of the retailing of such rumours as if they were thrilling details. He wrote in his book:

> There could be nothing heroic in Captain Smith or Murdoch putting an end to their lives. It is conceivable that men might be so overwhelmed by the sense of disaster that they knew not how they were acting; but to be really heroic would have been to stop with the ship – as of course they did – with the hope of being picked up along with passengers and crew and returning to face an inquiry and to give evidence that would be of supreme value to the whole world for the prevention of similar disasters. It was not possible; but if heroism consists in doing the greatest good to the greatest number, it would have been heroic for both officers to *expect* to be saved.

Meanwhile the embarrassment over the initial suicide report had led to the British press totally over-correcting to the point where no criticism of Captain Smith was possible thereafter. The *Daily Sketch* went into overdrive:

> High up on the bridge, at his post to the last, is the liner's captain. Waves sweep him off his feet, but he rises, And when the *Titanic* sinks beneath the waste of waters, Captain Smith dies like a simple hero, as a British sea captain should. Of all the cruelly heartless fabrications which the sensation-mongers have woven about this tragedy, the most stupid and senselessly false is the tale that Captain Smith killed himself on the bridge.
>
> The full story, in all its terrible truth, tells us what we had guessed to be true – that Death came honourably and nobly to all.

Thousands of messages of sympathy poured in to Smith's widow, Eleanor, mother of their ten-year-old daughter Helen, for whom he would surely have wanted to live. Mrs Smith had hand-written a message that she pinned up outside the White Star offices in Canute Road, Southampton, where hundreds of members of crew families flocked to read the hastily-pasted official messages proclaiming the names of survivors.

'To my poor fellow sufferers,' she wrote. 'My heart overflows with grief for you all and is laden with sorrow that you are weighed down with this terrible burden that has been thrust upon us. May God be with us and comfort us all. Yours in sympathy, Eleanor Smith.'

Such awareness of shared suffering was most touching and received widespread publicity, helping to foster the 'Smith myth' of fatherliness. By now all kinds of unreliable accounts were emerging as to the captain's edifying conduct at the end, sending his stock ever higher:

CAPTAIN SMITH'S BRAVERY

FIREMAN'S THRILLING STORY

'I THINK IT BROKE HIS HEART'

A very graphic story is told by fireman James McGann, who was on the bridge deck when the ship went down. 'When the water reached the captain's knees,' he said:

> ...the captain gave one look all round, his face firm and his lips hard set. He looked as if he might be trying to keep back the tears as he thought of the doomed ship. I felt mightily like crying myself as I looked at him. Suddenly he shouted: 'Well boys, you've done your duty and done it well. I ask no more of you, and I release you. You know the rule of the sea. It's every man for himself now, and God bless you.' Then he took one of the two little children who were on the bridge beside him. They were both crying. He held the child, I think it was a little girl, under his right arm and jumped into the sea. All of us jumped. I jumped right after the captain but I grappled the remaining child before I did so. When I struck water the cold was so great that I had to let go my hold of the kiddie. The next thing I knew I was swept towards the last collapsible boat. I clambered aboard. It was the intention of the captain to put the two little ones on the boat, but when it overturned it was swept away...'

When on the bridge, the Captain was all the time directing the lowering of the boats and shouting 'Women and children first.' Dead bodies were all around floating in the water when we jumped, and I think it broke his heart. I wasn't keen on living myself.

(*Derry Standard*, 24 April, 1912, p3)

Another fireman, George 'Paddy' McGough, said he saw Captain Smith at some distance, swimming towards another boat: 'When they reached out to help him, he shouted at them 'Look after yourselves men. Don't mind me. God bless you.' Then he threw up his hand and disappeared.'

But yet another member of the Black Gang, as stokers were called, seemed to corroborate the baby story. Fireman Harry Senior said: 'While I was swimming, I saw the captain in the water. He was swimming with a baby in his arms, keeping it out of the water as he swam on his back. He swam to a boat, put the baby in and then swam back to the ship.'

Senior had, like McGann, also gotten in on the act: 'I had also picked up a baby, but it died from the cold before I could reach the boat.' But the conclusion must be that the grappling of these three children – if any of them existed – was not so much unutterably sanctifying for all involved, but a disgraceful indictment of the failure to get any of those infants into lifeboats in the long hours before.

One report had lookout George Hogg seeing Smith in the water alongside a raft: '"There's the skipper," I yelled. "Give him a hand." They did, but he shook himself free and shouted "Goodbye boys, I'm going to follow the ship." That was the last we saw of our skipper.'

None of the above alleged witnesses gave evidence – except for Hogg, who did so both in America and Britain. Hogg left in the very first lifeboat and said he was half a mile away at the climactic moment. He thought about returning to the scene, but met a lifeboat that assured him nothing could be done.

Senator George Perkins asked him at the American Inquiry, after a perfectly routine recital of what he did and saw: 'Was there any other incident, that you can think of, that would be of interest to the public?' Hogg replied: 'No, sir.'

But the public curiosity was now being deluged with a wave of hagiographical material about the captain, as if his own mortality excused the enforced fatality of two-thirds of the people aboard his vessel, all of whom were in his charge.

Eventually the playwright George Bernard Shaw could stand it no more. He thundered with caustic indignation:

> The captain must be a super-hero, a magnificent seaman, cool, brave, delighting in death and danger, and a living guarantee that the wreck was nobody's fault, but on the contrary, a triumph of British navigation.
>
> The one thing positively known is that Captain Smith had lost his ship by deliberately and knowingly steaming into an ice field at the highest speed he had coal for. He paid the penalty; so did most of those for whose lives he was responsible. Had he brought them and the ship safely to land, nobody would have taken the smallest notice of him.

Arthur Conan Doyle, creator of Sherlock Holmes, could not abide what he saw as cheap point-scoring, and inveighed in the same publication Shaw had used, the *Daily News*, against the playwright's lack of compassion, arguing that the captain's heroism arose from his actions after the accident, and not what went before.

But Shaw was not to be moved, arguing that if going down with the ship was all that was required to achieve heroism, then a place in Valhalla should be cleared for the ship's cat, which had also gone down. In point of fact, Shaw is in error here – the only known feline aboard is reported to have seen discretion as the better part of valour. Fireman Joe Mulholland reported that 'Jenny' disembarked with her kittens in Southampton after giving birth in the stokehold on the delivery trip from Belfast, and therefore did not 'sign on' for the maiden trip.

Playwright George Bernard Shaw in 1912. Out of step with his time, Shaw decried what he saw as a titanic folly.

If the cat was denied a statue, the issue of whether Smith deserved one must go to the question of whether he was a guiding spirit towards catastrophe. The captain knew, as Bernard Shaw observed, that he was steaming straight into an ice zone. He had known about it for hours, if not days – and, as we know, had even handed an ice warning from the *Baltic* to Bruce Ismay, who treated it as an empty curiosity.

This gesture, to begin with, was unprofessional of Smith. An ice warning was not an amusement for Ismay or anyone else. The fact that Smith eventually recovered it some long time later, asking the managing director for it back, indicates that his conscience had reminded him that this was an important matter to be brought to the attention of the officers on the bridge.

Captain Smith seems to have been decidedly hands-off that day regarding how his ship was handled. A scheduled Sunday-morning muster for lifeboat drill had been cancelled without warning, although the practice would certainly have come in useful twelve or fourteen hours later when the lifeboats needed to be launched.

Meanwhile, even though the icefield loomed and many ships over previous days had indicated its whereabouts, it was planned without compunction that the *Titanic* would be doing her fastest speed of the entire voyage – 22 knots – at the time she neared the vicinity. This was twice as fast as the top speed of the ordinary Atlantic tramp, which comprised more than 95 per cent of the shipping on that ocean.

The figure of 22 knots is equivalent to 25 statute miles per hour. On the same day that the *Titanic* left Ireland, 11 April, three motorists were being stopped by police for 'excessive motor speed' in that country's capital. Frederick Baker was fined £1 for driving a car at 25mph in Lower Leeson Street, with similar penalties imposed on Laurence Doolin and William. Tribe for driving elsewhere at the even lower rate of 22mph. The White Star liner may not have been operating in a crowded thoroughfare, but it was heading for one – and the collision would prove the point. The speed of the vessel meant she could not avoid an iceberg that the British Inquiry believed had been spotted thirty-seven seconds prior to impact.

As the *Titanic* neared the danger waters, what did Captain Smith do? Why, he absented himself from duty on the bridge! Second Officer Charles Lightoller told the Inquiries that he estimated the *Titanic* would be meeting small ice from 9 p.m. and would be 'up to the ice,' meaning the larger stuff, at 11 p.m.

Lightoller, however, received just one fleeting visit from Smith during his entire time as officer of the watch, from 6 p.m. to 10 p.m. on the night of doom. The Doyen Commander of the White Star Line arrived on the bridge at 8.55 p.m. – having just come from a party in his honour below decks (at which he did not drink alcohol) – and sniffed that there was not much wind.

The second officer knew what was in Smith's mind – that the calm would mean no breakers at the base of the icebergs undoubtedly ahead. And yet the captain shrugged… when he should have ordered that an extra lookout be placed in the well-named 'eyes' of the ship, at the bow, for extra insurance. He did not give that order, a standard precaution at the time, and it may have been a grievous mistake.

It is worth examining this encounter between the captain and his officer of the watch, less than three hours before the collision, to see what it discloses about his general attitude and posture towards the ice, which he himself had informed his owner about through the passing-on of the *Baltic* warning,

'At five minutes to nine, when the commander came on the bridge, he remarked that it was cold,' testified Lightoller:

As far as I remember, I said 'Yes, it is very cold, Sir. In fact it is only one degree above freezing.' We then commenced to speak about the weather, He said 'There is not much wind.' I said 'No, it is a flat calm as a matter of fact.' He repeated it; he said: 'A flat calm.' I said 'Yes, quite flat, there is no wind.' I said something about it was rather a pity the breeze had not kept up whilst we were going through the ice region. Of course, my reason was obvious; he knew I meant the water ripples breaking on the base of the berg.

Lightoller says Smith perfectly comprehended that the flat calm could make an iceberg treacherously difficult to see. And they were going the fastest speed of the voyage:

He said 'Yes, it seems quite clear,' and I said 'Yes, it is perfectly clear.' It was a beautiful night, there was not a cloud in the sky. The sea was apparently smooth, and there was no wind. But at that time you could see the stars rising and setting with absolute distinctness.

We then discussed the indications of ice. I remember saying 'In any case there will be a certain amount of reflected lights from the bergs.' He said 'Oh yes, there will be a certain amount of reflected light.

Lightoller had misgivings about so-called 'blue bergs' – which could appear not brightly white, but as dark masses. Blue bergs were ice mountains that had capsized through the natural stages of melting, turning turtle so that the base – filled with dark seawater – could suddenly become a flank.

'Blue was said between us,' Lightoller explained, 'that even though the blue side of the berg was towards us, probably the white outline would give us sufficient warning, that we should be able to see it at a good distance, and, as far as we could see, we should be able to see it.' Here the officer is talking to his captain about the percentages... using phrases like 'probably', 'should', and 'as far as we could see'. Lightoller added:

We knew we were in the vicinity of ice, and though you cross the Atlantic for years and have ice reported and never see it, and at other times it is not reported and you do see it, you nevertheless do take necessary precautions, all you can.

What precautions did the captain take? We are about to see. In the meantime Lightoller was clarifying to his questioners that the absence of a breeze, as he had reported to the captain on approaching the icefield, would make it 'more difficult' to identify icebergs ahead. 'Naturally you would not see the water breaking on it if there were no wind; and so you would not have that to look for.'

If speed and the prevailing weather conditions made the identification of icebergs 'difficult', Captain Smith had it in his power to make it much less difficult. A reduction in speed would have given his vessel more time to locate and avoid any obstacles. The captain remained on the bridge about twenty-five minutes or half an hour, Lightoller said. Smith may have been mulling it over, but it was his decision. His navigating officers were only there to carry out instructions.

Question 13631: And during that time, whilst he was with you, was there any discussion between you at all as to speed?

Officer Lightoller: None.

Q. 13632: You were going full speed ahead at this time?

Lightoller: Yes.

Q. 13633: About 21½ knots as you think?

Lightoller: Yes.

Q. 13634: And no question was raised between you as to speed at all?

Lightoller: No question at all.

Q. 13635: The captain left you about 20 or 25 minutes past nine, you say. Did he say where he was going or where he had been, and so on?

Lightoller: Yes. The captain said 'If it becomes at all doubtful' – I think those are his words – 'If it becomes at all doubtful let me know at once; I will be just inside'.

The evidence indicates that it was already doubtful. Lightoller had said as much, and had gone as far as a conscientious officer could go with his commander. Smith had taken a chance. There was to be no diminution in speed.

Lightoller was later asked: (Q. 14355) 'Do you not think, then, it would have been desirable especially as you say the conditions were abnormal, to have slackened speed?' The officer sidestepped the question, although he had raised this very problem with Captain Smith on the night itself. His reply was: 'It has never been done in my experience.'

Just because ice has been reported does not mean it will be seen, much less collided with, was his general argument, with Lightoller effectively mounting excuses against what seasoned mariners might have seen as excessive caution. But the other extreme was excessive speed, and everything about the officer's encounter with Smith suggests he was offering his captain a middle road.

SOME NORTH ATLANTIC EXPERIENCES

To the Editor of *The Times*

Sir – May I give you some of my personal experiences gained as a marine engineer in a well-known line of cargo steamers from 1892 to 1900? Most of my voyages were on the North Atlantic. The risks taken by the captains on the ships on which I served, and they are no exception to the rule, were iniquitous.

Speed was the only consideration, speed through ice and fog at any cost, and it was not, and is not now, the captains who must bear the blame – it was and is the owners. Their instructions, very carefully veiled, were to save time and coal.

The loss of the ship and the crew (including the captain) was immaterial: ships are insured, men are plentiful, captains too. If the captain was too careful and time and coal were lost, then he had better ship as fourth officer, no doubt in some other line, if they would take him. And the result: Many of the ships then belonging to the company are now piled up on the rocks of Newfoundland and Labrador or sunk at the bottom of the Atlantic.

We struck icebergs on two occasions, and twice were saved from running on the rocks by a miracle.

I am Sir, yours faithfully,

Maurice C. Stubbs, Truro.

(*The Times*, 31 May, 1912, p4)

What cared the passengers for saving time and coal if it put their safety at risk? None cared about coal, certainly, although the speed of a ship was a prestige question to which the saloon passengers were not immune. A certain vigour in making the crossing was most appealing advertising, and none of the better-off cared to consider a much slower vessel. First class passengers placed bets of the extent of the daily run, the mileage covered in the previous twenty-four hours being posted every morning in the lounge. Large amounts were wagered, and there was general disappointment if the run should slacken.

In the steerage, the bottom of the ship where there was no natural access to lifeboats, there was no wagering on speed. The speed hardly mattered to emigrants who were thinking in terms of the rest of their lives:

CIVILISATION'S SHORTCOMINGS

The liner was travelling 21½ [nautical] miles an hour – the fastest of the voyage. All this racing is that the wealthiest and most idle class in the world may have two hours longer in New York, where nothing awaits them except the task of supporting the ennui and tedium of two more hours on their hands, but we may take it that for the emigrant from the west of Ireland, leaving sorrowing friends behind forever to face an uncertain and difficult future, the slowest liner travels fast enough.

(Editorial, *Connacht Tribune*, 27 April, 1912)

Mr William Dawson Harbinson, the legal counsel engaged in the interests of the third class passengers, argued in his speech on the twenty-ninth day of the British Inquiry that the most obvious precaution was to cut speed. Negligence was of the same quality while steaming on the Atlantic Ocean as when driving on the Thames Embankment, if life was lost as the result of excessive speed, he said.

If the driver of a motor-car were warned in advance that some obstruction was on the road ahead – a herd of cattle, for instance – could it seriously be suggested that he fulfilled his duty by going on at full speed in the hope that he might be able to detect the obstruction before he came up with it, he asked:

Now, whether it is navigating on the Atlantic Ocean or travelling in London on any highway, what is the rate that should guide those who are in command either of vessels or vehicles? It is this: that the speed should be such that they should have either the ship or the motor-car, or whatever it is, under such control as to avoid an object after being seen. And, as the result proves, my Lord, the *Titanic* was unable to avoid this object after it was notified from the crow's-nest.

The disaster to the *Titanic* was not the result of inevitable accident, he argued, and thus 'blame must attach to someone', since blame was at the root of negligence:

Blame must attach to someone, and my suggestion is that the vessel was not navigated with an adequate amount of care consistent with the warnings that had been received, and that blame undoubtedly attaches to those who were in charge of the navigation of the vessel. There was a breach of the duty to take care… to protect and preserve the lives of those who were on board. That breach of the duty to take care amounts to negligence.

Captain Smith went to his room, leaving the *Titanic* charging blindly, recklessly, ahead. His last instructions were effectively an endorsement of continued full speed into a treacherous stretch, with no additional posting of lookouts. His valedictory words 'If it becomes at all doubtful, let me know at once' essentially meant not only to maintain the speed which could give rise to difficulties, but for the officer of the watch to take no decision to moderate the rate of progress without prior consultation.

Lightoller, and his relief, First Officer William McMaster Murdoch, were thus left in the invidious position of having responsibility without power. Their precious reaction time had been cut away by a commander who had left the bridge.

When Captain Smith later rushed back onto the scene to blurt: 'What have we struck?' the temptation is to suggest that the answer readily supplies itself: 'You should know.' The duty of the captain's personal watchfulness cannot be palmed off onto underlings, particularly since it was the captain who had personally taken the decision to maintain top speed.

The following example suggests that Captain Edward J. Smith is culpable of negligent navigation, leading to the corporate homicide of 1,500 souls:

THE *TUNISIAN*
Reports seeing 200 Icebergs

Liverpool, Wednesday: The Allan liner *Tunisian*, which arrived at Liverpool yesterday, from Canada, reports on Saturday night speaking to the *Titanic* by wireless, sending a message, 'Good luck', to which the reply came, 'Many thanks; Goodbye'. The *Tunisian*, when 887 miles east of St John's, entered a huge icefield, through which she carefully picked her way for twenty-four hours, then stopped all night, eventually turning 62 miles south. No less than 200 icebergs were seen. The commander was on the bridge for a thirty-six-hour spell. The officers and passengers were afterwards greatly shocked on learning of the disaster to the *Titanic*.

(*Cork Constitution*, 18 April, 1912, p3)

Captain Fairfull of the *Tunisian*, 'one of the oldest commanders in the North Atlantic service' according to the *New York Times*, was on the bridge for a continuous thirty-six hours! Tired after his party, Captain Smith chose to step back from constant vigilance, leaving only a senior officer on the bridge as they approached a Gethsemane of bergs. *Could you not watch with me one hour?* It would seem that the 'fatherly' Captain Smith, on the night in question, failed not merely to earn the respect and devotion in which he was held, but abrogated his individual responsibility. That, in turn, becomes his responsibility, and it forfeits any 'heroism' that might arise from actions afterward.

Like a player in the daily mileage pool, Captain Smith gambled that evening. It matters not that the odds may have been heavily against the possibility of a collision, and that he suffered from sheer bad luck – such an excuse, as legal counsel Harbinson implies, would not have been tolerated for a moment from a motorist whose vehicle collided with a single beast in a herd of cattle. Nor would it safeguard the reputation of a motorist who struck a jaywalker, causing loss of life… yet the captain's risk in this case was one that bore with it the fate of the 2,200 persons aboard.

In that respect it is almost incidental as to whether there were sufficient lifeboats, except that knowledge of the latter shortcoming might point towards greater caution. Nor is it a mitigating factor whether the mere presence of the managing director aboard might have spurred Smith to take a chance – he remains, at all times, the captain of his own ship and of all the destinies enclosed within the hull. Smith, moreover, was close to retirement – all the more reason to exercise personal responsibility rather than cede to the temptation of posting a smart-looking voyage time.

His senior surviving officer, Lightoller, gamely attempted to muddy the picture by suggesting that it 'becoming doubtful' might have meant a haze descending on the clear horizon, thereby making the icebergs even harder to discern. But this is a canard, a distraction – Lightoller has already demonstrated to us that it was the very clarity of conditions that was making bergs an actual hazard earlier in the evening. The lack of breeze meant no telltale appearance of water breaking at their base. So the situation was *already* doubtful.

Commanders are paid to anticipate adverse conditions. Even if Smith did not comprehend the situation, it was brought to his attention by his officer of the watch. He then dismissed the danger, but failed to take responsibility for his decision while robbing others of their freedom of action. And the truth was that a reduction in speed, even had the managing director taken a dim view the next morning, could have been justified by the White Star Line's own regulations.

Specific instructions from the Line were prominently displayed in a framed notice in the chart room of the *Titanic*. The same injunctions were periodically circulated directly to the commanders of vessels in the company fleet. The notice read as follows:

WHITE STAR LINE

The Managers are desirous of impressing upon Commanders the importance of strictly adhering to the company's regulations, and attention is particularly called to the following points:

(1) The vital importance of exercising the utmost caution in navigation, safety outweighing every other consideration.

(2) Over-confidence, a most fruitful source of accident, should be specially guarded against.

(3) It cannot be too strongly borne in mind that any serious accident affects prejudicially not only the welfare of the company, but also the prospects and livelihood of the commanders and officers of the ships and, as every consideration is shown to those placed in positions of responsibility, the company relies upon faithful and efficient service being given in return, so that the possibility of accidents may be reduced to a minimum.

The company assumes the entire risk of insurance on its vessels, their freights, and on a considerable portion of the cargoes carried by them, whilst the large sum which is paid annually to its officers as a bonus for absolute immunity from accidents is additional evidence of anxiety to subordinate all other considerations to the paramount one of safety in navigation.

(4) No thought of making competitive passages must be entertained, and time must be sacrificed or any other temporary inconvenience suffered rather than the slightest risk should be incurred.

Captain Smith comprehensively broke the letter and spirit of these regulations. And since a further paragraph in the written regulations he was issued with recommended that: 'Commanders should be on deck and in full charge during thick weather,' he would be living dangerously to suggest the looming presence of icebergs did not constitute thick weather because the visibility was good.

Staying in his room in such circumstances still appears to lack care. And if he was tired after Mr and Mrs Widener's party in his honour, it may not have excused him to forget that the White Star regulations stated plainly that: 'Convivial intercourse with passengers is to be avoided.'

Under a section headed 'Responsibility', the Line's written regulations for captains declared:

Commanders must distinctly understand that the issue of these regulations does not in any way relieve them from responsibility for the safe and efficient navigation of their respective vessels, and they are also enjoined to remember that they must run no risk which might by any possibility result in accident to their ships.

It is to be hoped that they will ever bear in mind that the safety of the lives and property entrusted to their care is the ruling principle that should govern them in the navigation of their vessels, and that no supposed gain in expenditure or saving of time on the voyage is to be purchased at the risk of accident.

The company desires to maintain for its vessels a reputation for safety, and only looks for such speed on the various voyages as is consistent with safe and <u>prudent</u> navigation.

The word 'prudent' was underlined. Captain Smith may have been benign, venerable, beloved and solicitous to his passengers, as reported, but the extent of his imprudence was reckoned with terrible scales – the weights in the balance being human life to an unparalleled measure.

Second Officer Lightoller, who admitted the British Inquiry was a whitewash and who did his best to launder his company's dirty linen during it, was pressed whether it was reckless to proceed at 21½ knots into known ice. Defending Smith to the last, he replied: 'Then all I can say is that recklessness applies to practically every commander and every ship crossing the Atlantic Ocean.'

'Is it careful navigation in your view?' asked Thomas Scanlan for the National Sailors' and Firemen's Union. Lightoller replied defensively: 'It is ordinary navigation, which embodies careful navigation' – but clearly it did not.

There was simply no prudence shown by Smith, as officially demanded. Lightoller himself, when pressed in this same spell of evidence, significantly twice refused to state that in the same circumstances, were he in charge, he would not have slowed down. 'I should take every precaution, whatever appealed to me,' he managed.

The company's reputation for safety was greatly damaged by the risk, however small he considered it, that Smith chose to purchase that night. White Star was never quite the same, and, crippled by further losses in the Great War, would eventually be swallowed in a merger with Cunard, the company's great rival.

But Captain Smith was a Hero of the *Titanic* disaster. He went down and his statue went up. His character, the newspapers maintained, embodied the quintessence of Britishness. And he urged it upon others...

First class passenger Daisy Minahan, incidentally, denied that there had been any encounter between the captain and Officer Lightoller on the bridge. She stated in an affidavit to the American Inquiry: 'I read testimony before your committee stating that Capt. Smith had talked to an officer on the bridge from 8.45 [sic] to 9.25 p.m. This is positively untrue, as he was having coffee with these people [the Widener party] during this time. I was seated so close to them that I could hear bits of their conversation.'

She said Smith left the alcove in the dining room where he had been convivial with passengers between 9.25 and 9.45 p.m., when she herself departed. Nothing turns on this – either Minahan or Lightoller has erred in their timing, but the conversation on the bridge seems likely to have taken place, especially since the officer was so keen to contextualise it and explain it away. Alternatively, Ms Minahan is right, and Captain Smith retired to his room without going on the bridge at all, despite knowing the impending presence of icebergs. Such conduct would be absolutely inexcusable and entirely damning. It also appears inherently unlikely.

Captain E.J. Smith Memorial

A committee has been formed for the purpose of arranging for the erection of a suitable memorial to the late Commander Edward John Smith RNR, the Captain of the *Titanic*. It is proposed that it should take the two-fold form of a monument with inset medallion at Lichfield, in the county where he was born, and of a stained glass window and tablet in the new Cathedral at Liverpool. Queen Alexandra has been graciously pleased to express her sympathy and interest in this project. Lord Pirrie is a member of the committee.

(*The Times*, 27 September, 1913, p8)

The stained glass window in the Anglican cathedral in Liverpool features a portrait of St Cuthbert, with biographical details of Smith set out on a scroll beneath. Cuthbert is remembered in part for spending whole nights in prayer, up to his neck in the sea – and for miraculously saving five ships imperilled in a tempest at the mouth of the River Tyne.

The backers of the project evidently saw no irony in Smith's case. He was no redeemer – and if he made the greatest sacrifice, as conventional wisdom would have it, it should be remembered that he also needlessly sacrificed fifteen times one hundred others.

In Fairview Lawn cemetery, where many of the 300-odd recovered bodies lie, one grave marker has itself fallen victim to the glorification of enormous loss. To a twenty-four-year-old fireman named Everett Elliott, 'of the heroic crew, SS *Titanic*,' it displays the following verse:

Each man stood at his post
While all the weaker ones went by
And showed once more to all the world
How Englishmen should die.

Yet most of the people killed by one man's misjudgement have no monument at all – unless it be the permanent reminder that is the shifting slop of the sea.

THE BOARD AND
THE BETRAYED

OFFICIALDOM AND THE STABLE DOOR

Another single individual with moral responsibility for the enormous loss of life on the *Titanic* is one whose name has been all but lost to history. Sydney Buxton was President of the Board of Trade, and is possibly the *Titanic's* supreme survivor. How he managed to avoid political disgrace and the loss of his career over the failure to reform lifeboat provision over twenty years represents one of the great escapes from what passed for parliamentary accountability in early twentieth-century Britain.

What ought to have sealed his fate is the fact that he actively misled the House of Commons, usually a capital offence in politics. Instead Buxton went on to become an earl and the Governor-General of South Africa.

Born in 1853, the Right Honourable Sydney Buxton MP was a venerable fifty-nine by 1912. His career had already been illustrious. He first entered Parliament at the age of thirty, in 1883, a Liberal member for Peterborough. In 1886 he transferred to Poplar, and would occupy the London constituency's seat in the Commons for the next twenty-eight years.

Buxton's first promotion came when he was appointed Under-Secretary for the Colonies. It was reward for an already-demonstrated dexterity in politics – within two years of reaching Westminster, neophyte Buxton had confidently, even cockily, produced a book entitled *A Handbook To Political Questions Of The Day*. It argued the pros and cons of such subjects as Irish Church Disestablishment, Free Schools and whether the illiterate should be allowed to vote. It would go on to enjoy a dozen editions as Buxton developed new themes for changed times, such as the Home Rule question that would come sharply into focus by the time a new liner left Southampton in 1912.

An early photograph of Sydney Buxton, President of the Board of Trade at the time of the sinking. He managed to hang on to his political career, despite the repercussions over the loss of life, and later achieved an earldom. *Author collection.*

By then Buxton had penned a couple more books – including an appreciation of Cardinal Manning, an analysis of finance and politics over the previous century, a pamphlet on the Boer War, a study of Gladstone, and the apparently ill-sitting *Fishing and Shooting.*

It was this latter work that most endeared Buxton to his peers, for in spite of his erudition he was an immensely clubbable man. He forged alliances easily, was liked for his easy manner as well as his intellect, and became admired for the fact that this energetic and rigorous individual could also, apparently, relax.

It is doubtful whether his fishing tips helped him hook the important post of Postmaster General, but his overall reputation certainly did. He headed the Post Office from 1905 to 1910. Wireless telegraphy became one of his portfolios, and he entered into early dispute with the Marconi company over the compulsory acquisition of some coastal stations as the State muscled in on the exciting new medium for reasons of national security.

In 1910, Sydney Buxton became President of the Board of Trade, one of the most important posts in the Cabinet of Prime Minister Herbert Henry Asquith. Indeed, Buxton may still have harboured hopes of one day occupying 10 Downing Street himself.

He had lost none of his drive, although on entering the Board he became preoccupied with protectionism. A Copyright Act in 1911 was the highlight of his tenure before disaster struck in the North Atlantic. Immediately on the thunderclap of the *Titanic* sinking, some chickens began winging their way home to roost. Buxton had ignored reform of the shipping regulations, as had his fellow Presidents of the Board of Trade long before him. All of them had relaxed on the wrong issue, but he was the one left at bay.

Titanic had lifeboats sufficient for only half of those aboard, even though she had been half-empty in the first place. Although 2,208 placed their lives aboard her in April 1912, the new White Star liner had certified permission to embark no fewer than 3,547 passengers and crew. At the same time, her legally-permissible sixteen lifeboats provided accommodation for only 990.

The four additional collapsibles were not required by the Board of Trade. These optional – almost whimsical – extras contributed a theoretical 188 additional places. This brought the total number of lifeboat places on all *Titanic* boats to 1,178 (leaving a notional 2,369 to die in a case of maximum load).

Only 712 were saved as it turned out, while over 1,500 did actually go to their deaths; a survival rate of slightly less than one in three. When this became known, coupled with the fact that the *Titanic* had survived on a calm sea for more than two-and-a-half hours, the outrage became palpable.

Yet the *Titanic* exceeded, in all respects, what was legally required. The law had not been amended for eighteen years, having originally been framed for vessels up to a maximum envisaged displacement of 10,000 tons. The sunken White Star liner was four and a half times bigger.

At House of Commons questions on Thursday, 18 April, one MP hit the nail on the head when he asked: 'Having regard to the rapid growth of vessels between 1894 and 1911, have not the Board of Trade been slow in making regulations for vessels over 10,000 tons?'

Sydney Buxton 'did not reply to the question', the newspapers reported the next day. But its truth was abundantly clear. Buxton ought perhaps to have resigned at this point, even if he had only been carrying political responsibility for two years. The point was that ultimate accountability for the Board's prolonged failure rested with Buxton.

The *Daily Mail* screamed: 'The want of boats was the cause of the fearful tragedy on the *Titanic*, whereby 1,635 persons lost their lives, and the insufficiency of boats must be ascribed to the Board of Trade. No excuses, no special pleading, can get over this grim fact.'

It was in the same House of Commons, in which a defensive Buxton kept parroting that the *Titanic* had more boats than the law required (insensitive to the bereaved, one would think, even if instinctively protective of ship owners), that he strayed into an extreme parsimony with the truth.

Buxton said: 'In view of the increased size of modern passenger vessels, the Board of Trade last year (1911) referred to an advisory committee the question of revision of those rules. After considering this report, the Board was not satisfied the increased [lifeboat] provision recommended by the committee was adequate, and within the past few days referred the matter back to the committee for re-examination.'

The notable phrase is 'within the past few days.' Action to close the stable door came only after the horse had bolted. Yet the report had been with the Board of Trade since July of the previous year – nine months in which it had done nothing.

Buxton also blustered: 'Before this terrible disaster occurred, the Board had been carefully considering the question of the revision of the scale of lifeboat accommodation for large vessels.' But he had misled the House of Commons. He told MPs that the 1911 committee recommendations were 'not adequate'.

Yet, in fact, had they been implemented, it would have been a legal minimum requirement in 1912 that the *Titanic* should carry four more collapsibles or auxiliary boats than she did in fact carry. Although still falling far short of boats for all, another 188 boat places would have been provided for those *in extremis* in the ice of the mid-Atlantic.

And the truth was that it could have been, should have been, done at the stroke of a pen. The 1890 Merchant Shipping Acts allowed such matters to be governed by regulation. Buxton, the responsible minister, could have promulgated the recommended increase by decree, without further legislation. It could have been done in July 1911 as an interim step, while he referred the recommendations back to the committee. He might have pocketed the extra lifeboat accommodation they offered and sent them back to consider doing more.

Buxton's use of the careful phrase 'not adequate' suggested the committee's recommendations would not have made any difference. But the fact is that they would have made that difference of an extra four boats – as was discovered when the report of the committee was quietly printed by the Board of Trade two days later. In fact, the most senior adviser to the Board wanted to go even further, arguing for substantial increases in lifeboat numbers, pro rata, for the larger ships.

The RMS *Titanic* had plenty of deckchairs, but not enough boats. Pictured at Queenstown are second class passengers Elsie and Ada Doling, who nonetheless survived. Their escort, Frederick Wheeler, valet to millionaire Alfred Vanderbilt, did not. *Illustrated London News.*

It is well known that the White Star Line, resisting further lifeboats like other shipping lines and taking every advantage of bulkhead concessions on the argument that the ship would be her own lifeboat, knew that change was coming.

The *Olympic*-class ships were fitted with Welin double-acting davits. It is known that plans were drawn up to provide thirty-two lifeboats for the class of the *Titanic*, which were then shelved when the threat of action by officialdom receded. Papers in the British National Archives show exactly when that was – on 19 April, 1910, the question of requiring inboard boats beside those rigged in the double-acting davits was deferred 'for future consideration' by the Board of Trade.

In another document of 1910, a report submitted to the Engineer Surveyor-in-Chief at the Board of Trade, noted that the new White Star super-liners would have sixteen lifeboats immediately under davits, 'as required by the rules at present'. The internal memo added: 'This seems a very small number for such large ships, and it is for consideration whether it can be regarded as complying with the spirit of the rules.'

Politically, this is close to a smoking gun, particularly in light of what did happen – nothing – when the advisory committee reported a year later in 1911, many months before the *Titanic* sailed. The Board of Trade reply to this expression of concern from within would have been equally politically destructive, had it come out. It took the form of a note, forwarding the file to Sir Alfred Chalmers, the Nautical Adviser to the Board of Trade.

The note was from Alexander Boyle, the Engineering Surveyor-in-Chief. He wrote: 'We need not interfere further in this case [the *Olympic*] and the matter can be further gone into as soon as the proposed new [lifeboats] rule is settled.' He then added, in a more personal comment: 'This should be expedited, and it is not clear what we are waiting for.' Someone in the Board of Trade, higher up than its Engineering Surveyor-in-Chief (who communicated his own views in an aside) decided to capitulate to pressure from White Star. Both their immense new vessels went to sea with a fig-leaf of lifeboats.

Boyle was called to the British Inquiry. His testimony is seen, in light of the eventual opening of all Board of Trade files, as almost dark-comically brief. He was asked perfunctorily about a few issues. He was not asked about his views on lifeboats.

Nautical Adviser Alfred Chalmers took a different view when eventually called to give evidence, long after the initial public anger had subsided. He offered an obtuse argument that more boats would have required the shipping companies to carry more men uselessly across the Atlantic to operate them, who could be put to no other useful purpose. This claim is, of course, absurd. But Chalmers' fundamental attitude was the same one adopted in the immediate wake of the tragedy – that such an incident could not have been foreseen.

Prime Minister Herbert Asquith told the Commons on the day the extent of the North Atlantic tragedy became known that it was, 'one of those terrible events that baffle foresight'. Thus was provided a line of defence for the Establishment from the earliest moment.

In his first House of Commons utterances, Sydney Buxton, President of the Board of Trade, allowed that the disaster 'weighed heavily' with his bailiwick, as it must have done with him personally. In modern times, such a phrase would suggest the honourable member had taken the honourable course – and offered his resignation. But that might have wrong-footed the PM. It was not for a Cabinet colleague to resign and suggest that the accident had not baffled foresight. If offered, Buxton's resignation was refused by Asquith, who was looking to the larger picture of Government and national well-being. They were all in it together.

Internal Board of Trade documents from two years earlier, no less than persistent parliamentary questions since 1908, prove that instead of baffling foresight, the Board of Trade might have known of the possibility of disaster and *should have prepared*.

Buxton claimed to accept 'full responsibility' for what the Board of Trade may have left undone over the years, but he did not give practical effect to that sentiment. He also failed to disclose that four separate reports on lifeboat provision, each recommending that many more escape craft be provided on giant liners, had been received prior to the formation of the latest committee.

One of these reports comprised recommendations by William David Archer, the Principal Surveyor of the Board of Trade, who argued that for a ship of 45,000 tons [as with *Olympic* and *Titanic*, the new behemoths] there should be a minimum number of twenty-four standard lifeboats under davits. Not only this, but Archer urged that such ships should carry twenty-two 'additional boats' [such as rafts or collapsibles] sufficient to hold a total of 2,493 persons.

Here was the principal surveyor of the Board of Trade effectively calling on his boss, Mr Buxton, on February 28, 1911, to provide forty-six lifeboats (more than double the *Titanic*'s eventual number) on ships of 45,000 tons.

The *Titanic*'s complement in April 1912 was 2,200 passengers and crew and Archer's proposal would have provided 2,500 lifeboat spaces.

Of the three other reports, at least one called for lifeboat accommodation sufficient for all certified to be carried, a move which would have provided nearly two places for every one person on the *Titanic* on her maiden voyage.

But the Advisory Committee was asked to begin deliberations anew in April 1911. It came back in July with recommendations that were 'not adequate'. And still Buxton did not move.

This is the key to his personal dilemma. He is fixed with direct moral responsibility throughout. As the Attorney General later told the Mersey commission, if Archer's advice had been followed, 'that would give sufficient for all' on the *Titanic*.

Thus, Buxton's excuse for not implementing the committee recommendations – that they were 'not adequate' – falls far short of the truth. If this was the real reason, then Buxton's failure to make an interim order is all the more deplorable, and by his own standards. He is hoist on his own petard.

Aside from misleading the Commons, he might have resigned for what he patently omitted to do. Buxton had effectively stalled a series of recommendations. His inaction did not benefit the travelling public, even though the Board of Trade was charged with regulating the shipping industry and protecting travellers against unscrupulous operators.

As Horatio Bottomley MP, a long-time lifeboat campaigner (who had almost single-handedly forced referral to the advisory committee in 1911) would declare:

> I shudder at the thought of what must have been the reflections of the victims of this disaster when they looked wistfully and hopelessly for the lifeboats which were not there, and of what they thought of the British legislature, which is responsible for their safety.

The steamship companies and general public had long known the dangers posed by ice, even before a time when the speed of ships on the North Atlantic had been increasing in leaps and bounds.

In February 1911, repeated lifeboat questions by Bottomley and others in the House of Commons had resulted in the decision to appoint the advisory committee. As Lord Mersey succinctly remarked at the later Inquiry: 'Apparently the Board of Trade did not move of its own initiative.'

Referral to a committee is a classic time-wasting ploy. As far back as November 1910, Bottomley had asked a question in the Commons as to whether the President of the Board's attention had been called to the fact that the White Star Line's new super-ship, the *Olympic*, was to be provided with fourteen lifeboats only.

Mr Tennant, the Parliamentary Secretary of the Board, replied on Mr Buxton's behalf: 'I understand that the *Olympic* will be provided with fourteen lifeboats and two ordinary boats of an aggregate capacity of 9,752 cubic ft [sufficient for 975 persons] which is in excess of the requirements of the Statutory Rules.' The inadequate rules.

It is known that Sir Walter Howell, head of the Board of Trade's Marine Department, was opposed to extra lifeboats being made mandatory. He preferred the 'bigger picture' of trading lifeboat law for better superstructure integrity in terms of the provision of increased bulkheads. This was the canonisation of the argument that the ship should be its own lifeboat – and it led to what Lord Mersey would describe as 'bribing' ship owners to improve the watertight attributes of their vessels with a promise that if they did so, they need not provide as many lifeboats.

Nautical Adviser Chalmers held this view 'very strongly', and it happened to suit the steamship lines nicely. It thus became the infallible doctrine of the Board – yet everything then depended on the bulkheads, and the inviolability of watertight doors.

Even if the prevailing orthodoxy was unknowably faulty, however, the Board of Trade still failed to get the White Star Line even to provide the expected quid pro quo.

There is a document in the British National Archives entitled M-28910 (390) describing action taken 'as regards the bulkheads of SS *Olympic*'. On 25 April, 1910, a surveyor sent plans for the new ship to Principal Surveyor Archer, who noted that the collision bulkhead did not go up to D Deck, but terminated lower down, at E Deck. In addition, a forward bulkhead was too near the stem, at only 33ft behind.

Archer wrote in a memo: 'I advised the Board of Trade on 30 April that [it] should inform the builders that the collision bulkhead must be carried to D Deck, and that no part of it should be nearer the stem than 1/20th the vessel's length.'

But Archer had to write another memo on the same lines before his suggestions were made to White Star, who replied that the recommendations would be 'very difficult' to now carry out. Thus, nothing was done.

The toothlessness (or pliability) of the Board of Trade thereby became apparent to the powerful interests of the shipping lobby, if not the public. It all culminated in the *Titanic* sinking that much quicker – and with fewer lifeboats on her topmost decks.

How did Buxton, the great survivor, escape culpability for any of this? It scarcely seems credible, but get away with it he did – because the official Inquiry concluded that it had indeed all 'baffled foresight'.

Lord Mersey, despite his probing of the Board's shortcomings, concluded that the disaster was an Act of God, utterly unforeseeable, but that its recurrence would fix blame for any similar accident in the future. This finding essentially absolved the White Star Line and the Government from fault, much less actionable negligence. Nonetheless the courts would find a year later, in actions brought against the White Star Line, that the *Titanic* had been negligently navigated, despite Mersey's conclusion that she had not. No one, however, sued the Board of Trade.

Who had appointed Mersey to investigate the adequacy of lifesaving provision on British merchant vessels? Why, Sydney Buxton, President of the Board of Trade. Buxton's career may have been saved in the nick of time – by the prompt and deeply ironic action of the main steamship companies to *voluntarily* commit to provide boats for all within two days of the tragedy. His Board's tormentors had just cast him a lifeline. And who can blame him if he held on grimly?

The official British Inquiry, towards its end, summoned Archer, the internal critic of Board of Trade policy. He gave as his view that the *Titanic* had not complied with bulkhead requirements under Rule 12 that provided for lifeboat exemptions. The ship was not 'its own lifeboat' – not even in theory.

But by then the sting had gone out of the threatened political apocalypse. Recommendations would be duly made by the Inquiry, yet more recommendations... and an international conference on the safety of life at sea (SOLAS) in time would help to shore up the impression that the sinking of a ship had indeed evaded all anticipation. It did at least serve as political window-dressing.

In February 1914 Sydney Buxton was appointed Governor-General of South Africa and shipped off to the Cape. He was elevated to the peerage as a viscount two months later. In 1920 he retired, and on his return to the United Kingdom was made an earl. He died in 1934 at the age of 81.

FURTHER, GOOD MYTH, FROM THEE

MUSICIANS, ENGINEERS, AND SURVIVING CREW

'It was so close to us. That is why I rang them up,' said Fred Fleet, the lookout who first spotted the iceberg dead ahead of the *Titanic*. Although he also referred to 'the rate she was going', he was never asked at either Inquiry whether, had the speed been reduced, he would have seen the berg in time for it to have been avoided. Perhaps this was because the answer was readily apparent, it being only a matter of degree.

What he did say was that if he had been issued with binoculars, which he had on the trip from Belfast to Southampton, he could have seen the obstruction 'in time for the ship to get out of the way.' The glasses would have made all the difference between safety and disaster. But they had been borrowed from an officer in the first instance, and the lookouts were told on the maiden voyage proper that none would be provided for them.

Fleet's colleague in the crow's-nest, Reginald Lee, properly pointed out that the ship's speed 'has nothing to do with me. I am not on the bridge. I am a lookout man.' He did however estimate the berg as half a mile away at the time it was seen, adding that it could have been more, or equally, less.

Experiments carried out by the British Inquiry with the *Titanic*'s sister ship, *Olympic*, suggested that it would have taken thirty-seven seconds at 21½ knots for the ship's head to turn two points to port, as it did when the collision occurred on the starboard side of the bow.

This shows the distance to the berg when she was first seen to have been a whisker over a quarter of a mile away. Lee's half-mile in thirty-seven seconds would have had the *Titanic* travelling at double that speed, 42¼ knots, even if his half-mile was only a reference to the shorter, statute (land) mile, instead of the slightly longer nautical mile.

It is a matter of guesswork whether an extra fifteen seconds would have bought the further turn to port that might have avoided the berg. But the remarkable figure — if it is right — is that of thirty-seven seconds, which must represent an astonishingly poor reaction time. Such unwieldiness simply demands that any ice report be regarded with the utmost seriousness. And the *Titanic* had been sent many.

'The captain,' said Chairman of the American Inquiry, William Alden Smith, in his speech to the Senate, was 'strong of limb, intent of purpose, pure in character, dauntless as a sailor should be,' and walked the deck of his majestic structure as Master of her keel:

> Titanic though she was, his indifference to danger was one of the direct and contributing causes of this unnecessary tragedy — while his own willingness to die was the expiating evidence of his fitness to live.
>
> Those who knew him well, not in anger but in sorrow, file one specific charge against him: overconfidence and neglect to heed the oft-repeated warnings of his friends. The mystery of his indifference to danger, when other and less pretentious vessels doubled their lookouts or stopped their engines, finds no reasonable hypothesis in conjecture or speculation.

The British Inquiry verdict on Captain Smith was far more muted. The lookout was not sufficient 'in view of the high speed at which the vessel was running', the report found, and under the circumstances an extra lookout should have been placed at the stem or bows. The speed was deemed excessive, yet not negligent (a potentially highly costly finding, had it been made) — although future excessive speed in the vicinity of ice would be negligent in light of what had happened to Smith.

This gymnastic reasoning, which nonetheless seems to equate to the American Inquiry's finding of overconfidence, was explained in tortured and bizarre logic:

> The question is what ought the Master to have done. I am advised that with the knowledge of the proximity of ice which the Master had, two courses were open to him: The one was to stand well to the southward instead of turning up to a westerly course; the other was to reduce speed materially as night approached. He did neither...
>
> Why, then, did the Master persevere in his course and maintain his speed? The answer is to be found in the evidence. It was shown that for many years past, indeed, for a quarter of a century or more, the practice of liners using this track when in the vicinity of ice at night had been in clear weather to keep the course, to maintain the speed and to trust to a sharp lookout to enable them to avoid the danger. This practice, it was said, had been justified by experience, no casualties having resulted from it.

I accept the evidence as to the practice and to the immunity from casualties which is said to have accompanied it. But the event has proved the practice to be bad. Its root is probably to be found in competition and in the desire of the public for quick passages rather than in the judgment of navigators. But unfortunately experience appeared to justify it. In these circumstances I am not able to blame Captain Smith.

He had not the experience which his own misfortune has afforded to those whom he has left behind, and he was doing only that which other skilled men would have done in the same position...

The evidence shows that he was not trying to make any record passage or indeed any exceptionally quick passage. He was not trying to please anybody, but was exercising his own discretion in the way he thought best. He made a mistake, a very grievous mistake, but one in which, in face of the practice and of past experience, negligence cannot be said to have had any part; and in the absence of negligence it is, in my opinion, impossible to fix Captain Smith with blame.

It is, however, to be hoped that the last has been heard of the practice and that for the future it will be abandoned for what we now know to be more prudent and wiser measures, What was a mistake in the case of the *Titanic* would without doubt be negligence in any similar case in the future.

One can just imagine the motorist on the London Embankment, having had sight of a pedestrian half-a-minute ahead of collision, being told at his subsequent trial by Lord Mersey that while he had made a 'very grievous mistake,' in light of his previous fatality-free driving record, and that of others not before the court, he should go and sin no more...

And so the iceberg brushed the *Titanic*, which drank its fill, and lifeboats were lowered. The official reaction to it all was to strike up the band, beat the drum of heroism, trumpet individual acts of alleged valour – and to point, also, to the playing of the actual band.

The *Titanic* orchestra, we know, played soothing music to calm all fears. But behind this fact, accepted universally as the hallmark of impossible glory, may lie an uncomfortable truth. Because in the early part of the night the playing of such graceful airs must have provided a psychological reassurance to passengers that likely impeded the filling of boats.

It would have therefore been better had the band not been asked to play, but since they did, and since none escaped, they must also be judged as heroes rather than as the victims they also were, even if they may have been the unwitting authors of needless extra fatalities.

'Bandmaster Harley was a man with the highest sort of a sense of duty,' John S. Carr, the cellist of the White Star liner *Celtic* told the *Edmonton Daily Bulletin*:

I don't suppose he waited to be sent for, but after finding how dangerous the situation was he probably called his men together and began playing. I know that he often said music was a bigger weapon for stopping disorder than anything on earth. He knew the value of the weapon he had, and I think he proved his point.

Carr may be putting a brave face on things, as Hartley undoubtedly tried to do on behalf of his employer. But while celebrated for nearly a century for their undoubted gallantry, any rounded assessment of the actions of the band that night should be tempered by the realisation that their playing had subtle effects – which encouraged at least some passengers to choose death instead of life.

The strains of classical music early in proceedings surely conveyed the message that everything was as near normal as could be. Every wafting note spoke sweetly that the emergency was not what it was – an emergency – but instead a temporary inconvenience. The playing of the band ran directly counter to the entreaties of officers and crew that women and children should enter the boats. As such, whoever asked for or instigated the music made a terrible mistake.

Titanic passengers were at first unsure, undecided, hesitant, about the offer being made to them. They were being asked to enter tiny boats, to exchange light for darkness, warmth for cold, and apparent safety for danger. And the music in their ears was all the while speaking seductively to their souls; music that was light; music that was warm.

Second Officer Lightoller, at Lifeboat 6, commented: 'They were not at all eager to get into the boat, anyway, any of them. I had to sing out. Naturally, no one looked on it as serious and they were not in any hurry to go down to the sea in a boat.'

Music probably ought not to have been played by the *Titanic* band that night. Whether hymns were appropriate at the end or not is of little importance when set against the larger question of what the playing signified in the first place. *Titanic* passengers ought not to have been given auditory reassurance that all was well. A sense of unease would have served them far better than a sense of well-being. Unease would have helped to fill lifeboats.

It is important to stress that the 'music effect' was at first relatively minor. But if one person in a hundred was irrevocably influenced a particular way in their answer to the overwhelming question – Should I stay, or should I go? – then the band certainly cost lives.

The musicians, booked aboard as second class passengers and provided by the agency of C.W. and F.N. Black, literally set the tone at first. They began playing indoors, in the first class areas, as people assembled. At this point the band was only killing time – because the passengers were not yet wanted outside, as the boats had yet to be uncovered and cleared away.

When the evacuation was ready to proceed however, the band should have stopped playing. Putting away their instruments would have acted as a potent visual signal. The time for relaxation and detachment was already over by a short time after midnight.

But instead the band kept playing. No-one ever told them to stop. And in the absence of any form of public address system aboard the vessel, the music continued to transmit blithe reassurance – even as the unseen wireless was flashing silent and desperate appeals for assistance.

Vital time was thus wasted trying to fill early boats. Passengers were asked to enter, but the music was asking them to tarry, just as it persuaded them on other nights of the voyage to wait a while after dinner, to listen and luxuriate, rather than retire to their staterooms.

Had the early boats filled more quickly, with passengers stepping forward in the icy grip of silence, then precious minutes would have been made available later in the night when it was most needed. Heroism is all very fine, but in this case it didn't fill boats.

Joseph Conrad wrote in the *English Review* in July 1912:

I, who am not a sentimentalist, think it would have been finer if the band of the *Titanic* had been quietly saved, instead of being drowned while playing – whatever tune they were playing, the poor devils. I would rather they had been saved to support their families than to see their families supported by the magnificent generosity of the subscribers.

Passenger and author Archibald Gracie said the band continued to play 'while the boats were being lowered,' adding that he and others considered this,'a wise provision, tending to allay excitement'. Here he misses the point of the influence of music among the undecided at the very margins of decision-making. When the invitations to first enter the boats were being made, there was no tell-tale list and little discernible forward tilt. The ship seemed steady as a rock, the night magnificently clear.

In such circumstances it was easy to trust in the certainties of rescue, with only seventy-three passenger lives lost on the North Atlantic in the ten years to 1901, and fewer still in the ten years thereafter. Perhaps they heard that other vessels were already responding to the distress calls, or remembered the emphasis on safety and security in White Star advertising.

'Don't you hear the music playing?' asked passenger Arthur Ryerson of his wife, as probably others did the same. The whiff of fear was banished by the 'cheerful tunes' described by Gracie. The music was thus nothing more than soporific. It sapped, instead of strengthened, the will to take action.

The playing of the band emphatically did not save lives, as was claimed in further frothing of press sentiment when the body of bandleader and violinist Wallace Hartley was recovered. Instead it had cost lives and exacted further human sacrifice.

Nowadays we hear of the *Titanic* band only in the context of the hymns, sacred strains that some doubt they played at all. Gracie says that if such had been the case, he would have regarded it as a 'tactless warning of immediate death to us all'.

The corollary is that the cheerful tunes were the very opposite – what might be termed, 'tactless promises of swift and amusing cancellation of the problem'. Yet the problem did not go away, but grew steadily worse.

That the 'band played on' is regrettable, not another heroic aspect of the affair. If Wallace Hartley and the others *at the very death* wrote for themselves a page of ineluctable honour, then they were surely achieving a triumph of the human spirit over what they may have realised had been colossal miscalculation to begin with.

At least they were now deciding for themselves, if they did play when all boats were gone and death very near, whereas in the crucial early stages they had answered to their paymasters. That independence of action might symbolically have undone a little of what their earlier playing actually did do – which was to interfere in deadly manner with the independence of action of others. Just as Smith had done with his: 'call me if it becomes at all doubtful.'

How foolish it was to play music! How sad that it helped to encourage jibes at those who did enter the boats – 'You'll miss breakfast!' 'You'll need a pass to get back in the morning!' 'We'll see you in New York' – such that those who risked entering them also risked being ridiculed later. 'How innocent you were, my dear. Danger, indeed! Why, we had a lovely time here all night, listening to the orchestra.'

The risk was in staying, not in going, yet it was made psychologically more difficult for passengers to enter an early lifeboat by a shipping line that compounded reckless navigation with misplaced complacency.

Someone was needed who could have assessed clearly the importance of example when it came to the band. If only someone in authority could have seen also that the band was talismanic of the true situation… and persuaded them not only to cease playing, but to be seen trooping to a lifeboat…

The effect might have been powerful indeed. Sending away the reassurance would have sobered up the jokers. The band was indeed emblematic of the *Titanic* that night and could be seen as a key asset that was badly used. An opportunity was thereby missed and a 'glorious' failure followed.

The mistake was too subtle to be appreciated at the time – or even afterwards. It is only with modern understanding of music-induced psychology that the outlines of the error can begin to be seen.

Enough, then, of *Nearer my God to Thee* – especially since, closer to home and the hearts of those musicians, filthy lucre was having its say:

TITANIC MUSICIANS

Sir – In justice to all concerned, we shall be grateful if you would kindly give publicity to the following:-

These men were insured with the Legal Insurance Company Ltd, who took steps to ascertain the dependents, and in two cases where dependency was evident settlements were immediately made.

They were compelled to repudiate certain claims on the grounds of 'doubtful dependency,' and matters were delayed in consequence.

Although the court held that no legal liability held at all, the company have generously made *ex gratia* payments to the amount of nearly £700. [£100 per man]

In addition to the above, £1,555 has been distributed from a fund organised by ourselves for the benefit of the relatives, and to our knowledge they have further benefited by a sum of over £1,200 raised by concerts and from other charitable sources, making an approximate total of £3,450.

We are further in a position to state that their needs will be still further sympathetically considered by the distributors of the National Fund.

We wish to give publicity to these facts to refute the suggestion in various papers that the dependents of these brave men have been in any way badly treated.

Yours faithfully,

C.W. & F.N. Black,
Music Directors to the White Star Line

(*Cork Examiner*, 23 December, 1912, p8)

The company also wrote to the family of the dead violinist John 'Jock' Hume, in Dumfries, demanding settlement of an amount outstanding on his purchase of a uniform in which to perform.

But over 30,000 people did attend the funeral of bandmaster Hartley in Colne, Lancashire, after his floating body was recovered. And his grave would be duly marked, in the heroic style, with a proud bust of his likeness.

Other supposed heroes were the engineers. The last lie of *Titanic's* extensive mythology is that the engineers died down below in the belly of the ship. That they fought to give the opportunity of life to others until walls of water overcame them.

Propelling the *Titanic*: 'That not one [engineer] was saved is a tribute to the devotion and heroism of those buried deep in the engine room of the mighty vessel', said the *Daily Sketch*. Memorials still claim they all died incarcerated in the bowels of the ship, but Officer Lightoller admitted in his 1935 memoirs that the engineers evacuated to the open deck. Photo shows Harland & Wolff workers.

They didn't. The engineers made it topside like everyone else, able to throw their eyes to a starlit heaven in hope of deliverance instead of death. Then they waited for a seeming eternity – and eternity is what they entered. Not one survived.

It is startling how material and corroborated evidence about the near-total escape of the *Titanic* engineers – save for the unfortunate Jonathan Shepherd (who broke his leg in a boiler room manhole and could not be taken up an escape ladder) – was rigidly ignored in order to foster the blatant untruth that this class all died in the greasy canyons of the engine entrails.

The British establishment and public entered into a pact of self-deception about the engineers, preferring delusion to plain attested facts. In East Park, Southampton, the inscription on their special monument says the engineer officers of the *Titanic*, 'showed their high conception of duty and heroism by remaining at their posts'.

A brass tablet in the London entrance hall of the engineers' professional association announces that their members on the *Titanic*, 'gave their lives at the post of duty when the vessel sank'. And there is an eternal flame obelisk to the engineers in Liverpool which further conveys the impression that they remained to the last, keeping to the stokehold caverns until swallowed in the final plunge.

As late as 1992, the Institute of Marine Engineers' Guild of Benevolence produced an 80th Anniversary brochure entitled '*A Tribute to the Engineering Staff*', in which the chairman wrote that it was an 'undeniable fact' that the engineers were 'still at work in the depths of the ship, keeping the ship's lights ablaze until three minutes of the vessel sinking.'

None of this is true. The chairman was spouting the same 'undeniable' hogwash that first gushed forth in 1912. If the engineers all died at their posts, how is it that newspapers reported in the wake of the *Titanic* crew's return on the *Lapland* that Joseph Bell, the chief engineer no less, had been implored by some mates to climb onto a raft, replying: 'No, my extra weight would sink it.' Why wasn't he entombed fathoms deep with the rest of his noble lads?

The engineers of the *Titanic* undoubtedly did their full duty and more. Their selfless courage in toiling steadily below as the ship was taking huge amounts of water is not in question. But words have lost all their meaning if the claims of men 'dying at their posts' are intended to be interpreted as some form of metaphysical reality after they had given up the unequal fight and gone above.

Second Officer Charles Lightoller, the senior surviving officer, did much to foster the myth of the altruistic engineers, telling the American Inquiry [p. 90]:

Lightoller: All the engineers and other men and many of the firemen were down
  below and never came on deck at all.
Senator Smith: They never came on deck?
Lightoller: No, Sir; they were never seen.

But this same Lightoller, in his 1935 autobiography (Titanic *and Other Ships*) admitted the truth as he directly knew it while standing on the Boat Deck:

About this time [about 1.50 a.m.] I met all the engineers, as they came trooping up.
  Most of them I knew individually... much earlier on, the engine-room telegraphs
  had been 'rung off'... which conveys to the engine room staff the final information
  that their services below can be of no further use...

This revelation of *all* the engineers gaining the outside deck would come nearly a quarter of a century into the future, demonstrating in passing how Lightoller was prepared to perjure himself in 1912 in order to paint the servants of the White Star Line in a favourable light.

The British Inquiry at that time, while eulogising the engineers, bemoaned the fact that none survived for the valuable evidence they might have furnished. They thus overlooked fireman Thomas Dillon, who was a *virtual* engineer because he was seconded to the engine room under engineering direction. Dillon said the personnel in the engine room eventually got the order: '<u>All hands</u> on deck; put your life preservers on.' This order came at a quarter past one, he said – an hour before the sinking.

Dillon makes it clear (Q. 3902) that the engineers came aft 'in a bunch' from the boiler rooms (located forward of the engine room) where they had been fighting the influx.

The implied fate of the bunch, from Dillon's testimony, is that they evacuated, made it up onto the poop deck with him, and waited 'about fifty minutes' for the ship to go down. So much for remaining at their posts in romantic tradition.

On his own, Dillon might be dismissed. But his story is almost exactly paralleled by another who was down below until the suspension of operations. Greaser Fred Scott told an even more explicit story about the fate of the engineers:

Q. 5640: Did you get an order to go up on deck?
Scott: Yes, the engineer came down and told everybody to go out of the engine room... I think it was one of the senior engineers.
Q. 5645: Then did you go on deck?
Scott: Yes, up the working alleyway. [dubbed 'Scotland Road', on E Deck]

So far Scott agrees with Dillon, who had also been in the engine room. Scott told how those who now evacuated had to scour for lifebelts (Dillon: 'put your life preservers on'), and the very act of scavenging for buoyancy aids shows that no-one at all was intent on dying at their posts.

'We got them (lifebelts) at the Third Class,' said Scott at Q. 5647. He was refer-ring to a storeroom all the way aft on E Deck, reached after the men had climbed to the main crew passageway from below. 'From there we went up on the Boat Deck,' he added, citing the aft third class stairs.

Lest anyone should choose to interpret Scott's 'we' as conceivably referring only to greasers or firemen (as Scott and Dillon were, respectively), Scott helpfully spelt out who was near him on the Boat Deck in response to Q. 5685: 'All the engineers and firemen and all that.'

'All the engineers?' gasped the Attorney General, Sir Rufus Isaacs. It was Sir Rufus himself who had told Commissioner Lord Mersey only the day before (May 9) during the evidence of George Cavell: 'All the engineers were drowned. They all remained at the bottom of the vessel.'

Now Scott was apparently saying that the engineers did not remain at the bottom of the vessel to fulfil the hallowed role ascribed to them by the press, by virtue of their mass decease. One can imagine the question hanging in the air:

'All the engineers on the Boat Deck?'

'Yes', declared Fred Scott.

'Do you mean the officers?' persisted the Attorney General.

'Yes, the engineers that were on watch', replied Scott.

'Then, if I understand it aright' (Q. 5688), said the Attorney General, holding out a last hope that such was not the case, 'all the engineers had come up too?'

This was Scott's last chance. Many an eye must have swung in his direction and locked onto his face.

'They were all at the top', Scott insisted, in front of the most senior legal adviser to the British Government, the bench, journalists, and disappointed all.

'Did they come up when you came up?'

'Just afterwards, but some of them went up on the Boat Deck with me. They came up the ladder just behind me.'

These men, having secured their lifebelts aft, had climbed the third class stairs from E Deck onto the open steerage well deck at the stern of the *Titanic*. Evidently 'some of them' went from there up onto the Boat Deck with Scott – via the ladder leading to second class, as he says.

Q. 5690: When you say they were standing there, where were they standing?

Just against the electric crane aft.

Q. 5692: On the Boat Deck?

On the Boat Deck.

Q. 5693: That is the last you saw of them?

That is the last I saw of them.

None of these responses was satisfactory for anyone seeking to find another gleam of sacrifice to redeem a hopelessly futile marine casualty, an accident whose sheer fatuousness was also marked out by massive loss of life. The Attorney General retired hurt, but Mr Roche entered the fray for the Marine Officers' Association, apparently intent on throwing those engineers back down again:

Q. 5706: I want you to tell me with regard to the engineers you saw on the deck, when did they come up?

They came up just after I did.

Q. 5707: How long was that?

It was twenty minutes past one when I left the engine room. [Agrees broadly with Dillon's 1.15 a.m.]

Mr Roche was still not happy. But now he thought he could call Scott's bluff:

Q. 5710: Which of the engineers did you see? Can you tell me their names?

Mr Farquharson. I do not know the names of the others.

It is important to stop here to dwell on the importance of this answer. Not only was Scott supplying the surname of an engineer, but one who happened to be second in rank only to Chief Engineer Joseph Bell. Farquharson was the Number Two. He could not have been a runaway. His presence on the Boat Deck, along with the best available references to Bell at the sinking, shows that the senior command had led an evacuation *en masse* of the engineers.

None stayed back. Because there was nothing to stay back for. The battle for Boiler Room 4 (close to the tipping point for the *Titanic*'s stability) could not be won, it had obviously, eventually, been decided. And so the battleground had been rightly abandoned.

Farquharson's presence on the Boat Deck chimes with Scott's earlier utterance that a *senior* engineer had entered the engine room to order all hands up top. At 1.20 a.m.

Roche, meanwhile, for the Marine Officers' Association, wanted to dent Scott's testimony as much as he could:

Q. 5711: How many of them did you see?

I should say there were about eight of them [who made the highest deck via the ladder from the well deck.]

Q. 5712: There are 20 or more in the ship?

Yes.

Q. 5713: You think you saw eight, of whom you can remember the name of one?

Yes.

Q. 5723: Did you get any summons to go on deck, or did you go on your own account?

No, we were ordered up out of the engine room.

Q. 5724: Who by?

The Senior Engineer, I think it was.

Q. 5725: Who was in charge of your section, the turbine room?

One of the juniors I think it was, about the sixth. [William McReynolds]

Q. 5726: What is his name; do you know?

No.

Q. 5727: Do you know the name of the engineer who ordered you out?

I think it was Mr Farquharson.

Q. 5728: The gentleman you did see on deck afterwards?

Yes.

Q. 5429/30: And were the other engineers you saw on deck those belonging to your section, the turbine room?

Yes.

There is something odd about counsel for the engineers seeking to drown as many of his members down below as possible. But Roche could get little change out of Scott, who said he eventually got to the Boat Deck about 1.40 a.m. He then climbed out over No. 16 Davit when a lifeboat drifted close, plunged into the water nearby, and was pulled in.

Scott helped to save his own life by being proactive, but Dillon went down with the ship on the poop deck, presumably with a large body of the remaining engineers. Dillon could have chosen to go to the Boat Deck. He appears not to have done so because a departing boat on the port side cried out that it was the last one, and that any more women should get in quickly.

Dillon and others then 'chased' two women from the well deck up the ladders in answer to the boat's appeal, by his own account. For most of the engineers in the well deck there would thus have been no point in going to the Boat Deck, as they believed the last boat was leaving with all available women. Dillon said: 'We stopped where we were. It was no use us going there.'

Dillon was most fortunate to later regain consciousness in a lifeboat – under two others plucked from the sea. Both Dillon and Scott cheated the odds, just as the random odds cheated every single engineer of his life. But Dillon and Scott, remarkably, were in the engine room as non-engineers, and survived. They knew and told the truth as to what the engineers did. The fact that engineer bodies, clad in blue overalls, were later recovered by search ships was further eloquent evidence that they had made it to topside.

But the truth was not wanted. A varnished version was being created in an extraordinary pooling of interests, to which many lent their assent, even if unconsciously.

The reasons flimsily adduced in the press for engineers 'dying at their posts' amounted to only two – the need to either 'keep the pumps providing every inch of draught', or to ensure they 'kept the lights blazing 'til the last'.

The engineers did have 'all hands to the pump' in the crucial battle for Boiler Room 4, a fascinating struggle about which there is only circumstantial evidence.

But there swiftly came a point at which pumping would simply not have any effect, and neither could it be carried out in safety, or even at all. Edward Wilding, naval architect to Harland & Wolff, gave evidence to this point (Q. 20373): 'If the damage existed in No. 4, it was only a question of delaying it perhaps an hour. The evidence is that it rose in spite of their pumping… I have no doubt that the engineers in No. 4 were doing their best.'

Pumping was a strategy that failed early. There was nothing to be gained by persisting in pumping, particularly when the flooding had already gained the advantage. That fulcrum was Boiler Room 5, the one ahead of No. 4, since they counted backwards from the bows.

As to lights, engineers were simply not needed down below at all times to maintain electric illumination for those above. Engineers ran the engines, although a small proportion of their number were electricians. The ship's lighting circuit worked off a generator, which did not require any direct input by engineers. If the main supply should fail, the electricity needed to maintain lights was provided by the immediate start-up of a stand-by battery. This secondary source of power was introduced by means of an automatic switch in the circuit. No human hands were involved.

The generator was aft in the ship and late to be immersed. The lights flashed off – and then came back on again – when the stern was in the process of upending. This is widely testified, and is evidence of the stand-by battery coming automatically into effect. The remaining engineers were topside at the time.

The engineers did not keep the lights 'blazing 'til the last' because the state-of-the-art lighting system meant they were largely out of the equation. The mythmakers are thus robbed of any credible reason for all the engineers to remain at their posts. In effect, those 'posts' vanished relatively early in the night.

Lord Mersey avoided all reference to the engineers in his final report of the British Inquiry, in what may have been a clever move. He left the public to their rose-tinted glasses and sentimental inscriptions.

But marine engineers are not romantics. They are practical men in the most practical of trades. Chief Engineer Joseph Bell had a wife and four children; his deputy, William Farquharson, a wife and three children. The only reason they were in the tough old way of the sea was to make a living and to live, so that their children might be clad.

Their duty, after it was paid in full to the ship, was to their families. So big men put on their lifebelts and went up top. Their discipline was born of a very flinty realism, and they did not abandon their higher calling.

They owed no duty of drowning to the penny press, but their funeral bower was nonetheless a confection of posies and paeans, founded on ignorance. The syrup that has oozed ever since is a grave disservice to men who knew valour, but knew it honestly, in its workaday clothes.

The engineers, other crew and the steerage waited in the after well deck as the ship pitched ever more steeply in its ghastly throes. As far as they could see, the lifeboat falls hung limply and empty, straggling ropes that signified a minority had made good their escape.

It is a curiosity of this disaster, however, that the press coverage in Britain (rather than in America) seemed to transform the fundamental question as to why the *Titanic* had been so undersupplied with lifeboats into another question entirely – that is, why individual lifeboats had not gone back to the scene of the sinking in order to rescue more people.

The British Inquiry seemed to take fiendish delight in putting such questions to the harrowed and now harassed survivors. Virtually no passengers were called as witnesses, but the issue was exhaustively examined with lowly crew, who offered a variety of explanations and justifications.

It was as if a court martial into a military offensive that resulted in disastrous slaughter had confined itself to asking why individual soldiers who returned to the lines had not brought more wounded comrades with them. The idea that appalling fault might lie with those further up the chain of command who had caused the entire affair was somehow overlooked.

Newspapers will always gladly accept a 'thrilling' eyewitness account, while bureaucracy is almost by definition faceless; human interest comes down to the exploits or suffering of individual humans, which is part of the broad public's preference for encapsulations, easy answers and even distortion, if the latter should prove more palatable than reality.

Why this happens, or how precisely it happens, is beyond the scope of this work, but the fact remains that certain subtle tones – whether understood or recognised, consciously prompted or not – tended to guide whole currents of thought in relation to the aftermath of the *Titanic* sinking.

If there was a popular mood, channelled by whomever, it was quickly to the effect that Britain had not erred by sending a vessel to sea with lifeboats that would only save one-third of those aboard a relatively under-booked new vessel. Instead the majesty of individual conduct that night had demonstrated, on the contrary, the superiority of British discipline and order, while the dead had ennobled the entire race.

It could not be that the greater number had let down the few. The individual was duty-bound to uphold the ideals of Empire. Great Britain, inseparable from her people, was still great and in every way undiminished by what had happened. Britannia ruled the waves, and it was unpatriotic, churlish and plain wrong to suggest she ruled them clumsily, with idiocy, in blood.

The alleged selfishness or cowardice of individuals, as with heroes, is then seized upon for the reassurance, if not the distraction, of the country as a whole – the only constituency that matters. A few villains identified at low level, properly decried, shows that the corrosiveness of misdeeds can never, will never, be allowed to climb higher. Standards are rigidly enforced at the local eruption. It is therefore inconceivable that treachery and venality might already reside at the heart of the system.

MADNESS TO GO BACK
To the Editor of *The Times*

Sir – There have been so many opinions expressed as to whether the boats of the *Titanic* should have gone back when the vessel went down that it is interesting reading the evidence of two of the officers stating that it would have been madness to go back.

There is no doubt they were correct. I am one of those who actually saw the sinking of the *Grosser Kurfürst* in 1878 [Sunk with the loss of 269 lives after a collision with her fellow German naval vessel, the *Konig Wilhelm*], and I actually saw boats that were filled with disciplined German sailors pulled down by those struggling in the water. One large ship's cutter, with the crew pulling away, was pulled down.

It will be remembered that the *Grosser Kurfürst* floated for some time and then suddenly gave a dive and went to the bottom, an explosion taking place at the same time. Having seen this it would appear that if the *Titanic* boats had gone back they would have gone to the bottom also.

Your obedient servant,

G. Bruce Lambert
Carlton Club, Pall Mall, 23 May.

(*The Times*, 24 May, 1912, p54)

'After she went down we heard them calling,' steward William Ward, saved in Lifeboat 9, told the American Inquiry. 'Our boat was too full. It would have been madness to have gone back.' There was a 'swarm' of people in the water where the boat had gone down. Over-enthusiasm in the rescue attempt, or simply accidentally rowing into the crowd, could have been fatal. It was also, important to note, pitch dark – there could be no picking and choosing among swimmers. The night indeed held many terrors.

Many boats justified their staying off from the ship, even though they were not full, on the basis that they would have been prey to the forces of suction if they had returned to the settling leviathan's side. In fact there was very little suction, and the whole vortex argument evaporated as soon as the ship went down. Still they stood off – paralysed by the prospect of the grip of a drowning man multiplied many times.

Is this cowardice? Hardly, since the passivity and covering of ears, while unedifying, at least guaranteed the saving of those lives already in the boat. Were they to be visited with guilt for surviving, simply because so many died? What understanding did those who sat in judgement have when they implied a responsibility for the super-filling of lifeboats among those already evacuated, rather than focus on those who ought to have provided more lifeboats in the first place?

Odder still was the sudden alteration in outlook for the officers. Whereas the whiff of cordite had been aromatic, even heady, to the newspapers when reporting lurid tales of swarthy steerage passengers being shot down by men in ship's uniform in the immediate aftermath of the tragedy, by the time the Inquiries came around the suggestion was being aired that those same officers who had spattered bullets about ought really to have returned to the wreck – in order to admit as many of their original targets as the boats could possibly hold.

Officers Lightoller and Lowe admitted firing shots, but only into the air, to impose discipline. Lowe said he fired shots, and had also heard them fired elsewhere. Yet Lightoller made an adjustment in his evidence, to suggest he had only ever been brandishing an empty gun. Shots were also ascribed to First Officer Murdoch and others who were lost, while, as we have seen, some even put a gun in the captain's hand.

Lightoller was not in a position to go back after the sinking, being spreadeagled on an overturned, drifting collapsible with others who clambered aboard the sanctuary. Lowe, to his immense credit, did go back – but only when the 'people had thinned out' and he could deal with one exhausted person at a time.

His waiting, with an empty lifeboat, having distributed his passengers into a flotilla of boats that he had organised, may seem callous. But he told the British Inquiry that it would have been 'suicide' to go back until death had reaped a wide harvest.

Heroism should not mean stupidity, after all. And it was a lack of warranted caution, if not recklessness, that had brought them to this pass in the first place. Losing first ship and then lifeboat to a double-dose of impulsiveness would just have compounded catastrophe with calamity. Although Officer Lowe might have been granted a statue.

Yet he still suffered the indignity, after his practicality (he picked up four men from the water, one of whom died), of imputations that he had waited too long for the thinning out, that it was blameworthy, and that had he gone back earlier 'it would have been impossible for these people who were floating about to have swamped your boat, because you could have detached them'.

Steerage passenger Thomas McCormack, from Co. Longford, Ireland, who, together with Bernard McCoy insisted he was severely beaten in an attampt to prevent his boarding a lifeboat from the water. McCormack went on to serve in the Great War and ran a bar in New Jersey until shortly before his death, aged eighty-two, in 1975. See also p193. *Irish Independent.*

How could you detach them? Lowe neatly asked, turning the dilemma on counsel. Both, of course, knew about stories of 'detachment' of individuals, and it had even been raised – unsuccessfully – towards the beginning of the British Inquiry:

J.P. Farrell MP (for a number of Irish third class passengers):

Thomas McCormack alleges that when swimming in the sea he endeavoured to board two boats and was struck on the head and the hands and shoved back into the sea, and endeavoured to be drowned. That is one charge.

Commissioner Mersey: That gentleman who did it may be guilty of manslaughter for aught I know.

Farrell: McCormack was not drowned, my Lord.

The Commissioner: Very well, then he may be guilty of an attempt to commit manslaughter, but I cannot try that.

Farrell: Is it not a question for investigation by this Court?

The Commissioner: I do not think so.

It would surely be unfair if the sole officer to go to the rescue after the sinking (a few boats pulled in stray swimmers while the *Titanic* was still afloat) should be faced with manslaughter charges if his efforts were to get into difficulties – yet he was also being encouraged to just that resort if he would otherwise use it as an excuse for waiting!

This nasty doublethink indicates how survivors could only ever win grudging respect. Those in charge of lifeboats, whether officer, quartermaster or steward, were allocated a kind of accountability for their remaining partially empty – when they had been lowered that way in the first place, largely out of the ignorant assumption that the boats would buckle up and break in the falls if loaded full. In fact each standard lifeboat could take sixty-five occupants, yet the average comple-ment of those reaching the *Carpathia* was only thirty-nine-and-a-half persons.

The twenty boats launched saved 712 souls, including a handful of swimmers. Eighteen lifeboats reached the rescue vessel, with two collapsibles (of smaller capacity to standard lifeboats) abandoned after their survivors were taken aboard other boats in the later morning.

An artist's impression of the eventual rescue of the survivors by the Cunard liner *Carpathia*. But this sketch also neatly demonstrates how the *Titanic's* lifeboats were intended to be further loaded once in the water. The escape craft drew off and ignored impassioned calls to return. Both images from *The Graphic*.

Captain Smith apparently had the half-formed idea of filling up the boats from gangway doors at the lower decks. But one party sent down to open the gangways disappeared completely, although it seems at least one door was opened. Smith is reported to have called lifeboats back by megaphone, but they failed to respond. A gangway door stands open on the wreck today.

CALIFORNIAN

A GLEAM IN THE
NIGHT

AND OTHER ONES ELSEWHERE

One of the excuses or justifications used for not returning to the wreck site was the requirement to 'follow the captain's orders'. This meant a particular instruction given to a couple of lifeboats, mainly on the port side, before they were lowered. They were to pull for a light in the distance.

A light! A ship!

Alfred Crawford, a bedroom steward, had been put in charge of Lifeboat 8, launched from the port side at an early stage. He said he was ordered by Captain Smith to use his oars to row to the nearby vessel, estimated at only 5 miles away, in a direction two points off the port bow.

'During the pull across, one sailor offered to return to the ship, but all the ladies said: "Why not obey the captain's orders?"' Crawford related to the British Inquiry. They called out: 'Obey the captain's orders!' – rather than have the lifeboat turn back in the direction of cries of anguish.

Thomas Jones, in the same boat, said he wanted to return to the ship, 'but the ladies were frightened, and [said] I had to carry out the captain's orders and pull for that light, so I did so. I pulled for about two hours, and then it started to get daybreak, and we lost the light.'

Similar reminders about the captain's orders were made in Lifeboat 6, and possibly others. It is unlikely that any of the occupants seriously believed that the greater good would be served by reaching the ship some miles away and returning with her to assist those in the water. They must have known instinctively that most of those left screaming after the *Titanic* went down would be dead within minutes.

But those were indeed the orders – 'Make for those lights. Put your passengers on board that ship with those lights and then come back here.' (Q. 17965 to Crawford). The occupants of Lifeboat 8 got them directly from the captain, and those in Lifeboat 6, alongside, were handed identical instructions, on the captain's behalf, by Second Officer Lightoller.

There was doubtless a ship within 5 miles of the sinking *Titanic*. This staggering truth, when it finally emerged in evidence, caused a profound sensation.

The first description of a potential saviour standing so close came from Fourth Officer Joseph Boxhall, the man tasked by Captain Smith with watching the nearby vessel and attracting her attention. His bombshell revelations about a tantalising sanctuary for passengers and crew alike came early in the American Inquiry, on Monday 22 April, 1912.

The twenty-eight-year-old officer, with no less than thirteen years experience at sea, remarked matter-of-factly: 'I was around the bridge most of the time, sending off distress signals and endeavouring to signal to a ship that was ahead of us.'

The first time he said it, the assembled Senators missed it. So he repeated it a few minutes later: 'My attention until the time I left the ship was mostly taken up with firing off distress rockets and trying to signal a steamer that was almost ahead of us.' This time the Chairman of the American Inquiry, Senator William Alden Smith, sat up and took immediate notice:

Smith: How far ahead of you?
Boxhall: It is hard to say. I saw his masthead lights and I saw his side light.
In what direction?
Almost ahead of us.
On the same course, apparently?
No; oh, no. [*Titanic* had been steaming west]
On the same general course?
By the way she was heading she seemed to be meeting us.
Coming toward you?
Coming toward us.
Do you know anything about what boat that was?
No, sir.
Have you had any information since about it?
None whatever.
You say you fired these rockets and otherwise attempted to signal her?
Yes, sir. She got close enough, as I thought, to read our electric Morse signal, and I
     signalled to her; I told her to come at once, we were sinking; and the captain was

standing... I told the captain about this ship, and he was with me most of the time when we were signalling.

Did he also see it?

Yes, sir.

Did he tell you to do anything else to arrest its attention?

I went over and started the Morse signal. He said: 'Tell him to come at once, we are sinking'.

You were sinking already, you say?

Yes, sir.

Come at once, we are sinking?

Yes... It was sent in the Morse key, the Morse code.

And you did that?

Yes, sir.

And did you get any reply?

I cannot say I saw any reply. Some people say she replied to our rockets and our signals, but I did not see them.

Was any attempt made to get in wireless communication after you saw this boat, what you took to be a boat?

I do not know what was transpiring in the wireless room.

These signals you utilised were Morse signals?

Yes.

Are they recognised as standard for the sea?

Oh, yes.

Did you see any signals from this ship at all?

No, I cannot say that I saw any signals, except her ordinary steaming light. Some people say they saw signals, but I could not...

From what you saw of that vessel, how far would you think she was from the *Titanic*?

I should say approximately the ship would be about 5 miles.

What lights did you see?

The two masthead lights and the red light.

Were the two masthead lights the first lights that you could see?

The first lights.

And what other lights?

And then, as she got closer, she showed her side light, her red light.

So you were quite sure she was coming in your direction?

Quite sure.

How long was this before the boat sank?

It is hard to tell. I had no idea of the time then; I do not know what time it was then.

Can you recall about how long it was after the collision?

No.

Was this information communicated to the wireless operators?

Not to my knowledge.

Did you know that they had sent out a distress signal?

Oh, yes.

And you would expect that this boat would pick it up if they had a wireless on it?

If she had a wireless installation.

You busied yourself with the Morse signals?

Yes, sir... I would signal with the Morse and then go ahead and send off a rocket, and then go back and have a look at the ship, until I was finally sent away.

The newspapers were full of the 'Mystery Ship' the next day. She had been coming towards the *Titanic*, but had not arrived – instead the lifeboats were picked up by a vessel that had received the SOS and turned around when almost 50 miles away, not five.

Alfred Crawford in Lifeboat 8 stated that he was a mile and a half from the *Titanic* when she went down. He said his complement pulled for over two hours towards the mystery ship. They made no headway, and she 'disappeared' – whereas they had substantially cut the initial distance between the two ships. The vessel that had offered so much hope had moved off.

Fourth Officer Boxhall confirmed the crushing departure in his evidence before the Senators:

Boxhall: I am covering the whole thing by saying the ship was meeting us.

Senator Theodore Burton: Your impression is she turned away, or turned on a different course?

Boxhall: That is my impression.

Burton: At a later time, when you were in the boat after it had been lowered, what light did you see?

Boxhall: I saw this single light, which I took to be her stern light, just before I went away in the boat, as near as I can say.

The stern light was obviously showing that the vessel had turned through 180 degrees and was facing back the way she had come. She was departing the scene. Earlier both Boxhall and Crawford (and by extension, Captain Smith) had seen the red and green sidelights of a steamer approaching head-on. Crawford said he saw the red light (on the port side) and the green light (starboard) 'very distinctly'. These sidelights were baffled, or blinkered, meaning they were shaded off from showing behind – they could only be seen head-on, or separately side-on.

Second Officer Lightoller admitted to the British Inquiry that he had been calling the attention of many of the passengers to the approaching steamer, 'pointing it out to them and saying there was a ship over there, that probably it was a sailing ship'. He added (Q. 14138): 'I was perfectly sure it was a light attached to a vessel, whether a steamship or a sailing ship I could not say.'

Third Officer Herbert Pitman, sent away in Lifeboat 5, confirmed Boxhall's later analysis. He saw a white light from the water, 'which I took to be the stern light of a sailing ship'.

The much-maligned Quartermaster Hichens, in Lifeboat 6, said: 'We expected it to be a steamer from the ship, but when I got into the [life]boat and could not get nearer to it, and being calm weather, then we expected it to be a fishing boat, a cod-banker, as we call it.'

His fellow quartermaster, Arthur Bright, (saved in Collapsible D) also thought it looked like a sailing ship or fishing boat, as did Quartermaster George Rowe (Collapsible C): 'I think there was a ship there. Indeed, I am sure of it, and that she was a sailer.'

Rowe had been attempting to contact the visitor with a Morse lamp, which itself is indicative of how close the stranger came. Later he told how it was his impression the other ship had 'hauled off from us' towards daylight.

Lookout Fred Fleet was in the same boat as Robert Hichens and Major Arthur Peuchen (No. 6). He commented: 'It might have been a fisher sail, or something; it was only just one bright light. I couldn't say what it was... it might have been a sailing ship, or it might have been a steamer.'

THE MYSTERY OF THE SHIP SIGHTED

Underwriters yesterday were considerably mystified by that part of the evidence of Mr Boxhall, the fourth officer of the *Titanic*, before the United States Senate Committee which relates to signalling for assistance by the *Titanic* to a vessel directly ahead of her after the collision with the iceberg had occurred

The most serious part of the evidence was, of course, that signals in answer were reported to have been seen by several persons, for as a rule Masters of ships, with an eye to salvage awards, are always ready to render assistance, if they understand it is acceptable. In the present case there can hardly have been any misunderstanding on this score, for the Morse Code is generally known by the mates of all ocean ships.

There are at present, therefore, two suggestions: (1) That the lights seen were a reflection; and (2) that another vessel really was, as described, about 5 miles distant, but she also came to grief through striking an iceberg. Though the *Titanic* took some hours to sink, a small vessel might, of course, have gone down very quickly. Unfortunately, the names of missing vessels have lately been rather numerous, though it is generally supposed that they met their fate in heavy water. Should this theory, which is not entirely improbable, prove to be the correct one, the truth will be suspected before very long.

(*The Times*, 24 April, 1912, p10)

The newspapers were struggling to deal with the enormity of what had been disclosed. Another ship had been within a few miles of the sinking *Titanic* – so close that the latter attempted to contact her by flashes of Morse lamp; so close that Captain Smith believed lifeboats could row to her and return with her for a greater redemption; so close that the vessel could still be seen within the hopelessly reduced horizon of a lifeboat on the Atlantic deep, quite apart from the height of the Boat Deck of an admittedly sinking, but enormous liner.

It was inconceivable to many that the other vessel could have missed the Morse signals – indeed, some *Titanic* witnesses felt she had responded with flashes of her own – and it was impossible to believe that she had failed to see rockets. Thus the perplexity of why this craft had turned on her heel, as it were, rather than riding to the rescue as she had earlier implied she was doing.

The idea that the lights were a reflection can be dismissed. Reflections do not approach, and neither the moon nor any other celestial presence is known to cast both red and green lights and masthead lights in imitation of a steamer – else steamers would be coloured otherwise.

That the mystery ship might herself have struck an iceberg, subsequent to the *Titanic* doing so, seems enormously far-fetched – doubly so when the wounded steamer or sailing vessel should not herself fire rockets, or burn a tar barrel on her deck, to indicate her plight. Nor did she make a sound with a fog-signalling apparatus or fire a gun at regular intervals, all part of the alternatives in a compli-cated set of regulations for indicating distress at night.

The evidence is unfortunately clear only to be unclear – the mystery ship approached after the *Titanic* collision (neither lookout in the latter having seen any indication of a ship before the iceberg impact, despite scanning all over the horizon), lay quietly within a very short radius for a time, then turned and steamed away. As Boxhall told the Americans:

Senator Duncan Fletcher: Apparently that ship came within 4 or 5 miles of the *Titanic*,
    and then turned and went away in what direction, westward or southward?
Boxhall: I don't know whether it was southwestward. I should say it was westerly.
Fletcher: In a westerly direction, almost in the direction which she had come?
Boxhall: Yes, sir.

What she did thus seems clear, why she did it, totally unclear. Could it be that she had mistaken the rockets for a warning, that she could not understand the Morse flashes, that she could not see that a gigantic ship nearby was not halted on an even keel, but drinking her death water?

The puzzle of why that ship worked her way so close, then waited, then wandered away, has existed for nigh-on a century. Her conduct, at first glance, seems blameworthy – especially in light of the huge prize on offer, that of saving everyone on board the stricken maiden voyager. Hindsight in particular would seem to cast a sinister light on her actions and inactions, but her state of knowledge is the key to any condemnation... and it is not known what she knew, leaving aside what she might reasonably have guessed...

Boxhall had an early theory of his own as to why she did not continue to proceed and eventually come joyously alongside his own ship:

Senator Theodore Burton: Is it your idea that she turned away?

Boxhall: That is my idea, sir.

Burton: She kept on a general course toward the east, and then bore away from you, or what?

Boxhall: I do not think she was doing much steaming. I do not think the ship was steaming very much, because after I first saw the masthead lights she must have been still steaming, but by the time I saw her red light with my naked eye she was not steaming very much. *So she had probably gotten into the ice*, and turned around.

Burton: What do you think happened after she turned around? Do you think she went away to avoid the ice?

Boxhall: I do not know whether she stayed there all night, or what she did. I lost the light. I did not see her after we pulled around to the starboard side of the *Titanic*.

Officer Boxhall went away in Lifeboat 2 quite late that April night, considerably more than an hour after he first saw the approaching ship. He believed that she had been blocked in approaching the *Titanic* because of an ice barrier that ran north to south, blocking progress between the east and west. The *Titanic* had struck a 'scout' berg on the eastern side of the barrier.

Boxhall says the mystery ship eventually turned away 'westerly', back the way she had come. His suggestion is that the mystery ship had been approaching on an easterly course, when she had 'probably gotten into the ice' that was extending in a north-to-south field.

Boxhall's description may imply that the stranger was aware of the *Titanic*'s predicament. She appeared about fifteen minutes after the White Star liner had first sent out distress messages by wireless. Had the other ship received them? If so, necessarily being equipped with a wireless herself, why did this visible vessel not transmit messages of her own to the frantic *Titanic*?

On the other hand, fifteen minutes or so is extraordinarily early for a ship to respond, and her appearance may simply be a coincidence. If she had any degree of knowledge of *Titanic's* distress, and then came upon a ship firing rockets, it seems reasonable that she would have taken steps to indicate her awareness – and the difficulty she had in proceeding. If her wireless had suddenly somehow packed up after receiving the SOS, such that she was unable to transmit, it seems she ought to have fired a rocket or two herself, in order to indicate that she was striving to bring succour.

ROCKETS AS DISTRESS SIGNALS

Lieutenant J.O.Williams, RN, hon. secretary of the Aldeburgh branch of the National Lifeboat Institution, writes, with reference to the use of star rockets at sea as signals of distress, that the practice of sending up rockets has become, roughly speaking, not uncommon when the condition of matters hardly warrants this extreme course. The result is that they are sometimes not regarded with the gravity attaching to them. Lieutenant Williams thinks that the proper penalty attaching to the improper use of rockets at sea ought to be increased, so that in the discretion of the court the irresponsible firing of rockets should be made a criminal offence.

It is not an unknown event, Lieutenant Williams says, for lifeboats to go out in response to a rocket signal, to cruise about for hours, and to find nothing. This means worry, trouble and expense, which the Lifeboat Institution can ill afford.

(*The Times*, 27 June, 1912, p4)

The fact that the mystery ship did not respond in any discernible way (no-one on the *Titanic* could read anything out of claimed flickers in response to their Morse lamp, hinting strongly that it might have been a wishful illusion, or only a masthead light twinkling) suggests that the mystery ship did not appreciate what was actually meant by the rockets. Or else, if she did, she must have provided an emphatic and unmistakable response…

If she found herself 'into the ice' and trapped, but realising distress on the other side of the field, she ought to have lowered her boats – empty save for dedicated crews of muscular men. If the ice was impassable, it was likely traversable on foot. Men have pulled boats by rope over ice for generations in those latitudes.

Indeed the annual seal hunt, held every year around this time, saw steamers landing crew members on 'pans' of ice to go clubbing seals. These ships, from Nova

Scotia and particularly Newfoundland, hunted out the ice floes on which colonies of seals would be drifting south. Parties from the same vessel were often dropped in different spots. Such sealing ships also fired rockets at night to call their dories, or small boats, back to the ship.

There is no compelling evidence from her behaviour to suggest that the mystery ship – which Boxhall described as likely a three-mast or four-mast vessel, with 'beautiful lights' – discerned distress from the *Titanic* rockets erupting in front of her, unless her disregard of them, and her subsequent departure, were entirely callous acts.

There is a fellowship of the sea. Those whose business in done in great waters must render assistance to one another, for assuredly their own time might come when help is needed. Any seafarer who would propose leaving another to his fate, while hardly worthy of the name seafarer, might expect an instant mutiny from his fellows – unless all sensibility and civilisation has passed from the mind of man. And even if it had, such that only pirates existed on the Mystery Ship, there was always the question of salvage, as noted in the theory of the underwriters reported in *The Times*.

Huge riches awaited those who could make good a sinking ship and its cargo. It is no exaggeration to note that a boarding party that saved a valuable vessel could make many thousands of times a man's monthly wages. And a captain who passed up a crew's attempt at a prize would be worthy of denunciation in every waterfront tavern where a ship made landfall.

But what, in the end, was meant by rockets? Rockets, in 1912, did not automatically mean distress. They could be used as a night signal that a ship was 'not under control'. They were also fired, at night, as company identification signals. They could be sent up in sheer celebration, or for illumination, as flares, in uncertain waters. They could be a warning off, rather than an invitation onward.

Today the use of rockets has been restricted at sea to indicate distress and distress only. Furthermore, distress rockets are red in colour and red alone. Neither of these singular qualities was in operation at the time of the *Titanic* disaster, and in fact they were only adopted after she had gone down, the red colour being a particularly late refinement. The actual regulations for indicating distress aboard a ship were various and cumbersome in 1912:

The following signals numbered 1, 2 and 3 when used or displayed together or separately shall be deemed to be signals of distress at night:

(1) A gun fired at intervals of about a minute. (2) Flames on the ship as from a burning tar barrel, oil barrel, etc. (3) Rockets or shells of any colour or description fired one at a time at short intervals.

Rockets were option three. Traditionally the most commonly used had been a constant display of flames, since fire at sea was never less than serious – distress imitating real distress, as it were, while the problem might only be a broken rudder. Again, the definition of 'distress' was imprecise; it was treated as 'wanting assistance' and there was no sole signal for a case of extreme urgency, such as to demonstrate imminent danger of sinking.

Many vessels that sink go down in less than a minute, particularly when broached by an exceptional wave. The regulations may have been framed before the advent of wireless (only installed on the first ocean liner, Cunard's *Lucania*, in 1903), but it was still optimistic to imagine that 'distress' – meaning a dire emergency – could be indicated at sedate intervals of one minute at a time, unless that case of 'distress' were one of wanting a tow, or a top-up of drinking water.

It is very difficult for the modern reader, raised on the exclusive use of rockets to indicate immediate danger at sea, to understand the concerns of Lieutenant Williams, the Royal National Lifeboat Institution, and others in 1912, about the 'not uncommon' use of rockets at sea for all manner of purpose.

Like the boy who cried wolf, the result had been that they were, 'sometimes not regarded with the gravity attaching to them'. Yet the option of rockets, under the regulations, also suggested it was not so much their visibility that was important to those framing the guidelines as their *audibility*... they were not so much rockets, per se, as substitute minute signals (option 1), or shells. A steady drumbeat of noise was what was sought, almost as if there was a distaste for over-ostentatious display!

Sound and fury, of course, may signify something – and at least do it rather better than sound alone, or visual effects on their own. It is striking, once more speaking with hindsight, that rockets were not 'elevated' at the time to become the preferred, or only, option for indicating distress at night. But the fact remains that they were not, and sailors, being traditionalists at heart, tended to be wedded to what they had always been told.

Then we look at the options, as specified in the regulations, and note that it is not one choice or another, each being mutually exclusive. The regulations state explicitly that the various ways of indicating distress can (should?) be 'used or displayed *together*'.

It is also true that in the years leading up to 1912, many British vessels in extreme danger had relied on *every* option available in the regulations – firing guns, firing rockets, sounding with a fog apparatus, even setting a brazier of flames, and doing them all simultaneously when the sea threatened.

Newspaper columns are littered with cases of all indicators used at the same time. However the *Titanic* simply did not use a multiplicity of effects, the way these other ships did, unless the Morse lamp is somehow added as a signal of distress; albeit officially unrecognised. She only used rockets, one method alone.

And yet she had them all. The Belfast surveyor of the Board of Trade reported to his superiors after the accident about the rockets and lights aboard the *Titanic*. But he also detailed the separate mechanisms aboard for indicating distress audibly in an emergency. These included steam whistles on two funnels, a hand-operated mechanical fog horn, and socket distress signals for noise (as well as silly flags and 'collapsible shapes' for display in the daytime). The Establishment did not want to know about these other factors. The surveyor also noted that there was 'no gun carried'.

The audibility element was in fact removed from a draft Parliamentary reply to a question on why the *Titanic* had not managed to attract the nearby ship. Instead mention was made *only* of rockets and pyrotechnics, as if the distress regulations were neat and tidy, which they assuredly were not. The surviving document for the Government side of the House of Commons shows the line about the fog horn crudely struck out in someone's hand – leaving the clear impression that the *Titanic* that night had done absolutely all that anyone might have been expected of her.

Meanwhile the fact remains that the Mystery Ship went away; whether to search for another way through the ice or not, we do not know. When the sun came up at around 4 a.m. she was not seen by any of those who had pulled energetically towards her. They had to turn around and head instead for the Cunard liner *Carpathia*, which had come up, alerted by the SOS, from the ice-free southeast.

The American Inquiry, at length told the story of the nearby ship by Boxhall, at once set about trying to find out who it could be that had apparently ignored the rockets, as well as the Morsed messages to 'Come at once. We are the *Titanic* sinking.'

Initially the Chairman, Senator W.A. Smith, seemed to think the steamer with the 'beautiful lights' must have been a foreign vessel. He may have thought that she had not comprehended the Morse code message stabbed out in English through long and short flashes of light. Smith asked questions about the German Norddeutscher Lloyd vessel *Frankfurt*, and the Danish passenger liner *Hellig Olav*. But he soon switched his attention to a British ship when he heard that a particular steamer had seen rockets.

Of course rockets are designed to be seen, and seen over the visible horizon. An unseen ship, or ships, may see them over the curvature of the earth – besides a ship well within the visible horizon, which for a ship of the *Titanic*'s height was at least 10 miles that night and probably more. In short, the mere witnessing of rockets does not make the seeing ship necessarily as the vessel in view within 5 miles.

Rockets fired from the bridge of the *Titanic* must have risen to the height of at least 300ft above sea-level, and should therefore have been visible at a distance of 19 miles. From the bridge of another ship they would be visible at a greater distance still.

(*The Times*, 23 May, 1912, p6)

But seeing rockets was something to go on. The name of this new ship was the *Californian*.

WIRELESS operator Cyril Evans had been asleep all night, his instrument powered down. His vessel, *Californian*, did not receive news of the *Titanic* SOS until around 5.30 the following morning. Three hours later she reached the side of the *Carpathia*, when the last of the lifeboat survivors had just been taken up. She was the second ship on the scene.

The *Californian* came to prominence because of lights seen low on the horizon during the night that were soon established to be rockets. Her captain, Stanley Lord, had retired to the chart room, fully dressed, following a tiring seventeen-hour day on duty. He fell asleep about 12.40 a.m., as the ship's middle watch was underway on the flying bridge, open to the air, overhead.

Captain Lord did not see rockets himself, but his officer of the watch, Second Officer Herbert Stone, did. So too did an apprentice, James Gibson, who joined Stone on the bridge some little time into the watch after attending to other duties.

The Master realised the potential significance of the sightings the next morning, and later asked Stone to write out a report on all he had seen. Composed while still at sea (the *Californian* was bound for Boston, where she would arrive a few days after the sinking), it is still the most immediate summation of what happened:

On going up to the bridge [just after midnight] I was stopped by yourself [Captain Lord] at the wheelhouse door, and you gave me verbal orders for the watch. You showed me a steamer a little abaft of our star[board] beam and informed me that she was stopped. You also showed me the loose field ice all around the ship and a dense icefield to the southward. You told me to watch the other steamer and report if she came any nearer and that you were going to lie down on the chartroom settee.

I went on the bridge about eight minutes past twelve, and took over the watch from the third officer, Mr Groves, who also pointed out ice and steamer, and said our head was ENE and we were swinging. On looking at the compass I saw this was correct and observed the other steamer SSE dead abeam and showing one masthead light, her red side light, and one or two small indistinct lights around the deck, which looked like portholes or open doors.

I judged her to be a small tramp steamer and about 5 miles distant. The third officer informed me he had called him up on our Morse lamp but had got no reply. The third officer then left the bridge and I at once called the steamer up but got no reply. Gibson, the apprentice, then came up with the coffee about 12.15. I told him I had called the steamer up and the result. He then went to the tapper with the same result. Gibson thought at first he was answering, but it was only his masthead lamps flickering a little. I then sent Gibson by your orders to get the gear all ready for streaming a new log line when we got under weigh [sic] again.

At 12.35 you whistled up the speaking tube and asked if the other steamer had moved. I replied, 'No' and that she was on the same bearing and also reported I had called him up and the result. At about 12.45 I observed a flash of light in the sky just above that steamer. I thought nothing of it, as there were several shooting stars about, the night being fine and clear with light airs and calms.

Shortly after I observed another distinctly over the steamer which I made out to be a white rocket, though I observed no flash on the deck or any indication that it had come from that steamer; in fact, it appeared to come from a good distance beyond her.

The *Californian* with a tug on her starboard quarter. She was a freighter of 6,200 tons. *Shipping World.*

Captain Stanley Lord at a lifeboat, teeth clenched on his trademark pipe, during his later career. He had no idea the *Titanic* had sunk and rushed to the *Carpathia*'s location the next morning with all his lifeboats swung out and ready to lower. *Author collection.*

Between then and about 1.15 I observed three more the same as before, and all white in colour. I, at once, whistled down the speaking tube and you came from the chartroom into your own room and answered. I reported seeing these lights in the sky in the direction of the other steamer, which appeared to me to be white rockets.

You then gave me orders to call her up with the Morse lamp and try to get some information from her. You also asked me if they were private signals and I replied, 'I do not know, but they were all white.' You then said: 'When you get an answer let me know by Gibson.' Gibson and I observed three more at intervals and kept calling them up on our Morse lamps but got no reply whatsoever.

The other steamer meanwhile had shut in her red side light and showed us her stern light and her masthead's glow was just visible. I observed the steamer to be steaming away to the SW and altering her bearing fast. We were also swinging slowly all the time through S and at 1.50 were heading about WSW and the other steamer bearing SWxW.

At 2 a.m. the vessel was steaming away fast and only just her stern light was visible and bearing SW a half W. I sent Gibson down to you and told him to wake you and tell you we had seen altogether eight white rockets and that the steamer had gone out of sight to the SW. Also [to tell you] that we were heading WSW.

When he came back he reported he had told you we had called him up repeatedly and got no answer, and you replied: 'All right, are you sure there were no colours in them?' and Gibson replied: 'No, they were all white.'

At 2.45 I again whistled down again and told you we had seen no more lights and that the steamer had steamed away to the SW and was now out of sight, also that the rockets were all white and had no colours whatever.

We saw nothing further until about 3.20 when we thought we observed two faint lights in the sky about SSW and a little distance apart. At 3.40 I sent Gibson down to see all was ready for me to prepare the new log at eight bells.

The chief officer, Mr Stewart, came on the bridge at 4 a.m. and I gave him a full report of what I had seen and my reports and replies from you, and pointed out where I thought I had observed these faint lights at 3.20.

He picked up the binoculars and said after a few moments: 'There she is then, she's all right, she is a four-master.' I said: 'Then that isn't the steamer I saw first,' took up the glasses and just made out a four-master steamer with two masthead lights a little abaft our port beam, and bearing about S, we were heading about WNW. Mr Stewart then took over the watch and I went off the bridge.

Second Officer Herbert Stone.

The first point to be made is that the *Californian* was stopped. Her progress had been arrested by an icefield, suddenly seen in front. The way came off the ship at 10.21 p.m. ship's time and she lay still, drifting imperceptibly. At this point she sent out a wireless message saying she was 'stopped and surrounded by ice'. The *Titanic*, still surging ahead, replied: 'Shut up, shut up, I am working Cape Race', meaning she was trafficking messages and snippets of news with a land-based station in Newfoundland.

The *Californian* was stopped, and remained so for the duration of Stone's watch. Yet the mystery ship that approached the *Titanic* was undoubtedly moving, as we have seen. Nonetheless, this glaring impossibility for any equation between the *Californian* and the *Titanic's* mystery ship tends to be ignored, even defied, because of the Great Coincidence.

Left: Californian second officer, Herbert Stone. Known to the firemen as 'Stoney', he would go on to have a long career at sea, despite originally intending to become a schoolteacher. He performed well at the British Inquiry and was unshakable in his evidence as to the nearby visitor eventually steaming away to the southwest. *Author collection.*

Below: Californian apprentice officer James Gibson. *Daily Sketch.*

Another view of the *Californian*, this time of her port side, showing her steering-gear house all the way aft. She was approximately one-eighth the displacement of *Titanic*, and saw another vessel on the Boston track that was 'something like ourselves'. *Author collection.*

The coincidence is that the *Californian*, stopped at the icefield, was later joined by another vessel, 'about 5 miles distant', that also stopped at the barrier. The *Californian* was on course for Boston – and the New York course of the *Titanic* was many miles away to the south. Yet the similarity of the separation between the latter and her mystery ship, and the *Californian* and her partner, has led to a tendency among some to see them as one and the same – so that instead of two pairs of ships, behaving differently, over the horizon from one another, there was only one pair, *Californian* and *Titanic*.

Captain Lord's ship was undoubtedly one half of a local pair, by Officer Stone's account, and indeed the captain himself had seen 'something like ourselves' approaching before he left the bridge. But could this other vessel have been the mighty *Titanic*, largest moving object ever built?

Look at Stone's assessment – the other steamer was: 'showing one masthead light, her red sidelight and one or two small indistinct lights around the deck, which looked like portholes or open doors. I judged her to be a small tramp steamer.'

There is no reason to disbelieve Stone on this point. Portholes and open doors are consistent with a good view, through binoculars, of a small freighter. It seems inconceivable that Stone could have missed deck upon deck upon deck, the sheer tiers of the towering *Titanic*. In any case, the apprentice, James Gibson, was also asked to prepare an account while still at sea, and his opinion was also that she was merely a tramp steamer. Gibson wrote:

Looking over the weather-cloth, I saw a white light flickering, which I took to be a Morse light calling us up.

I then went over to the keyboard and gave one long flash in answer, and still seeing this light, flickering, I gave her the calling-up sign. The light on the other ship, however, was still the same, so I looked at her through the binoculars and found that it was her masthead light flickering. I also observed her port side light and a faint glare of lights on her after deck. I then went over to the second officer and remarked that she looked like a tramp steamer. He said that most probably she was, and was burning oil lights.

Ah, another coincidence! Gibson thought the other ship's Morse light was calling them up – just as *Titanic* had desperately Morsed to her approaching steamer. But it should be remembered that the third officer, Groves, had previously tried to Morse the other steamer and failed to get a response, just as Officer Stone had done a second time, with the same lack of result.

A failure to respond bears no similarity to the *Titanic*, which was vigorously flashing after midnight. Here Gibson confirms inactivity – not feverish activity – when he detects for himself that the apparent Morsing was only 'her masthead light flickering'. Like Stone, Gibson saw that she only had indistinct lights – a faint glare on her after deck. His remark to Stone, which the latter immediately agreed with, was that she looked like a tramp steamer. The *Titanic*, with 10,000 electric lights throughout and no oil lights, certainly did not resemble anything of the sort.

These facts, and this agreement between the two men, should be borne in mind before the rush to consider the rockets. Haste in jumping to conclusions would lead a person to also miss the salient fact, described by Stone and later supported by others aboard, that the *Californian* was pointing ENE (east-northeast) at the crucial time.

In other words she was only ever showing her green light (on her starboard side) to any vessel to the southward, or SSE in this case. Yet *Titanic* observers saw both red *and* green lights on their approaching steamer, before she slowed and apparently turned, showing – as Boxhall described, a 'red light most of the time.' This mystery ship of the *Titanic* would also, as seen, later display a white stern light as she departed.

Meanwhile Stone initially detected 'a flash of light in the sky just above that steamer', and thought nothing of it. The next he made out to be a white rocket, 'though I observed no flash on the deck or any indication that it had come from that steamer'. Stone writes, of his own accord: 'In fact, it appeared to come from a good distance beyond her.'

Again this shouldn't surprise. The *Californian* is on a Boston track north of the *Titanic's* New York track (and the *Titanic* wreck site today shows she drifted south of the New York track, 20 miles from the Boston track, after she struck her berg). The rockets seen by Stone, and later Gibson, undoubtedly came from the *Titanic*. But she was felled by a scout berg, east of the icefield. A southern track and an eastern impact give SE or SSE – the same vector on which the *Californian* would and should see rockets, beyond their 'coincidental' steamer.

Stone's earliest prepared statement shows that Captain Lord had been initially concerned lest his vessel's nearby and incommunicative stranger should move at all, or come closer. When Stone called down by voice-tube to his sleepy skipper and mentioned these 'lights in the sky in the direction of the other steamer', he has immediately linked the two (lights and steamer) for his captain – just as the latter was exclusively concerned about the proximate 'tramp'. Because he could not have had any prior concerns about any unseen vessels the wide world over.

Stone mentions that the lights 'appeared to me to be white rockets', but he is saying nothing about the small steamer's condition, and Lord must assume that she is still the same, as indeed Stone had indicated to him earlier. Besides mentioning nothing untoward about her, apart from this display, Stone signally fails to mention to his captain that the lights/rockets 'appeared to come from a good distance beyond her'.

Lord, with no knowledge of anything but a steady stranger making lights – after previously failing to reply to a Morse lamp from the *Californian* – may be only mildly puzzled. He asks if they are 'private signals', meaning the type of rockets fired to convey company allegiance. In his mind, it may be that the other vessel is trying to identify herself by other means.

Captain Lord seems to prescribe further Morsing: 'When you get an answer let me know by Gibson.' There is no particular urgency to this task; it has become a curiosity rather than a routine exchange, but the *Californian* is bobbing gently, engines stopped, and the men on watch have little else to do.

And so the captain dozed off again in his steam-heated room. Stone and Gibson saw more rockets, but they also saw the small steamer actively move away – steaming from the SSE to the SW and 'altering her bearings fast'.

As Stone later remarked (Q. 8037 at the British Inquiry): 'A steamer that is in distress does not steam away from you, my Lord.'

At 2 a.m. Captain Lord was informed that his ship's stranger had shown more lights or rockets and had steamed away. Company signals 'usually have some colours in them', the captain said later, which was why the apprentice heard a question as to whether they were all white. It was a further curiosity, merely.

Captain Lord would later remark that he understood that 'some companies have white' as identification rockets, but it appears he couldn't readily think of any at the material time.

The distress regulations, as seen, establish that distress rockets could be 'of any colour or description', meaning that whiteness was utterly irrelevant, although the later British Inquiry tried to paint a picture that equated distress with white

The 46,000 ton RMS *Titanic* at Cherbourg in the dusk of April 10, 1912. Although retouched (the aftermost funnel. left, was for ventilation only) this represents the only indication of what the largest vessel in the world looked like at night. Captain Lord testified that he had once seen the sister ship, RMS *Olympic*, at a distance of 5 miles and that such monsters were 'impossible to mistake'. His apprentice, James Gibson, said passenger ships were 'generally lit up from the water's edge'. *L'Illustration*.

rockets and vice versa. But the evidence would actually be that the *Titanic* also fired rockets of different colours, even if they were principally white – with only the latter colour being seen by the *Californian* on the Boston track.

Stone's 'portholes and open doors' had by now resolved themselves into a light in the distance. At 2.45 a.m. that light disappeared in the opposite direction to that in which the rockets had first been seen.

The *Titanic* only began firing rockets, however, after she had stopped for the last time. She obviously could not, thereafter, move to any other part of the ocean – except to its very bottom.

SHADOW AND SUBSTANCE

THE FICTIONS IN FINDINGS OF FACT

Despite the contradictions between a Boston-bound yet stopped *Californian* (showing a green light to southward) and a vessel that approached the *Titanic* on the New York track (before turning to show a *red* light), the seed of similarity had been planted by an estimated distance of 5 miles between vessels in each pair – and by the sighting of rockets.

No other ship admitted to seeing rockets – although at least one other was charged with doing so in the newspapers – and it is possible the *Californian* might not have disclosed the sightings had not her rendezvous at the rescue scene with the *Carpathia* drawn reporters to her berth in Boston.

The Cunard vessel had asked the *Californian* to continue the search as she prepared to make for New York with survivors. The fact that the Leyland liner was remaining behind for a time was wirelessed to land, and led to speculation that the *Californian* may have picked up bodies. In fact she had not done so.

But an assistant donkeyman, who had been working on the engines below decks, immediately took the opportunity to tell the press on landfall that everyone aboard the *Californian* had been discussing the lights seen and whether they could have been the *Titanic*'s rockets. This man, Ernest Gill, went further – telling, in return for a $500 fee, how he had personally been on deck and seen a large steamer rushing along at full speed. He had also, he said, later seen rockets.

This story is now discredited. The *Titanic* could not have been the claimed 'large steamer', because she was not rushing anywhere at the time Gill said he went on deck (for a prodigiously long time smoking a single cigarette – and then stayed for five minutes after he had finished, wearing only thin flannel clothes in sub-zero temperatures).

Gill was not seen by either Stone or apprentice Gibson, and despite seeing rockets which he claimed he 'knew at once meant distress', Gill did not identify himself to anyone on watch to double-check that the rockets had been seen and distress discerned.

The sensational tale told by Gill nonetheless prompted the summoning of Captain Lord and his wireless operator, Cyril Evans, to the American Inquiry hearings. Here Gill, who had deserted the ship as a result of his riches, told yet more of his lurid tale – with further obvious defects, such as why a large liner should be steaming rapidly when there was an ice barrier in front of her.

Captain Lord was the next witness called, but was remarkably never asked about Gill's account – the latter having the effect, of course, of putting the *Californian* within sight of a large steamer. Seeing such an ocean monarch may have assisted Gill's marketability – his article fee amounted to a couple of years' salary – but it hardly did anything for his skipper.

Lord was soon asked whether he had seen any distress signals on Sunday night, either rockets or Morse signals. He replied: 'No sir; I did not. The officer on watch saw some signals, but he said they were not distress signals.'

He related how that officer, at 1.15 a.m., had called down on the voice tube to say: 'I think she has fired a rocket.' Stone had added: 'She did not answer the Morse lamp and she has commenced to go away from us.' Lord responded: 'Call her up and let me know at once what her name is.' So, he put the whistle back, and, apparently, he was calling. I could hear him ticking over my head. Then I went to sleep.'

It will be seen that there are slight differences with Stone's account, but they broadly agree. What did not help Captain Lord was his claim to be only half-awake when Gibson came down to him at 2 a.m. He did not remember speaking to the apprentice, who actually entered his room to report that the steamer had fired eight rockets altogether, and had steamed away. Lord said he could only recall the banging of the door and his asking: 'What is it?'

The captain could, of course, have claimed to have been fully awake – the apprentice was reporting that the steamer had moved off and was now out of sight. Lord, told of only one rocket earlier by his account, was now told of eight. But the puzzle had removed itself. He could perfectly well have shrugged and gone back to sleep.

Captain Lord, had he been given reason to think that something was not quite right – rather than merely unusual – could naturally have woken the wireless man. But he had only one operator (the *Titanic* had two), who slept at night. With the Marconi apparatus installed only the year before, the captain appeared to assume that other operators would only have been transmitting during the day. The wireless operator was asleep throughout, and his evidence is of little importance.

The officer of the watch, Stone, was fully awake however – and had the direct evidence of his eyes as to what he saw. It was open to him to personally wake the wireless operator if he had the slightest misgivings. The fact that he did not do so indicates beyond reasonable conjecture that Stone was truthful in saying that he never at any stage feared that a ship was in trouble. If he had done so, a short walk to the Marconi shack, a matter of a few seconds' initiative, would have cost him nothing.

Captain Lord later made a further point along these lines in an article penned in March 1914 for the *Savannah Morning News*: 'It is also a fact that this apprentice, Gibson, called the chief officer at 3.45, talked to him about fifteen minutes about making a new log line in place of [a] log line lost when we backed out of the ice, but said nothing whatever about the signals he had seen while on watch with the second officer from 12 to 4, showing of what little importance Gibson or the second officer considered them.'

Lord finished his evidence to the Inquiry and was soon on a train back to Boston for the *Californian*'s homeward sailing. In the meantime, however, the US Inquiry would be hearing from Navy Hydrographer, John J. Knapp, who drew up a hypothetical sketch of where the *Californian* could have been *if* she were the ship seen from the *Titanic*.

This breathtaking assumption apparently deeply impressed Senator Smith, the Chairman. The drawing indicated the two vessels were 14 miles apart, not five, but the whole construct was entirely whimsical. When the notion was put to a recalled *Titanic* fourth officer, it was swiftly dispelled:

Senator Smith: We have been figuring the distance the *Californian* was away from the *Titanic*, and from the positions given we have concluded – that is, we have evidence to support the theory, that the *Californian* was but 14 miles distant from the *Titanic*. Do you think that under those circumstances you could have seen the *Californian*?
Officer Boxhall: I do not know, sir. I should not think so.

Yet the *Titanic* officer was later pushed again, this time in a session with Senator Theodore Burton:

Boxhall: ...I have already stated, in answer to a question, how far this ship was away from us, that I thought she was about 5 miles, and I arrived at it in this way. The masthead lights of a steamer are required by the Board of Trade regulations to show for 5 miles, and the [side lights, either red or green] are required to show for 2 miles ...I could see quite clearly.
Senator Burton: You are very sure you are not deceived about seeing these lights?
Boxhall: Not at all.

Burton: You saw not only the mast light, but the side lights?

Boxhall: I saw the side lights. Whatever ship she was had beautiful lights. I think we could see her lights more than the regulation distance, but I do not think we could see them 14 miles.

Boxhall was not told that the *Californian* was on the Boston track, nor that the usual separation between that course and the New York track had been notionally massaged down to 14 miles. But he could still smell a rat as the investigators tried to fit a theory to the facts.

More interesting, perhaps, in the wider scheme of things – as to whether the *Californian* should have taken action on seeing rockets, wherever she was – Boxhall had this to say:

Senator Duncan Fletcher: It seems that an officer on the *Californian* reported to the commander of the *Californian* that he had seen signals; but he said they were not distress signals. Do you know whether or not under the regulations in vogue, and according to the custom at sea, rockets fired, such as the *Titanic* sent up, would be regarded as anything but distress signals?

Boxhall: I am hardly in a position to state that, because it is the first time I have seen distress rockets sent off, and I could not very well judge what they would be like, standing as I was underneath them, firing them myself. I do not know what they would look like in the distance.

Fletcher: Have you ever seen any rockets sent off such as you say are private signals?

Boxhall: Yes, sir.

Fletcher: Under what circumstances?

Boxhall: Ships passing in the night, signalling to one another.

This is exactly what *Californian* assumed, conditioned by a nearby steamer, intended communication of their own, and low pyrotechnics in view. It is safe to assume it was the first time Stone and Gibson had 'seen distress rockets sent off', thus not realising their true nature or actual distance.

Captain Lord and his crew had completed their voyage back to Britain before the Chairman of the American Inquiry produced his report into the *Titanic* disaster. Remarkably, it had this to say:

The Steamship *Californian*'s Responsibility

The committee is forced to the inevitable conclusion that the *Californian*, controlled by the same company, was nearer the *Titanic* than the 19 miles reported by her captain, and that her officers and crew saw the distress signals of the *Titanic* and failed to respond to them in accordance with the dictates of humanity, international usage, and the requirements of law.

The only reply to the distress signals was a counter signal from a large white light, which was flashed for nearly two hours from the mast of the *Californian*. In our opinion, such conduct, whether arising from indifference or gross carelessness, is most reprehensible, and places upon the commander of the *Californian* a grave responsibility.

The wireless operator of the *Californian* was not aroused until 3.30 a.m., New York time, on the morning of the 15th, after considerable conversation between officers and members of crew had taken place aboard that ship regarding these distress signals or rockets, and was directed by the chief officer to see if there was anything the matter, as a ship had been firing rockets during the night.

The enquiry thus set on foot immediately disclosed the fact that the *Titanic* had sunk. Had assistance been promptly proffered, or had the wireless operator of the *Californian* remained a few minutes longer at his post on Sunday evening, that ship might have had the proud distinction of rescuing the lives of the passengers and crew of the *Titanic*...

In point of fact, the wireless operator, roused at 5.20 a.m. ship's time the next morning, was only called after Captain Lord had ordered it. And the captain, now fully conscious, had done so after consultation with the chief officer, who had come to him concerned – having heard from Stone that a vessel had fired several rockets during the period of the middle watch.

The result, from starting up the wireless and sending out a general call, had been reports that the *Titanic* had described herself as sinking. No other ship but the *Carpathia* knew she had sunk. So Captain Lord had next ordered all his lifeboats swung out and readied for lowering, placed extra lookouts, and ordered immediate haste for the transmitted distress location, which he estimated at 19½ miles away – the *Californian* having drifted a little closer in the hours of darkness.

But Chairman Smith was not to be detained by mere detail in an overblown speech to the Senate to mark his report's publication. He told his listeners: 'It is not a pleasant duty to criticise the conduct or comment upon the shortcomings of others, but the plain truth should be told... Captain Lord stated that: "from the position we stopped in to the position in which the *Titanic* is supposed to have hit the iceberg was 19½." I am of the opinion it was much nearer than the captain is willing to admit, and I base my judgement upon the scientific investigation of the Hydrographic Office of our Government.'

There was just one problem with this 'scientific' investigation. The Hydrographer had placed the *Titanic* in her SOS location – meaning the co-ordinates of longitude and latitude she specified in her transmitted distress messages. He then located the *Californian* in that hypothetical position of 14 miles away.

But the astounding truth is that the SOS location was wrong. Oceanographer Robert Ballard discovered the wreck of the *Titanic* 13 nautical miles to the east (and a little to the south) of the transmitted position, the huge error being the reason she had eluded discovery for so long. The wreck is now on a line consistent with where the *Californian* said she saw low-lying rockets – and the distance from the wreck site to the *Californian* stop position is precisely 22.8 miles.

The British Department of Transport, knowing the wreck site, estimated in 1992 that the *Titanic* had collided in a location 20.1 miles from the *Californian* – drifting further south in the two hours and forty minutes she took to sink. Hydrographer Knapp's ideas were thus demonstrated to be utter fantasy.

But Senator Smith, eighty years earlier, was in full flow:

Why did the *Californian* display its Morse signal lamp from the moment of the collision continuously for nearly two hours if they saw nothing? And the signals which were visible to Mr Gill at 12.30 and afterwards – and which were also seen by the captain [*not true*] and officer of the watch – should have excited more solicitude than was displayed by the officers of that vessel.

And the failure of Captain Lord to arouse the wireless operator on his ship places a tremendous responsibility upon this officer from which it will be very difficult for him to escape. Had he been as vigilant in the movement of his vessel as he was active in displaying his own signal lamp, there is a very strong possibility that every human life that was sacrificed through this disaster could have been saved. The dictates of humanity should have prompted vigilance under such conditions…

The conduct of the captain of the *Californian* calls for drastic action by the Government of England and by the owners of the vessel… contrast if you will the conduct of the captain of the *Carpathia* in the emergency, and imagine what must be the consolation of that thoughtful and sympathetic mariner, who rescued the shipwrecked and left the people of the world his debtor as his ship sailed for distant seas a few days ago.

By his utter self-effacement and his own indifference to peril, by his promptness and his knightly sympathy, he rendered a great service to humanity. He should be made to realise the debt of gratitude his nation owes to him, while the Book of Good Deeds, which has so often been familiar with his unaffected valour, should henceforth carry the name of Captain Rostron to the remotest period of time.

There it was – the public had been presented with a hero, and with a coward. Where one had shown 'knightly sympathy', the other had allowed human life to be sacrificed and had failed to measure up to the fundamental principles of mankind. Captain Lord's name was bound to be carried eternally in the Book of Evil Acts.

Chairman Smith rounded it all off by summoning once more that image of the vessel that had gone down. Here was a lyrical vision of wholesomeness and fortitude that could only cast Captain Lord's humble freighter in a yet colder light:

> We can see again the proud ship, instinct with life and energy, with active figures again swarming upon her decks – musicians, teachers, artists and authors; soldiers and sailors and men of large affairs; brave men and noble women of every land…
>
> At the very moment of their greatest joy, the ship suddenly reels, mutilated and groaning. With splendid courage the musicians fill the last moments with sympathetic melody. The ship wearily gives up the unequal battle… upon that broken hull new vows were taken, new fealty expressed, old love renewed. And those who had been devoted in friendship, companions in life, went proudly and defiantly on the last life pilgrimage together.

There wasn't a dry eye in the house. How beastly for someone to have inflicted such a blow on all that innocent, upstanding and effortlessly charming elite!

Smith was regarded as a buffoon by the British papers – with the British Ambassador, Sir James Bryce, describing him in official correspondence as: 'a person always anxious to put himself forward where any passing notoriety can be achieved.' Bryce had also written to his Foreign Secretary, Sir Edward Grey, referring to the Chairman of the American Inquiry as a person of 'singular incompetence'.

Elsewhere he referred to 'conspicuous incompetence' and questions of an 'irrelevant character' which were already being lampooned in the British press. Even the American Merchant Marine Association was moved to denounce the 'farcical inquiry'. A list of Senator Smith's errors and demonstrations of ignorance would fill a chapter in its own right, and the notorious question as to what an iceberg was made out of ('ice', replied Officer Lowe) was joined by one to Third Officer Pitman – whom he called 'captain' – as to whether the cross marked 'ice' on a chart indicated ice? ('Ice, yes sir.')

Smith also thought the 'weather side' of a ship meant to leeward, had no grasp of basic nautical terms, and seemed to think *Titanic* passengers and crew could have been saved in her watertight compartments. He thought *Titanic* left Southampton at midnight (she left at noon), referred to 'knots per hour' (a knot is one nautical mile per hour), and voiced some bizarre theories about meteorology, such as whether icebergs could explode. And all this in the course of a single day.

The *Daily Mirror* of 26 April, 1912, devoted its page nine to 'Strange Questions at the *Titanic* Inquiry', with a large photograph of Senator Smith and samples of the questions he asked:

Where do icebergs come from?
Of what are icebergs composed?
Did you fire horizontally upwards?
Did she go down by the bow or the head?
Don't icebergs expel rays of light?
Could the passengers take refuge in the watertight compartments?
Is 46 degrees Fahrenheit above zero?

The Chairman of the American Inquiry had pushed President Taft for it to be held, and in that initiative alone he deserves credit, since it ultimately elicited much useful evidence about the tragedy. Senator Smith personally is too easy a target to waste time upon, yet it is a further shortcoming that he was not sufficiently self-aware to deny himself the headlines likely to be achieved by casting another's good name into the blackest of disrepute.

Smith's parable of good and evil, in the final analysis, was too powerful to resist. Even if it incorporated the most extraordinary maligning of the character of an individual they had examined as a witness for precisely an hour and a half on a single afternoon, with most of that questioning taken up with the most mundane of matters.

Thus was a shadow cast over the substance of Captain Stanley Lord's entire career. He was a thirty-five-year-old who had first gone to sea as a cadet aged thirteen, qualifying for Master ten years later at the exceptionally young age of twenty-three. He further possessed an Extra Master's Certificate, superior to the qualifications of many the officers of the *Titanic*. And Lord had already been honoured by his King, receiving the Transport Medal (along with 1,800 others) for the carrying of troops and horses to South Africa at the time of the Boer War.

And in that vein:

A THOUSAND TO A LIFEBOAT
To the Editor of *The Times*

Sir – The British Government has never provided such a number of boats on its ships as were carried on the *Titanic*, nor anything approaching such a number.

I can give the name of a liner employed during the South African War in which the number of crew and troops and other passengers was over 3,000 persons. The number of boats carried was *three*.

Yet there was no wireless apparatus on board at that time, and the sea-track to South Africa is a lonely one, and not a crowded route like that of the *Titanic*, within likelihood of assistance if disabled.

Similar conditions prevailed on all the other troopship liners, and do so today.

I am Sir, faithfully yours,
Herbert Trench
Athenaeum Club, London.

(*The Times*, 29 April, 1912, p11)

In 1904, Lord found himself as chief officer of the *Antillian* in a flotilla conducting a major land-sea military exercise. Some 4,000 soldiers were put ashore by ships' boats onto the Essex coast during the manoeuvres. Lord's vessel had then also picked up hundreds of troops in small boats during the withdrawal – at night – meaning he actually had experience of the very scenario that *Titanic* passengers found themselves yearning for, eight years later, in the bitter cold of the Atlantic dark.

Lord was a teetotaller, a man who had put in a seventeen-hour day before lying down fully clothed on a settee in the chart room on the night that would ruin his career. He had a wife and a toddler son. He was frugal in habits, tall and weather-grained, yet almost painfully thin. His lack of personal hubris may perhaps be deduced from the fact that his son, throughout his long life, never saw his father wear his decorations – Captain Lord, in 1919, being also awarded the British War Medal and the Mercantile Marine Medal for services at sea during the Great War.

Lord never read the American Inquiry findings. Before they came out, he had returned to Britain – where a separate *Titanic* inquiry was being set in train. A proper one, as the British sniffily saw it. The Marquess of Lansdowne told the House of Lords: 'The proceedings here will be more regular in form and more satisfactory in substance than those which are going on in Washington.'

Indeed Captain Lord's position had been sympathetically considered that very same day (25 April, 1912) by the *Daily Sketch*: 'The good fortune that enabled the *Carpathia* to pick up the *Titanic*'s distress signal – the *Carpathia*'s wireless operator was off duty and had gone into the wireless room on unofficial business – is offset by the harrowing ill-luck which prevented the *Californian* from getting to the scene of the disaster before the liner sank. Had the *Californian* caught one of the early distress signals, everybody on the great White Star liner might have been saved.'

The *Californian* arrived in Liverpool on Friday 10 May, 1912, on her return journey, having made a 160-mile deviation to the south of her usual course to avoid all possibility of ice. She was berthed in the Huskisson dock and her officers prepared to attend the British Inquiry.

Yet her 'harrowing ill-luck' was about to get worse. The local Receiver of Wreck took depositions from all forty-seven crew aboard (there were no passengers) and these were sifted elsewhere for anything that might throw light on her circumstances and conduct. Depositions had also been taken from each of the returning *Titanic* crew, yet it already seemed there were only two ships involved in the official investigation…

The British Inquiry, held in London, was presided over by Lord Mersey, the former barrister John Bigham, who had been retired two years from his previous role of hearing cases in the divorce division of the High Court. A Liverpudlian, Mersey was an enthusiastic advocate of shipping interests and a regular speaker at the Chamber of Shipping annual dinner. In 1908 he told his fellow diners: 'that those connected with the industry had to see that nothing was done by legislation, or in other ways, which would decrease the carrying power of this great country'. So reported *The Times* on 17 February that year.

Captain Lord appeared as a witness on the seventh day of the Inquiry. As a witness, he was not legally represented in his own right, but he had been introduced before the session to Robertson Dunlop, a barrister watching proceedings on behalf of the Leyland Line, Lord's employer. Of Ernest Gill, the story-seller who fancied he saw a 'too big' ship charging to the westward a few miles from the stopped *Californian*, there was no sign. Gill would instead be produced on the sixteenth day of the Inquiry, long after the other *Californian* witnesses had gone home.

What impression did Lord Mersey leave on Captain Lord? 'Hostile, at once', the latter replied in a taped interview in 1961. 'He had made up his mind before he started the Inquiry. That's my opinion. Whether that's the right thing to say or not, I don't know… Mersey wasn't sympathetic at all.'

Lord was examined by no less a figure than Sir Rufus Isaacs, Attorney General of the United Kingdom, the first holder of that office to sit at Cabinet. The questioning soon drew out that the *Californian* had been bound for Boston, and in advance of the *Titanic* accident, had seen three icebergs south of her course – transmitting this information to all shipping by wireless.

These were the same three bergs seen by another vessel in the same vicinity, proving that the *Californian* had been on the Boston track some five hours before the *Titanic* collided on the New York track, much further to the south.

At some point, therefore, the *Californian* would have had to journey to the south, leaving her track, to become the mystery ship seen approaching by the *Titanic*, if Captain Lord's vessel were indeed to be that ship. Yet Lord had received 'numerous ice reports' that day of hazards to the south of his course line.

Right: John Charles Bigham, later Lord Mersey and Viscount Mersey, had made his name taking shipping cases for the big lines in Liverpool. He was anxious to limit the scope of the British Inquiry, which excluded all passenger evidence but for J. Bruce Ismay and a society couple rumoured to have bribed lifeboat crew to stay away from the tumult of the dying. *Author collection.*

Below: A photograph taken on the deck of the *Carpathia* soon after the rescue. Visible over the shoulder of the woman in the fur coat, right, are the bows of the *Californian.* She had been above the 42nd parallel, on course to Boston, when she met field ice the previous night and decided to stop. *Library of Congress.*

With the wreck site now known, the *Californian* could barely have reached the location of *Titanic's* sinking in the timeframe in which the mystery ship was seen – but she would have had to steer a diagonal southwest course, no matter the inherent danger, practically immediately after transmitting the warning about the three icebergs.

But the *Californian*, bound west, did not stop until 10.21 p.m., Captain Lord told the Attorney General, and he proceeded to give his overnight stopping place. This position was a crucial assertion, and a huge distance away from the transmitted SOS coordinates – at four times the separation from the *Titanic* of the mystery ship!

It may be helpful at this point to think of that testified *Californian* position as the apex of a pyramid, with the *Titanic's* course line as its base. At opposite extremities along the baseline are the SOS position, to the left, which the maiden voyager never reached, and the wreck site – or at least the actual collision point, to the right.

The British Inquiry completely accepted the reliability of the *Titanic* SOS position, even though it would be shown to be hopelessly wrong seventy-three years later with the 1985 discovery on the seabed.

If the *Californian* stop position were correct, therefore, the British Inquiry would expect *Californian* witnesses to see *Titanic* rockets flying diagonally to the southwest... whereas the evidence in America had been that they had seen them to the southeast... where the wreck would eventually be discovered.

This meant the two positions claimed by the *Titanic* and the *Californian* in 1912 could not both be correct... or else two vessels were firing rockets at the same time. In this clash of positions, as the British Inquiry saw it, the sinking maiden voyager, with 2,200 aboard, would have every incentive for transmitting her position as accurately as possible.

The obvious next step in this unfortunate logical fallacy was to pronounce the *Californian* stop position a falsehood. And if it was false, it meant the *Californian* could be anywhere. She need not have been *stopped*. She could have been *moving*, as the most reliable *Titanic* witnesses openly asserted.

And so, one quarter of the way through Captain Lord's evidence – before any other *Californian* witness has been heard (and even before any *Titanic* officer or White Star Line official had been called to give evidence!) the President of the British Inquiry made this pronouncement:

Lord Mersey: What is in my brain at the present time is this, that what they [*Californian*]
  saw was the *Titanic*.
Attorney General: I know.
Lord Mersey: That is in my brain, and I want to see whether I am right or not.
Attorney General: It certainly must have been very close.

(Br p148. Q. 6804-5)

There were simply no grounds for saying, at this stage of the evidence especially, that the only two ships under consideration 'must have been very close'. There were six more *Californian* witnesses who would be called after Captain Lord, and the fact remained that the depositions of all crew aboard were unassailably to the point that their vessel had been stopped.

Indeed, had the British Inquiry been inclined to dismiss any *Californian* testimony that didn't fit the theory first created in America, they could simply not have ignored the reality of the prior wireless warning of ice transmitted by the *Californian* – and heard by the *Titanic*:

We are stopped, surrounded by ice…

The Marconi operator aboard, Cyril Evans, was employed by the wireless company and owed nothing to either Captain Lord or the Leyland Line. Indeed he had been transferred in any case, and replaced by an operator named Hancock, by the time of the *Californian's* next voyage. Evans says he transmitted the 'stopped' message as instructed by his captain, only to be rebuffed angrily by the still-speeding *Titanic*.

The depositions taken in Liverpool all agreed that the *Californian* had been idle for over an hour and a half before midnight and had not moved again until long after daybreak. The clash between a moving Mystery Ship and the *Californian* could not be more stark.

As Captain Lord declared on tape in 1961:

There are two things I've always stressed. The *Californian* stopped in the ice at 10.20 and her engines never moved. The *Titanic* came up, stopped. There was nothing in sight when she hit the berg. Nothing, by two lookout men and two expert officers on the bridge. They saw nothing. Now how could it possibly have been the *Californian* that they saw?

Californian never moved. This steamer approached them. You don't want any technical adviser to point it out. It's all bunk, isn't it? Those two things would prove to me, and any nautical examiner, that the *Californian* couldn't have been the ship. They proved she never moved after 10.20, and they proved that the *Titanic* never saw anything after she hit the berg, and the steamer they saw steamed towards them. Dammit, that clears everything, doesn't it? Clears everything…

But there were still the rockets. Captain Lord testified that he had a responsible officer of the watch on duty, on whom he was entitled to rely. Second Officer Stone had told him the next day they were not distress rockets that he had seen.

Charles Groves, third officer of the *Californian* and her fourth-in-command. Groves never saw rockets, but had noticed a ship displaying both 'a lot of light' and 'a few minor lights' stopping nearby the night before. By landfall in Liverpool, he told investigators he had concluded it muct have been the *Titanic*, even though he could subsequently cast no light on the size, height or length of the stteamer seen. Groves conceeded that if the *Californian's* own position was even approximately right, 'then of course I am wrong'. *Author collection.*

'Did you question your second officer as to why you had not been called,' Lord was asked at the end of his British evidence. 'I did', he replied, having realised the *Californian* might have been seeing the *Titanic* rockets, even at a great distance. In light of the discovery of the wreck site, it is now certain that they were indeed *Titanic* rockets, intended to signal distress – but horribly confusing for Stone through their appearance in the direction of a nearby tramp steamer.

Q. 7374: What was his explanation to you?

Captain Lord: He [Stone] said that he had sent down and called me. He had sent Gibson down, and Gibson had told him I was awake and I had said: 'All right, let me know if anything is wanted.' I was surprised at him [Stone] not getting me out, considering rockets had been fired. He said if they had been distress rockets he would most certainly have come down and called me himself, but he was not a little bit worried about it at all.

Q. 7375: If they had been distress rockets he would have called you?

Lord: He would have come down and insisted upon my getting up.

1 Captain Edward John Smith of the *Titanic* in confident pose. This arms-folded attitude was used as the model for a statue of Captain Smith erected in a park in Lichfield, even if it is unconsciously emblematic of his hands-off approach to the navigation of his ship that night. Nowadays a Master whose vessel took the lives of 1,500 passengers would be more likely to be cited in a corporate manslaughter charge than to be immortalised in bronze. *The Sphere.*

2 *Left:* A magazine representation of the moment when the aftermost starboard lifeboat, No. 15, nearly lowered onto No. 13. The iceberg impact triggered a largely ill-coordinated abandonment of the *Titanic*, with little evidence of a properly organised evacuation. Each lifeboat departed one-third empty, on average. *The Graphic.*

3 *Below:* Captain Smith swimming with a baby to the overturned Collapsible B. Yet only men were rescued from this perch. The artist depicts Second Officer Lightoller in the background, blowing his whistle to summon help. *Illustrated London News.*

4 *Opposite above:* Harold Cottam, wireless operator on the rescue ship *Carpathia*, was curiously overlooked for hero status, despite operator Jack Binns winning all the plaudits three years earlier in the case of the *Florida–Republic* collision. He received a cheque for just £10 from the Liverpool Shipwreck and Humane Society, whereas his Captain received one for $10,000 from an American newspaper. Cottam died in relative obscurity in Nottingham in 1984, aged 93. If he had not stayed up later than usual that night the *Titanic* SOS would not have been heard. *Illustrated London News.*

THE MAN WHO SAVED OVER 700 LIVES THROUGH SITTING UP A LITTLE LATER THAN USUAL:
·'·MR. COTTAM, THE WIRELESS OPERATOR OF THE "CARPATHIA," AS A STUDENT.
It will be remembered that the "Titanic's" wireless call for help was received by the "Carpathia" some time after the hour at which the latter's operator, Mr. Cottam, usually retired. Had he gone to bed that night at his usual time, it is said, the call would not have been heard, and probably few, if any, of the "Titanic's" people would have been saved. After the wreck, Mr. Cottam worked for days without sleep under extraordinary tension. Our photograph shows him as a student at the British School of Telegraphy in Clapham Road, where Mr. Harold Bride also studied.

5 *Above left:* *How the* Titanic *went down.* Press coverage of the disaster was described by playwright George Bernard Shaw as an 'outbreak of braggartly lying'. *Illustrated London News & Author collection.*

6 *Above right:* Shoes attributed to the Unknown Child, retained by former Halifax police sergeant, Clarence Northover, and kept in a drawer of his office desk until his retirement. All other clothing from unclaimed *Titanic* bodies was burnt. Body number four was buried with a brass plaque inscribed *Our Babe,* the funeral paid for by crewmen of the *MacKay-Bennett,* a search vessel. *Maritime Museum of the Atlantic.*

7 *Above:* Captain Arthur Henry Rostron of the *Carpathia* was awarded a special Congressional medal, knighted, and made an aide-de-camp to the King. He became Commodore of the Cunard Line. Here he is being presented with a commemorative loving cup by survivor Margaret Brown on behalf of *Titanic* escapees. Later known as the 'unsinkable Molly Brown', she enjoyed heroine status despite the basis for her celebrity lying in an apparent exchange of threats with the crewman in charge of her boat. *Library of Congress.*

8 *Left:* Major Arthur Peuchen, a Canadian passenger who descended dangling ropes to reach Lifeboat 6 and provide further seamanship for her. Despite being praised for his bravery by *Titanic* officer Lightoller, Peuchen had to endure a snide whispering campaign for years afterwards. *Courtesy Alan Hustak.*

9 Major Archibald Butt, military attaché to President William Howard Taft in 1912. Nothing is known of Butt's behaviour on the night of the sinking, but the American press still assumed that he had been to the fore in suppressing panic by force of arms. *Library of Congress.*

10 *Left: Titanic* Second Officer Charles Herbert
Lightoller, seen here on the bridge of the *Oceanic*,
warned Captain Smith that the conditions might
make icebergs difficult to detect. Captain Smith
failed to take any resultant precautions.
Courtesy Tim Lightoller.

11 *Below:* Senator William Alden Smith
of Michigan, Chairman of the US Senate
subcommittee on commerce's investigation into
the sinking, which was deemed by much of the
British press to be a gross impertinence. Smith was
out of his depth in nautical affairs. *US Senate.*

12 Captain Lord and his wife Mabel on the deck of the *Californian* in early 1912. Son Stanley Junior is clasping his father's binoculars. They are on the liner's starboard side, looking forward. Picture has some surface damage. *Author collection.*

13 The terrible reality of the *Titanic* disaster: canvas-wrapped bodies piled on the fo'c'sle of the cable ship *MacKay-Bennett*. The vessel had simply run out of coffins, which were reserved in any case for saloon-passenger remains. 125 caskets were stacked on the vessel's after deck. *Collection of Alan Ruffman, Nova Scotia.*

14 *Right:* A ship's boat from the *Minia* attending to one of the seventeen bodies she recovered. Over 300 were found but four times as many were not. *Illustrated London News.*

15 *Below:* William Harbinson, counsel for the third class passengers, walking to the British Inquiry in the company of Sir Robert Finlay, for the White Star Line. Unlike the American Inquiry, no steerage or second class passengers were allowed to testify. *Southampton City Collection.*

16 *Above:* The British Inquiry was presided over by Lord Mersey of Toxteth, then aged 71, some of whose dictums in the case were disproved by the discovery of the *Titanic* wreck in 1985.
Illustrated London News.

17 *Left:* Captain Stanley Lord as a young officer. A brilliant student, he won all available qualifications exceptionally early and was awarded command while still in his twenties. *Author collection.*

18 *Opposite above:* The *Californian*, docked at Boston while under lease to the Dominion Line. Newspaper reporters vied to get her story a few years later when she arrived in the same port from the scene of the *Titanic* disaster. *Author collection.*

19 *Opposite below:* Officers of the *Californian* posing with two child passengers during a voyage to New Orleans on 10 February, 1912. Second Officer Herbert Stone and Third Officer C.V. Groves stand behind Captain Lord and Chief Officer George Stewart. The girls will have to give back the binoculars and telescope. *Author collection.*

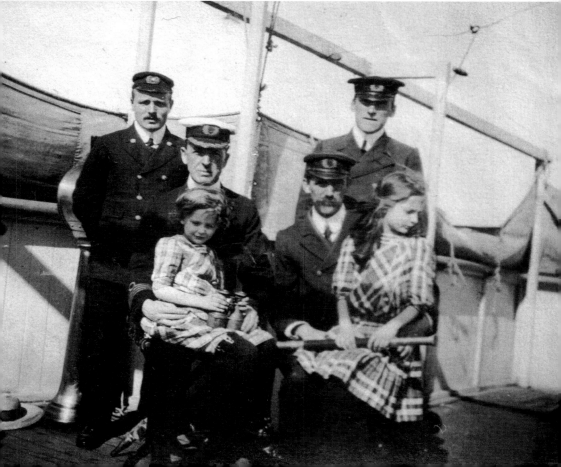

20 Two more in the series of photographs by a passenger family outside the steering gear house, all the way aft on the *Californian*. Captain Lord is seen amid the cheerful group and standing smiling at the stern. Two months later, a patent log trailed from here was snapped away by ice as the liner made a sudden turn on the night of 14 April, 1912. Its recovery would positively establish the *Californian's* whereabouts at the time. *Author collection.*

21 *Above:* Captain Lord, right, in white uniform, poses with American passengers aboard the *William Cliff*, wearing a straw hat he has temporarily accepted in exchange for his own. The man second from left is wearing the Captain's uniform cap. *Author collection.*

22 *Left:* Prime Minister Herbert Henry Asquith told the House of Commons that the *Titanic* disaster had baffled foresight. It had been eighteen years since the Government last significantly addressed the question of lifeboat provision, although the size of passenger ships had been increasing exponentially. *The Graphic.*

23 *Below:* White Star Line MD J. Bruce Ismay mournfully contemplates blueprints of the lost *Titanic* at the US inquiry. Many believed that honour dictated that he should have been lost too.

24 *Above left:* The leader of the *Titanic* orchestra, Wallace Hartley, was celebrated by the newspapers of the day for playing soothing music as the ship sank – even if this psychological reassurance likely impeded the filling of early boats. *Illustrated London News.*

25 *Above right:* The funeral of bandmaster Hartley on Saturday 18 May, 1912 in Colne, Lancashire, was attended by over 30,000 people. They flocked to 'pay their last tribute of respect to the memory of the central figure of one of the most touching incidents in the history of the sea' – after widespread reports that the band had played a final hymn as the ship sank. Scene outside the town hall on Albert Road. *Daily Graphic.*

26 A contemporary postcard of a Leyland liner of about *Californian's* size under way at sea, with another vessel off her starboard bow. Captain Lord said if he had known of any steamer in distress he would naturally have responded, if only because there was 'everything to gain and nothing to lose'.

27 Steerage passengers in the tender *America* at Queenstown on their way to join the *Titanic* for New York, Thursday, 11 April, 1912. Many in this photograph died, including bearded Frank Dwan, centre. Piper Eugene Daly, lower left, holding his instrument, played Irish patriotic airs on the journey to the ship. A few days later, according to an account he gave on the *Carpathia* and in a 1913 court case, he saw men shot down in the scramble for survival. *Irish Examiner.*

28 The same Eugene Daly (sitting, with blanket) a few days later on the *Carpathia*. Daly survived hours of exposure on an upturned collapsible boat, but lost his pipes, for which he was later paid $50 compensation. *Library of Congress.*

29 A May 1912 portrayal of the icefield *Titanic* had been warned about, with a cross to the western side representing the transmitted SOS position – making it apparent to a number of mariners that *Titanic* could not have sunk there. Two crosses to the eastern side are an estimate as to where the *Carpathia* picked up boats. The British Inquiry nonetheless trusted in the accuracy of the distress co-ordinates – which would later prove in error, being some 13 nautical miles from where the wreck was found in 1985. *Illustrated London News.*

30 Cutaway of half the length of the RMS *Titanic*, showing a warren of decks and rooms populated by thousands. 'Social inequality at its most extreme and at its most vertical.' Built at enormous cost, all grades of grandeur went to the bottom because of someone's carelessness. *Illustrated London News.*

This is surely the logic of the position and the proof of Stone's attitude to the rockets at the time. He did not regard them as indicative of distress because he did not go down at any stage to fetch the captain.

'The second officer, the man in charge of the watch, said most emphatically they were not distress rockets,' said Lord, recalling the conversation he had with Stone the next day. Unfortunately, as we know now, they were *Titanic's* rockets. And Lord, for his part, made it clear he would have responded, if he had any inkling of a ship in distress: 'Most certainly I would have made every effort to go down to her.' The record shows that he responded with alacrity the next morning, when the wireless operator returned to duty and sought news.

Stone, in evidence, was unshakeable that he had not discerned any emergency. He pointed out, with regard to the small tramp nearby that: 'a steamer in distress does not steam away from you, my Lord'. That near ship had changed her bearings, moving at least 5 miles out of sight, or 8 miles as Captain Lord thought from Stone's descriptions.

This movement contrasted completely with the immobility of the sinking *Titanic*. Furthermore, the Stone account was supported by the apprentice officer, James Gibson. He testified that he and the second officer had watched as the tramp steamed out of sight, specifically mentioning that she was moving, until she disappeared. But Lord Mersey was having none of it, immediately countering: 'Oh yes, a ship goes out of sight when she goes down to the bottom.'

Gibson suggested that he and Stone knew there was something not quite right with the situation, but he did not imagine there was anything critical – being focused on the ship he could see. The youngster, aged twenty, corroborated that Stone had not suggested the word 'distress' to him at any stage.

The growing suspicions of the British Inquiry found their breakthrough with the next witness, Third Officer Charles Victor Groves. He had been on duty with the captain when Lord detected an icefield ahead and the ship was ordered to a halt. Groves then stayed on watch aboard the stationary *Californian* until midnight.

He first offered that the recorded *Californian* stop position was, 'bound to be [accurate] if the captain put it in', but the Inquiry did not want to hear that. The Attorney General immediately suggested sarcastically that the third officer would not know whether it was or not.

Groves went below after midnight, once he had handed over duty to Stone, and had not seen any subsequent rockets. Thus he was not thereafter witness to anything at all. But he now found himself in a witness box in London faced by the country's top legal eagles, with a huge fuss being made of what had been seen that night.

Unlike his colleagues, who had watched her far more closely and for longer, Groves announced his opinion that the steamer he had noticed approaching was a passenger steamer, because she had been showing 'a lot of light'. He could not, however, make out either her length or her height. Towards the end of his evidence, Groves succumbed completely.

He was asked (Q. 8440): 'If this vessel which you did see was only some 4 or 5 miles to the southward of you, do you think she could have been the *Titanic?*' Lord Mersey immediately interrupted: 'That is a question I want this witness to answer.' He addressed Groves:

> Mersey: Speaking as an experienced seaman and knowing what you do know now, do you think that steamer that you know was throwing up rockets, and that you say was a passenger steamer, was the *Titanic?*
> Groves: Do I think it?
> Yes?
> From what I have heard subsequently?
> Yes?
> Most decidedly I do, but I do not put myself as being an experienced man.
> But that is your opinion as far as your experience goes?
> Yes it is my Lord.

Robertson Dunlop, counsel for the Leyland Line, immediately tried to recover the position: 'That would indicate that the *Titanic* was only 4 or 5 miles to the southward of the position in which you were when stopped,' he noted, going to the point that the *Titanic* would have been colossally off-course to have been that close to the Boston track. In fact, her wreck now proves her to lie south of the New York track!

But Lord Mersey interrupted once more: 'If his judgment on the matter is true, it shows that those figures, latitudes and longitudes, that you are referring to [the *Californian's* testified stop position] are not accurate. That is all it shows.' Dunlop replied through clenched teeth: 'The accuracy we will deal with, my Lord.'

But the accuracy was not his to decide, and instead fell to Lord Mersey – who would go on to ignore a key observation made by Captain Rostron, the Master of the Cunard liner *Carpathia*, to which vessel fell the honour of picking up the *Titanic* survivors: 'At five o'clock it was light enough to see all round the horizon. We then saw two steamships to the northwards, perhaps 7 or 8 miles distant. Neither of them was the *Californian.'* Rostron testified to the Senate Inquiry.

And the *Californian* had still not moved. If she was within sight of the *Titanic* and the *Titanic* lifeboats, she could not have got out of sight by the following morning because she did not even engage engines until 5.15, nor move before 6 a.m.

Despite all this substance, the shadow still fell. In his final report, Lord Mersey declared himself satisfied that the *Californian* stop position, which claimed to see rockets in the 'wrong' place, was 'not accurate'.

His only concession was that there were 'contradictions and inconsistencies in the story as told by the different witnesses', going on to make it clear which construct he preferred. The circumstances convinced him that the ship seen by the *Californian* was indeed the *Titanic*, 'and if so, according to Captain Lord, the two vessels were about 5 miles apart at the time of the disaster'.

That was a direct reference to Captain Lord's response to Q. 6992, about the separation of his ship from the steamer that was 'something like ourselves.' But Lord's response to the question immediately before – Q. 6991 – was that 'a ship like the *Titanic* at sea it is an utter impossibility for anyone to mistake'. He had once seen her sister ship, *Olympic*, at 5 miles.

Lord Mersey had been guided that the *Titanic* would indeed have looked enormous so close. Thus, although he next remarked that: 'the evidence from the *Titanic* corroborates this estimate' of 5 miles, he continued: 'I am advised that the distance was probably greater, though not more than 8 to 10 miles.' More somersaulting.

Mersey concluded:

> The ice by which the SS *Californian* was surrounded was loose ice extending for a distance of no more than 2 or 3 miles in the direction of the *Titanic*. The night was clear and the sea was smooth. When she first saw the rockets the *Californian* could have pushed through the ice to the open water without any serious risk and so have come to the assistance of the *Titanic*.

> Had she done so she might have saved many if not all of the lives that were lost.

Captain Lord, commander of the eventual second ship on the scene (while the two steamers that Captain Rostron had seen at 5 a.m. remained where they were), thus became a scapegoat – or more accurately a sacrificial lamb, since he himself had done absolutely nothing wrong.

IN BLACK
AND WHITE

---•-◆-•---

REPUTATION AND DEMONISATION

The British Inquiry reached its conclusions without throwing its net terribly wide on the issue of the Mystery Ship. Evidence was never called from other ships that could have acted as witnesses to some vital wireless transmissions that night.

For instance, Captain J.T. Gambell of the Allan liner *Virginian* spoke to the British press on landfall in Liverpool of his attempts to assist, although he was too far away. 'At 3.45 a.m. I was in touch by wireless with the Russian steamer *Birma*, and gave her the *Titanic*'s position,' he said.

Gambell added, with huge significance: 'At 5.45 a.m. I was in communication with the *Californian*, the Leyland liner. He was 17 miles north of the *Titanic* and had not heard anything of the disaster.'

Seventeen miles north of the New York course to the SOS position is not the 5 miles of separation described by *Titanic* officers; men who had height, binoculars and years of experience, who knew instinctively the distance to their horizon and whether a ship was moving or not. The *Californian*'s contact with the *Virginian* had resulted in her first knowledge of the crisis, and still her engines were idle, as they had been all night.

No one from the *Virginian* was called to give evidence. Yet this description of a huge distance between the *Californian* and the transmitted *Titanic* distress location happens to dovetail perfectly with a log kept by Joseph Cannon, the wireless operator of the Russian-America liner *Birma*, another vessel mentioned by Gambell.

The *Birma* log states that at 6 a.m., ship's time, she received a call from 'MWL' [the call-sign for the *Californian*], which 'informs she is only 15 miles away from the position given by *Titanic*. *Birma* 22 miles.' *Californian* was at this point under way and responding.

The mileage similarity between these two independent accounts, from *Virginian* and *Birma*, is striking indeed. Both ships could furthermore have provided compelling evidence (from their own experience with the icefield) to prove that the *Titanic* could not have sunk at the SOS coordinates, but must have done so considerably to the east.

In fact the British Inquiry did have other evidence to this point, with the captain of the *Mount Temple* having claimed the real sinking point was 8 miles to the eastward. But the Inquiry's misplaced trust in the SOS position remained absolute.

Since *Californian* was at the apex of a triangle, with the SOS position and actual sinking site located to the lower left and lower right respectively, it follows that the distances cited by the *Virginian* and *Birma* for Captain Lord's vessel broadly also apply in the opposite direction – to where the prestige White Star liner actually went down.

In a handwritten letter to the Board of Trade on 10 August, 1912, after the findings of Lord Mersey were made public, Captain Lord protested: '15 April, about 5.30 a.m., I gave my position to the *Virginian* before I heard where the *Titanic* sunk; that gave me 17 miles away.' He added: 'I understand the original Marconigrams were in court.' (National Archives documents MT9/920E, M23448, Kew.)

None of it made any difference. The Master Mariner's reputation had been shredded, and the Board of Trade, which had both licensed the *Titanic* to go to sea with too few lifeboats and then held the official inquiry under its own auspices, was not about to reconsider the verdict returned by the Wreck Commissioner's Court.

WRECK AND SAFETY REGULATION
To the Editor of *The Times*

Sir – On the way from Sydney to San Francisco in December 1905, from an American passenger ship in the Pacific Ocean, I wrote to you relating how, in compliance with the new marine law of the United States of America, I and every other passenger was individually instructed how to put on a lifebelt.

I told the captain that I was writing to you in the hope that a like regulation for better lifesaving at sea might be put in force on British ships. The captain's remark was prophetic: 'That's no good. Our folks never moved till we lost nearly 1,000 people in the *General Slocum*, and nothing but a big disaster will ever move yours.'

My letter appeared in your journal and others, which also had leading articles thereon. Considerable correspondence ensued, and the shipping companies were communicated with.

As that American captain has prophesied, so it has proved; that as with the Americans, so with the British; only a big disaster would move them.

Yours faithfully,

S.R. Timson, Lieut-Col,
The Kraal, Berkhamsted, Herts.

(*The Times*, 26 April, 1912, p10)

Captain Lord's case proved a useful distraction from the mild criticisms levelled at the Board of Trade by the Final Report, and from the absolution of Captain Smith from a charge of negligence, even though the *Titanic* was found to be travelling at an excessive speed.

Instead, having passed from weeks of idolatrous hero-creation in the immediate aftermath of the sinking, the British public in the summer of 1912 was offered a pantomime villain on whom to vent their spleen.

Indeed the change in mood had first been evident at the Inquiry, which became rather fevered in its often-gymnastic attempts to fix blame on the *Californian*. At one point (Q. 7245) Captain Lord had been asked whether he considered it reasonable that he should go off duty when his ship was stopped and a similar tramp stopped nearby.

'Perfectly reasonable,' replied Lord. 'I was looking after my own ship.' But if the insinuation was that it was somehow unreasonable to leave the bridge of a vessel because it was stopped and drifting imperceptibly in the presence of ice, then how much more unreasonable was it to absent oneself while charging at 21 or 22 knots towards that ice, with full knowledge and forewarning?

'The usual thing, on approaching ice, at night, is to stop and wait until daylight,' said Captain Moore of the *Mount Temple*, which was what the *Californian* had done. But the 'usual thing' for ocean greyhound passenger liners, the Inquiry also heard, was to keep going at full speed, even if warned of ice, so long as the weather was clear and the visibility good.

There was one rule, or at least practice, for the 'rich' ships and another for their 'commoner' or cargo cousins. Yet a single rule would soon be applied across the board – those freighters, with only one wireless operator (who slept at night), would be required henceforth to always carry two operators in order to maintain permanent wireless contact over twenty-four hours. Presumably lest another big passenger liner should ever need assistance.

Lord Mersey had concluded, from the powerful throne of a Government investigation, that the *Californian* was indeed the *Titanic*'s Mystery Ship and that Captain

Lord could have saved many, if not all, of the 1,500 lives lost – had he but woken the wireless operator.

Never mind that Captain Lord was of the opinion that the ship stopped near to him, 'something like ourselves' as he called her, did not possess wireless at all. And wireless was by no means widespread, since slow boats, carrying goods, rarely required it:

WIRELESS TELEGRAPHY

The rapid extension of the use of wireless telegraphy is shown by some figures in a report presented to the Conference [on wireless telegraphy at sea] by the German delegation. It appears that in the last four years the number of ships, excluding warships, equipped with wireless telegraphy has increased from fifty-two to 926, and that during the same period the number of coast stations from fourteen to 155. The total number of ships of all sorts equipped with wireless telegraphy is stated to be 1,577, and the total number of coast stations is 286.

(*The Times*, 13 June, 1912, p6)

The above appear to be worldwide figures. The number of wireless-equipped ships on the North Atlantic in 1912 may not have reached 200. At the same time, it is no exaggeration to say that there were thousands of ships plying that ocean between the Old World and the New. Wireless, if not exactly a luxury, was very much a minority installation.

Nevertheless, a month and a half later, at the end of July, *The Times* had:

...nothing but praise for the [British *Titanic* Inquiry] report, which is masterly, and will, we have no doubt, give general satisfaction. It is very thorough, lucid, dispassionate and firm. The severest blame is implied, rather than expressed, and it concerns the *Californian*. The proofs that the *Californian* saw the display signals of the *Titanic* and could have come to help her... are set out with a deadly conciseness and merciless logic.

Thus the so-called 'Thunderer', the voice of establishment Britain, editorialised. The popular magazine *John Bull* had meanwhile printed an open letter addressed to Captain Lord. It read:

Sir – Perhaps by this time you are thoroughly ashamed of yourself. Although you were called by the officer of the watch, by your apprentice Gibson, and through the speaking tube, and informed that a vessel was firing rockets of distress [sic], you took no heed of the signal.

No doubt it was a cold night, and it was not pleasant to turn out of a warm bed, to go on the bridge, and drive through the ice. But surely you might have taken the trouble to instruct somebody to call up the Marconi operator, and get him to try and find out what was the matter. Yet on your own evidence you slept on, and largely through your inaction 1,500 fellow creatures have perished.

There is no doubt that your officers saw the *Titanic* (it is quite evident that your vessel was within a few miles of her), and had you acted like a man, turned out at the first call, and driven your ship with all possible speed, you would have been able to save every soul on board.

I fear you are a remnant of an old type of skipper, and it strikes me that your officers were somewhat too timid in expressing their views to you. They should have insisted on your going to the assistance of the distressed vessel. They should have chanced your displeasure and pulled you out of bed.

Another matter I don't like is the utter absence of any reference to these distress signals in your log-book. Was the idea to say nothing about it, had the donkeyman not split?

Your whole action is, to say the least of it, reprehensible and un-British, and if the Board of Trade were a real live business body, I rather think they would take stringent action without waiting for the findings of the Court.

You have brought discredit on the fair name of the British Marine service. I rather fancy some of my American friends will give you a warm reception when next you reach New York.

(John Bull)

The portion of the report referring to the *Californian* 'stands out as a thing apart,' moreover wrote the *Daily Telegraph*. 'A horror, which in days to come, will wound the human instinct of the race whenever the story of the *Titanic* is recounted.'

This was indeed a prophetic remark. The horror, and the distortions of the likes of *John Bull* (Captain Lord in a 'warm bed' instead of lying fully dressed on a chartroom settee) would indeed persist with every retelling. Captain Lord was to *become* the horror, to counterbalance the heroes. He would be the default black in countless literary adventures in chiaroscuro.

The captain lost his job with the Leyland Line, at the insistence of one director, even though the company had earlier written to the British Inquiry, submitting the wireless log of its vessel *Antillian*, and pointing out, 'in justice to the captain of the *Californian*,' that the position transmitted by the Lord's vessel at 6.30 p.m. was consistent with her claimed stop position four hours later, when engines were shut down. She could thus not have intentionally prefabricated an alibi for her presence on the Boston track – she was either there or she was not.

Captain Lord himself wrote repeatedly to the Board of Trade protesting a miscarriage of justice that hot summer of 1912, saying in one letter:

> My employers, the Leyland line, although their nautical advisers are convinced we did not see the *Titanic*, or the *Titanic* see the *Californian*, say they have the utmost confidence in me, and do not blame me in any way, but owing to Lord Mersey's decision and public opinion caused by this report, they are reluctantly compelled to ask for my resignation, after 14½ years service without a hitch of any description, and if I could clear myself of this charge, would willingly reconsider this decision.

The Board, naturally, did not reconsider its own position. In fact it had internally been discussing whether to rescind Captain Lord's certificate or to pursue him through the courts for the misdemeanour indicated in Mersey's findings. The official report had included in its recommendations what amounted to a further smear:

> That the attention of Masters of vessels should be drawn by the Board of Trade to the effect that under the Maritime Conventions Act, 1911, it is a misdemeanour not to go to the relief of a vessel in distress when possible to do so.

This naturally implied a state of knowledge, whereas the testimony of all relevant personnel on the *Californian* that night was uniform in denying that any 'vessel in distress' had been detected or even seriously suspected.

The *Review of Reviews*, formerly edited by the distinguished journalist W.T. Stead, a first class passenger lost on the *Titanic*, went so far as to refer to Captain Lord as 'that thousand-fold murderer'. It called on the Board of Trade to take immediate steps to run him off the sea.

(It changed its mind in July, 1913, based on inconsistencies in the evidence. Captain Lord wrote eight months later: 'It is hardly to be supposed that that paper, above all others, would have accorded me the support it does in the article, unless fully convinced there had been a miscarriage of justice and that I have been wrongly condemned by public opinion.')

Meanwhile the Board of Trade, with plenty of legal advice, realised that a criminal prosecution would merely hand Captain Lord an important advantage he did not enjoy when called as a witness at the *Titanic* Inquiry. He would be able to call in his defence witnesses of his own choosing – and to cross-examine those offered by the prosecution. It was a risk too far, and the eventual decision not to proceed with a misdemeanour charge was couched – and cloaked – in sentiments suggesting that Captain Lord had already suffered serious opprobrium sufficient to meet the rankness of his offence.

Captain William Masters took over command of the *Californian*, and Lord went home to Liscard, Cheshire, and his wife and child. No action was taken against the officer of the watch, with the former Master of the ship left to become the sole embodiment of her sin.

It all seemed to offer the perfect 'morality play' fodder for authors, although the first to touch on the question – *Titanic* second class passenger Lawrence Beesley, a science master at a public school – was admirably circumspect in his use of language. Beesley's 1912 book about his *Titanic* experience contains comments which put the *Californian* '20 miles away' but which also acknowledge the findings of the US Inquiry.

Beesley, who actually saw the Mystery Ship, clearly felt he was not in a position – unlike some who stood on land – to judge her identity. He wrote:

Closer than any of these – closer even that the *Carpathia* – were two ships. The *Californian*, less than 20 miles away, with the wireless operator off duty and unable to catch the signal which was now making the air for many miles around quiver in its appeal for help – immediate, urgent help – for the hundreds of people who stood on the *Titanic*'s deck.

The second vessel was a small steamer some few miles ahead on the port side, without any wireless apparatus, her name and destination still unknown; and yet the evidence for her presence that night seems too strong to be disregarded. Mr Boxhall states that he and Captain Smith saw her quite plainly some 5 miles away, and could distinguish the masthead lights and red port light. They at once hailed her with rockets and Morse electric signals, to which Boxhall saw no reply, but Captain Smith and stewards affirmed they did.

The second and third officers saw the signals sent and her lights, the latter from the lifeboat of which he was in charge. Seaman Hopkins testified that he was told by the captain to row for the light; and we in Boat 13 certainly saw it in the same position and rowed towards it for some time. But notwithstanding all the efforts made to attract its attention, it drew slowly away and the lights sank below the horizon.

The pity of it! So near, and so many people waiting for the shelter its decks could have given so easily. It seems impossible to think that this ship ever replied to the signals: those who said so must have been mistaken.

The United States Senate Committee in its report does not hesitate to say that this unknown steamer and the *Californian* are identical and that the failure on the part of the latter to come to the help of the *Titanic* is culpable negligence.

There is undoubtedly evidence that some of the crew on the *Californian* saw our rockets; but it seems impossible to believe that the captain and officers knew of our distress and deliberately ignored it. Judgment on the matter had better be suspended until further information is forthcoming.

An engineer who has served in the trans-Atlantic service tells me that it is a common practice for small boats to leave the fishing smacks to which they belong and row away for miles; sometimes even being lost and wandering among icebergs, perhaps never found again. In these circumstances rockets are part of a fishing smack's equipment, and are sent up to indicate to the small boats how to return. Is it conceivable that the *Californian* thought our rockets were such signals, and therefore paid no attention to them?

Incidentally, this engineer did not hesitate to add that it is doubtful if a big liner would stop to help a small fishing boat sending off distress signals, or even would turn about to help one which she herself had cut down as it lay in her path.

In light of the last paragraph, above, consider the following:

TITANIC SPLASHED A 'DANGEROUSLY NEAR' TRAWLER

Our Boulogne correspondent writes that one of the last vessels to sight the *Titanic* was probably the Boulogne steamer trawler *Alsace*, which passed the liner on Thursday 11 April, off the south-west coast of Ireland. The trawler appears to have been rather dangerously near to the *Titanic*, passing so close in fact that she was splashed with spray from the *Titanic*'s bow. The fishermen cheered the liner, and their salutations were responded to by the officer on the bridge.

(*The Times*, 22 April, 1912, p12)

Here we see that it was the trawler, slow and ponderous, that was dangerously near to the *Titanic* – rather than the other way around. The officer on the bridge of the thrusting leviathan might have cut the fishermen mighty close, such that the salutation of a shaken fist might be understandable. Yet the composition of this brief report goes to the natural tendency that 'might is right,' that the strong have strength of character, that small-fry are to be lightly regarded and that inferiority in size is an inferiority that applies across the board.

There are undoubted elements of such thinking, no matter how subconscious or how well-suppressed in overt expression, in some of the treatments of the rival assertions made by the *Titanic* and *Californian* – as evidenced by the rejection of the latter's doubt (since vindicated) over the former's actual sinking location. Beesley, at least, tried to resist such conditioned bias.

There are minor errors with his account, however, such as his claim that Captain Smith thought he saw a response to their Morsing. What Boxhall actually stated in London was that he and the captain both studied her through glasses, and the captain did not see any answer. The second and third officers (Lightoller and Pitman) saw 'the signals sent', but Beesley presumably means the *Titanic's* own Morse flashes or rockets being discharged, as neither man testified to any action on the part of the Mystery Ship.

Yet Beesley is convincing about his own efforts to reach the vessel and how it instead 'drew slowly away' and disappeared over the horizon. This is a moving ship – which is why Beesley instinctively talks of two ships under discussion, the *Californian* being a vessel that must be distinct from the Mystery Ship.

His misgivings about the equation of the *Californian* and the tantalising masthead lights as being one and the same are subtle, but clear. It is not a conclusion he is able to draw, despite (or because of) his being there that night, and judgement should be suspended rather than rushed.

No further information as to the identity of the *Titanic's* nearby moving visitor was immediately forthcoming, however, and the inquiry findings thus seemed to gain ground – or at least become the truth by dint of the absence of other evidence.

The *Californian* was a British ship that had not complied with the 'Be British!' spirit but had instead been 'un-British', at least in the eyes of *John Bull*. But Beesley was also a Britisher, and one who found it impossible to believe that distress would be known about and deliberately ignored.

The fact that the *Californian* witnesses told of being entirely unperturbed, while the Mystery Ship seemed to behave in a like manner (sending no signals herself in Beesley's view), does not allow him to make any connection. Of course, at a facile level, if the Mystery Ship had verifiably sent Morse signals back to the *Titanic*, this would have been seized upon as a proof positive of her being the *Californian*, which had assiduously signalled her own stranger without success.

Similar shoddy logic had been evident at the British Inquiry, when Captain Lord volunteered that *Californian* Third Officer Groves had claimed to see two masthead lights on the steamer which came close to them and stopped – whereas Lord himself, Second Officer Stone and apprentice officer Gibson, three together, had each seen only one light:

Attorney General: If he did see two lights, it must have been the *Titanic*, must it not?

Captain Lord: It does not follow.

Attorney General: Do you know any other vessel it could have been?

Lord: Any amount.

The next *Titanic* book to be written by a passenger was that by Colonel Archibald Gracie, who had fought on the Confederate side in the American Civil War. *The Truth About the* Titanic appeared in 1913, after Gracie's death, and it evidently lacked the cautious consideration of Beesley on this question – albeit that Gracie, a fellow eyewitness, was again convinced that the Mystery Ship was moving:

> To reassure the ladies of whom I had assumed special charge, I showed them a bright white light of what I took to be a ship about 5 miles off, and which I felt sure was coming to our rescue. Colonel Astor [J.J. Astor, the richest man in the world at the time, who would not survive] heard me telling this to them and he asked me to show it, and I pointed the light out to him. In so doing we both had now to lean over the rail of the ship and look close in towards the bow, avoiding a lifeboat even then made ready with its gunwale lowered to the level of the floor of the Boat Deck above us, and obstructing our view. But instead of growing brighter the light grew dim, and less and less distinct, and passed away altogether.
>
> The light, as I have since learned, with tearful regret for the lost who might have been saved, belonged to the steamer *Californian* of the Leyland line, Captain Stanley Lord, bound from London to Boston. She belonged to the International Mercantile Marine Company, the owners of the *Titanic*.

Gracie gives no pause to consider why a Boston-bound steamer should be approaching ('meeting us', as Boxhall said) on the New York track. He goes on to echo not just Senator Smith's explicit findings, but also his grandiloquent mention of the 'brave men and noble women' aboard the *Titanic*. Gracie writes: 'It was not chance, but the grossest negligence alone which sealed the fate of all the noble lives, men and women, who were lost.'

And although acknowledging that the *Californian* had sent two of the six ice-warnings received by the *Titanic*, Gracie does not appear to grasp the significance of the second one, which he correctly reports as the message that: 'We [*Californian*] are stopped and surrounded by ice.' Gracie himself saw a *moving* ship, but reports the *Californian* to be stopped…

Gracie rushes to add that the *Titanic* had 'brusquely replied, "Shut up, I am busy. I am working Cape Race"' but the meaning of the stopped *Californian* totally eludes him. Yet he next goes on to report once more that Captain Lord's vessel was immobile at all material times:

> It appears from the evidence referred to, information in regard to which we learned after our arrival in New York, that the captain of the *Californian* and his crew were watching our lights from the deck of their ship, which remained approximately stationary until 5.15 a.m. on the following morning.
>
> During this interval it is shown that they were never distant more than 6 or 7 miles. In fact at 12 o'clock, the *Californian* was only 4 or 5 miles off at the point and in the

general direction where she was seen by myself and at least a dozen others, who bore testimony before the American Committee, from the decks of the *Titanic*.

The white rockets, which we sent up... were also plainly seen at the time. Captain Lord was completely in possession of the knowledge that he was in proximity to a ship in distress. He could have put himself into immediate communication with us by wireless had he desired confirmation of the name of the ship and the disaster which had befallen it.

His indifference is made apparent by his order to 'go on Morsing', instead of utilising the more modern method of the inventive genius and gentleman, Mr Marconi, which eventually saved us all.

Look at Gracie's obvious fudge – the *Californian* was 'approximately' stationary. He knows the ship he saw was moving. He also knows the thrust of the *Californian* testimony. But what he relies on completely is the finding of the Inquiry. The *Californian* was the Mystery Ship; ergo the correctness of the decision is only lacking in minor detail...

We know, however, that this detail is not minor. Gracie may have 'learned' much information after arrival in New York, but hearing and reading speculation is not the same as obtaining distilled knowledge or objective truth. He himself was there and knows what he saw – he has nothing to learn about his own experience, in New York or anywhere else.

And how can he know that Captain Lord was, 'completely in possession of the knowledge that he was in proximity to a ship in distress'. He does not know what was known or not known on a ship other than his own.

Beesley and Gracie reported near-identical things from the deck of the *Titanic* – a very near ship which 'drew slowly away and the lights sank below the horizon' [Beesley] or 'grew dim and less and less distinct and passed away altogether' [Gracie].

But while Beesley says judgement should be suspended, the Inquiry findings have surpassed and replaced Gracie's own experience – his subjective truth having now been replaced by the 'objective history', which he accepts and endorses (despite its wrong-headedness), that Captain Lord displayed 'indifference' and was furthermore guilty of the 'grossest negligence'.

These are statements purporting to be those of fact, with no qualification or 'approximation'... Captain Lord was a villain with an 'approximately stationary' ship.

Again, had it been the other way, had the *Californian* been cheerfully picking her way along (anywhere at all), then Gracie would have gladly grappled this fact to his bosom as proof of what his own eyes had told him. The American Inquiry, in those circumstances, certainly would have been even more triumphantly correct.

As it was, Gracie appears to believe that the Inquiry ringingly vanquished those who had sought to mislead it.

And so history is formed, not out of truth or detail, but of 'what everyone thinks'. Perceptions become the reality, and it matters not a whit that the accepted ideas might be those largely formed by Senators on land, rather than eyewitnesses at sea. Captain Lord was guilty – his ship may have been moving or stopped; 20 miles away on the Boston track or unexpectedly appearing on the New York track – but he was guilty.

This hypnosis even infected Lord's own acquaintances. A Captain J.D. MacNab, the Board of Trade chief examiner in Liverpool, wrote to that city's *Daily Post* on 3 August, 1912:

> I am not out to defend Captain Lord's inaction, but to ask for sympathy for his terrible misfortune of failing to realise that the signals seen by his officers indicated distress. His past life and character go to prove that, had he realised this, he would have braved the ice dangers which beset his own ship, and gone to the rescue.
>
> But seamen are only mortals, and especially when wearied with long watching, liable like other people to temporary dullness of apprehension of matters happening outside the limits of their own charge.
>
> Captain Lord passed all his Board of Trade examinations most brilliantly before me, his testimonials for good conduct and ability at sea being invariably of the highest order. Since then I have ever heard him spoken of as a humane and clever officer and commander, as well as a kind husband, a loving father, and a high-principled gentleman.
>
> His mental punishment, however, may be assuaged by the reflection that his sin was of omission, not of commission, and certainly in no sense intentional.

This tribute to Lord's past character acknowledged his present 'sin', one that brought punishment, even if it stemmed from 'temporary dullness' – as if the clever, even brilliant commander had somehow erred in assessing the circumstances described to him. Yet the describer, Officer Stone, was indicating no concern, and was reporting instead on a near ship that was safe and well and eventually steaming away.

The exertions of watch-standing were not so wearying as to stultify Stone on the appearance of something important – the rockets went up relatively early in his watch. Yet it may have been not only the obvious safety of the ship in whose direction he saw the rockets that blinded him to the reality of distress over the visible horizon (and as we now know from the wreck site, distress there was), but the unexpected calm, even the pleasure, of being on watch while his ship was stopped may have caused the very idea of risk elsewhere to have been banished utterly.

That Lord would have instantly gone to the rescue, had he but known, he repeatedly asserted himself. MacNab posits what Gracie will not believe – the fact of Lord's inaction proving his lack of awareness, since he would otherwise always have taken action. But this is no heroism, as Joseph Conrad noted in the *English Review* of July 1912:

> I am not a sentimentalist; therefore it is not a great consolation to me to see all these people breveted as 'Heroes' by the penny and halfpenny Press. It is no consolation at all. In extremity, the worst extremity, the majority of people, even of common people, will behave decently.
>
> It's a fact of which only the journalists don't seem aware. Hence their enthusiasm, I suppose.

How many lifeboats would Captain Lord have needed to pick up the next morning to have been breveted a hero? One?

Perhaps a single clutch of survivors might have guaranteed his being fêted as one of the favoured few who managed to perform another 'Marconi miracle' in the wireless age... so that rescuing even a shivering handful would have also rescued his own reputation.

We can imagine then his triumph, the laudatory headlines, despite an unlucky start. And nothing more would have been made of that initial inactivity but 'ill-luck' – rockets were simply misunderstood, and the wireless man had gone to bed; it was a damnable happenstance.

Captain Lord would thus have been accorded the basic presumption of a willingness to go to the rescue, which of course he later did demonstrate – but his misfortune lay in arriving minutes too late, when the *Carpathia* was just completing the rescue of survivors. 'I think he was taking the last boat up when I got there,' Captain Lord told the American Inquiry.

The fact that he did not rescue anyone saw him instead saddled with the presumption of an *unwillingness* to assist. And from there it was a shortcut to suppose that there existed a conscious callousness.

Consensus snowballs, gathering adherents. MacNab, in acknowledging Captain Lord's 'sin', was perhaps affected with the malady of 'Inquiry awe', entirely understandable as that particular condition is, even today, in relation to the outcome of any process. *I hadn't the time to go into the detail myself, but I must assume these other fellows got it right.* Presumption, and assumption, lie of course at the very heart of this particular problem.

Joseph Conrad, on the other hand, trusted to faith in his fellow man – the very quality on which seafarers rely among themselves. The majority of people will behave decently in any extremity. How much more likely is that when set against Captain Lord's status, recounted by one who knew him, as a 'kind husband, loving father, and a high-principled gentleman?'

Leaving aside the bonds and brotherhood of all those who occupy their business in great waters, if Captain Lord had known – or even suspected for a moment – that a passenger liner was in difficulties, what would he have done?

The *Daily Telegraph* spoke in its reaction to the official report about the 'high standard of conduct on the sea, accepted by sailors everywhere as a commonplace duty which none would dare escape even at personal peril'. Leaving this accepted code to one side, but bearing in mind the concept of 'commonplace duty' rather than any 'fanfare fearlessness', the answer to what Lord would have done supplies itself in the fact of his fatherhood, above all.

Any child is everyone's child – my child – when momentary danger should loom. Every parent knows this, and from the prompting of their own instincts. Parenthood bestows that obligation to intervene, irrespective of risk to oneself, when the child of even another individual should wander into harm's way. This is an automatic response, and not an audaciously brave or heroic one. It is the innate decency that Conrad talks about, springing eternal.

And Captain Lord was a father. There is a photograph of him taken on the deck of the *Californian* in early 1912, published in this book but never anywhere before. It shows him with his wife, Mabel, and his son, Stanley Junior. The three-year-old is seen gripping his father's binoculars.

Captain Lord is also a sea captain. He knows that a passenger ship will contain children by the score, if not the hundred, just as the *Titanic* did. His own son stood on his ship's deck just months earlier, and away at sea he must trust to the kindness of strangers himself. The man therefore does not choose the moment; the moment summons the man. The father-captain (as they would portray Captain Smith) is drawn to action and cannot resist.

How then is Captain Lord a villain? Why, only in cardboard cut-out portrayal, in the ridiculous reduction from flesh-and-blood man to bloodless, or cold-blooded, cur. It is a travesty of the reality, and indeed the commonplace matter of the monster possessing a family life is not wanted, and nor indeed is any humanising context that would subvert his allotted role as a hiss-figure of history.

And this is what consensus often does, robbing the truth of layers of meaning (sucking Gracie's own sense and his own sightings out of him, for instance), smoothing all 'distracting' detail away until what we want to believe is what we think we know, and folly finds a hallowed place hereafter.

In this process, a refusal of circumstances to be clear-cut is unacceptably wishy-washy. Grey areas are simply areas that are too cowardly to make up their minds as to whether they are black or white. And so it is done for them. We simplify, sum up, take a stab in the dark. It will do. The ferocious French fishing boat dangerously menaced the *Titanic*...

And so the books that followed thereafter followed Gracie. Not Beesley, with his commendable circumspection, for one cannot be cautious when setting out a cautionary tale. And in a deeply paradoxical sense, everyone loves a villain. Or at least they love the shared shudder of distaste, for again it becomes the collective – good – against the outsider, outcast.

Captain Lord was not cast out for long, spending four months at home with his wife and child before obtaining an appointment as a captain with the Lawther Latta line of steamships. Sir John Latta was evidently impressed with Lord's litany of testimonials and maximum qualifications, and had no hesitation in appointing the pariah not just to one of his ships, but to her command.

The 'thousand-fold murderer' described on tape in 1961 how he was forced to leave the Leyland company, but how his 'grossest negligence' was not long an obstacle to advancement:

I was asked to resign, not because the firm – the managing director – wanted it. It was settled in London, and I was told by Mr [Henry] Roper [managing director] that he had nothing at all to do with it. It was strongly against his wishes.

Captain [John] Fry [Leyland marine superintendent] came up to me and told me that Mr Roper was very sorry, but he couldn't give me another ship. Well, I thought to myself, that's rather strange, as it was only a few weeks ago, when I'd transferred from the *Californian*, that he'd said that I would get my own ship back again.

I said I would like to see him. He said, 'Yes, of course you can'. He went in, and I went in and saw Mr Roper, and told him I was very grieved to hear this, and he had said I would get the *Californian* back again. He said, 'Yes, I told you that, but it was taken altogether out of my hands. I had no say in the matter whatsoever. It was all settled without any opinion from me.'

I was out of work until the following January, and my wages were paid up to the particular day when I was asked to resign. And my bonus [normally only paid for days at sea], most unusual. Usually when a ship came into port, after a few days the captain went onto half pay. And the bonus was most certainly not running while she was in there.

My next appointment was with Lawther Latta. I received a letter from them one morning, telling me they'd heard from a friend of mine, Mr Frank Strachan of New Brunswick, Georgia, who spoke very highly of me, and was under the impression that I'd been very harshly treated, and if they had a ship he could highly recommend me for the appointment as Master.

So Mr Latta – he was Mr Latta in those days [later knighted] – said, 'If you feel like calling in here and have the opportunity, I will be very pleased to see you'. I wrote back and told him that there was nothing to bring me down to London that I could see, unless I came specially to see them. So he wrote back to tell me to come down and they'd stand all expenses, which they did.

I had a long conversation with him and told him I knew Strachan, I'd been all these years with Leyland, and my record. And he said, 'From what Mr Strachan tells us, if we have a vacancy – we probably will have, very shortly – we'll let you have command of her.' And about a couple of weeks after, I think it would be, I forget exactly, he wrote and told me that they'd appointed me Master of their steamer *Anglo-Saxon*.

The magazine *John Bull* may have expressed the hope that its American friends would give Captain Lord 'a warm reception' when next he touched New York, but in fact:

I went to New York a dozen times, oh a dozen times during the war. Never mentioned. Never mentioned. I was in New Orleans, a place I'd been trading to for years and years in Leyland's – [and was] received very well by everybody. 'Hello Cap, glad to see you back again', the boys on the wharf were always yelling to me.

So much for a storybook world in which the good are honoured forever and only the wicked are punished. Such indeed is the actual stuff of make-believe. Villains are simply not intended to live contentedly ever after.

A GATHERING DARKNESS

TIME, THE THIEF OF TRUTH

The world moved on, and soon became enmeshed in horrid conflict. The Great European War, as it was first called, would have a ruinous effect on shipping. Towards its end, in 1918, the rescuer of *Titanic* survivors, the Cunard liner *Carpathia*, was sent to the bottom of the Atlantic by three torpedoes in a position southwest of the Fastnet rock, off Ireland.

Two illuminated testimonials, presented by *Titanic* survivors to her former captain barely six years earlier, were also taken down to the inky depths:

It was at the main entrance to the saloon that we noticed the most striking proof of the feelings of the rescued people, for there framed in vellum, and meant to be retained as long as the *Carpathia* is voyaging, are two handsomely engrossed resolutions, one passed by the women saved by the *Carpathia* from the *Titanic* disaster, and which in part reads:

16 April, 1912
'We, the women passengers saved from the Titanic *by the* Carpathia, *wish to place on record permanently our undying gratitude to the* Carpathia's *captain, officers and crew. We shall ever remember their tender kindness, courage and generosity, and while life lasts the memory of their succour will never be forgotten by us.'*

The resolution goes on to refer to the awful night of grief which the passengers went through when the ship went down under them, and of that life-long parting with all who were dear to them – husbands, fathers, brothers and children, and of the fine gallantry which the chivalrous captain, officers and crew of the *Carpathia* displayed at a time of grief and despair, of the timely rescue made, and the sacrifices cheerfully undertaken, on board the heaven-sent *Carpathia*.

A somewhat similar resolution also is framed beside that of the women folk, and which gives praise to those of the *Carpathia* from the men saved from the *Titanic*.

(*Cork Examiner*, 8 February, 1913, p3)

Captain Rostron was not aboard at the time of his former ship's sinking, having moved to take command of the *Mauretania*. Five men were, however, lost in the *Carpathia's* destruction, and the rest were taken aboard HMS *Snowdrop*, one of the other vessels in convoy. In his later memoirs, *Home From the Sea*, Rostron remarked: 'It was a sorry end to a fine ship… she had done her bit both in peace and war, and she lies in her natural element, resting her long rest on a bed of sand.'

Also sent to the same grey and grainy berth was the Leyland Line's *Californian*. Converted to a troopship, she sailed from Salonika to Marseilles on 7 November, 1915, under Captain William Masters, the man taken out of the *Cuban* at short notice to provide a replacement for Captain Lord. She was torpedoed by U-35 two days later at 7.45 a.m., off Cape Matapan, Greece.

A French patrol boat tried to tow the stricken vessel, but the hawser parted. A second torpedo then struck at 2.15 p.m. and the *Californian* made water fast. As it turned out, she had both time and boats for all aboard – the latter an ironic by-product of the *Titanic* incident – and a total of 115 survivors, including sixty-one crew, were picked up. Only one life was lost.

George Frederick Stewart, Chief Officer of the *Californian*. Confident of his vessel's latitude, he naturally knew the *Titanic's* close-in mystery ship 'wasn't us'. Steward died in March 1940, a victim of a *Luftwaffe* aircraft's bombing of the *Barn Hill* off Beachy Head.

Captain Lord had spent four months of the war ashore, supervising the fitting-out of the *Anglo-Chilean*, newest and largest vessel of the Lawther Latta fleet. He was in Liverpool when he suddenly met his old chief officer of the *Californian* from the night of the *Titanic* sinking, George Frederick Stewart.

'I met Stewart about 1917 when I was waiting for this new ship,' says Lord in a recording made forty-four years later:

> I was home for two or three months, on pay all the time, and met him outside the Kardomah [a café in Whitechapel, Liverpool]. I said: 'Good lord, fancy meeting you. Come on, let's go and have a coffee.' We went down and had a coffee, and we talked and talked for about two hours. I said: 'What do you think of this [Mystery] Ship?'
> He [Stewart] said: 'I don't know; I don't think there's any question it wasn't us. But what the devil did Stone see? I've never been able to gather together what he did see yet.'

Lord eventually took charge of the *Anglo-Chilean*, loaded her with army stores at Tilbury, and began a voyage to Alexandria. In the Mediterranean he was chased by a U-boat (which had disguised herself with a sail) and was fired upon in a prolonged pursuit. The submarine fired altogether sixty-seven shells, and the *Anglo-Chilean* replied with seven of her own from a stern gun. Eventually they outran the U-boat, which was slower over the surface in any case, amid reports that one of the gunnery shots may have struck the German and damaged her.

Later that same year, in November, the *Anglo-Chilean* led to home waters a convoy from New York, with the Royal Navy commodore for the entire undertaking having joined Lord aboard his vessel. This officer, Captain W.H. Owen, later wrote to Lawther Latta expressing himself 'greatly indebted to Captain Lord for all his help'. He added:

> One hopes you will not consider it presumption on my part to express my appreciation of this splendidly-equipped ship, and still more of the loyal and able man in command... Pray forgive my writing to you, my only desire is to express admiration of a well-appointed ship and her able and courteous commander.

Lord received another testimonial ten years later when he acceded to medical advice that he should retire from the sea, in his fiftieth year, because of failing eyesight. Sir John Latta penned this reference:

> It gives us very great pleasure to state that Captain Stanley Lord held command in this company from February 1913 until March 1927, during the whole of which period he had our entire confidence, and we regard him as one of the most capable commanders

we have ever had. It was a matter of much regret to us that he felt compelled to retire owing to indisposition. He carries with him our grateful appreciation of his excellent services, and we earnestly hope that he will soon recover his wonted health.

Also soon retiring was Captain Rostron, whose memoirs would tell how *Carpathia* wireless operator Harold Cottam had been stooped, taking off his shoes, prior to going to bed – when he suddenly heard the *Titanic's* frantic SOS. If Cottam had turned in a fraction earlier, or taken off his headphones to attend to his feet, all the laurels would have fallen to Captain Lord.

Cottam himself received scant recognition, although all *Carpathia* crew were presented with medals and small purses, while Rostron went on to get his loving cup, a special Congressional medal of honour, and various accolades including a gold watch from the Austro-Hungarian Government, and a knighthood from the King, who also made him an aide-de-camp. Rostron in time also became Commodore of the Cunard Line and commander of its largest liner, the *Berengaria*.

In 1912 Rostron received hundreds of letters from admirers, and the widowed Mrs Madeleine Astor entertained both he and Dr McGee, the liner's surgeon, to a special lunch in the opulent family mansion on Fifth Avenue. The only other guest was Mrs John B. Thayer, whose husband, the late vice-president of the Pennsylvania Railroad, had perished with John Jacob Astor in the *Titanic*.

Going to a performance at the Winter Garden Theatre in the city, Rostron was recognised and compelled to make a speech to an enthusiastic crowd during one of the intervals. Nor was the proffering of very large amounts of money to him unusual at this time:

> Captain Rostron, the commander of the Cunard Liner *Carpathia* was today presented with a cheque for ten thousand dollars, raised by public subscription by the *New York American*, in recognition of his efforts in the rescue of the survivors of the *Titanic* disaster.
>
> Acknowledging the cheque, Captain Rostron declared that he would never forget the way in which he had been received by Americans, though he again maintained that the members of his crew were entitled to equal credit. 'I shall use this cheque,' he said, 'for the education of my three sons, whom I hope to bring up as worthy representatives of the Anglo-Saxon race.'
>
> (*Cork Examiner*, 4 June, 1912, p3)

'In those days,' wrote Rostron in his 1931 autobiography, 'wireless was but a recent addition to the equipment of ships at sea':

We were quite proud of our installation... and we carried only one operator.

This man should have finished duty at midnight. Yet here was half past twelve and he was still listening in. But he was on the very point of retiring. He was, in fact, in the act of bending down to undo his boots when the dread call came...

Rostron himself had already undressed and gone to bed, retiring earlier than Captain Lord – who, his ship being in the presence of ice, had resolved to lie down in the chartroom. 'A little pokey hole – the worst accommodation I've ever seen in a ship. I couldn't stretch my legs and I was fully dressed; boots, bridge coat, hat, collar, tie and everything on. Just snored, dozing off there. The light was on...'

Yet Cyril Evans, the *Californian's* wireless operator, had gone to his bunk earlier than Cottam, his opposite number on the *Carpathia*, no doubt encouraged by the *Titanic's* suggestion that he should shut up and keep out. He had shut down his instrument by midnight, ship's time.

What would Captain Lord have done if the wireless roles had been reversed, Cottam turning in, but Evans electing to stay up for a while to listen to traffic?

The answer is obvious. But the assertion from later critics, who seize on Stone's sightings and innocuous reports as if they were proof positive of wilful, selfish, cognisant cruelty on the part of the Master, is to claim that Captain Lord would actually have done nothing. Because he did nothing when rockets were seen.

This is to overlook both the confusing position surrounding rockets at sea at that time (when rockets did not necessarily or solely mean distress), the idea entertained that the nearby 'small to medium' steamer might have been signalling back after three separate Morsing attempts by the *Californian*, and the actually ordinary nature of Stone's communications with Captain Lord.

A specific wireless communication by a ship saying that she is sinking is entirely different to a 'low-lying' light in the direction of a close and secure (but uncommunicative) tramp. There was no sound to those rockets, whereas the distress regulations emphasised sound over visibility, even if those aged regulations ought to have been radically overhauled long before in order to give pride of place to both qualities.

The first option when signalling distress at night, by the regulations then in force, was to fire a gun at minute intervals. This meant making a sound, a regular crack or boom, with no flashes needed. The second option was to light a barrel of pitch on deck to show flames... and only the third option turned out to be rockets, 'of any colour or description, fired one at a time at short intervals'.

The *Titanic* carried socket signals, a particular type of rocket, whose principal function was to make a large bang aloft. They were specifically certified to be carried 'in lieu of guns'. None of the witnesses on the *Californian* at any stage heard a crack synchronous with a rocket, or even a delayed detonation, since sound travels much more slowly than light.

All this would tend to show that those rockets, as Stone first suspected, were indeed emanating from much further off than the visible steamer, the sound being lost. The *Titanic* wreck site shows how much further, and why nothing at all was heard.

Absence of sound helped Stone honestly believe nothing was awry. Again, the real blame for this confusion must actually go to the Board of Trade – they could have specified rockets alone as a signal of distress at night, combining both audibility and visibility. Yet their preferred methods of conveying nocturnal distress were, in order, 1) sound, 2) light, and 3) sound and light. The fourth option, incidentally, was sound again – 'a continuous sounding with any fog signalling apparatus'.

Stone and Gibson had only light, and it didn't come from flames in a barrel on anyone's deck.

Again, the practice in emergencies at this time – specifically encouraged by mention in the regulations of methods being used singly or *together* – was to use every available resource to indicate distress. The small steamer under observation from the *Californian* absolutely did not do anything of the sort.

Meanwhile, in separate consideration, if the Board of Trade had revised its regulations for signalling distress at night – even while maintaining eighteen-year-old regulations that created such a paucity of lifeboats aboard ocean liners – then the Board itself 'may well have saved all aboard.'

The Board of Trade was the agency specifically chartered with the establishment, upkeep and enforcement of precautions for the safety of life at sea, and it demonstrably failed in that primary function.

If rockets had been expressly forbidden from being fired at sea for any purpose other than distress, and if the old tar-barrel of centuries gone by had been scrapped, along with the absurd Royal Navy-informed reliance on guns, then Stone would have acted immediately. A light in the dark on its own would have been a direct spur to action.

And what would Lord have done? The proof is actually in the testimony. Captain Lord consulted his Chief Engineer, William Mahon, when he decided to stay at the ice rim until daylight. From his American evidence:

Captain Lord: The engines were stopped; perfectly stopped.

Senator Duncan Fletcher: But you could have gone to the *Titanic*?

Lord: The engines were ready. I gave instructions to the Chief Engineer and told him I had decided to stay there all night. I did not think it safe to go ahead. I said 'We will keep handy in case some of those big fellows come crunching along and get into it.'

He would stay ready to respond in case he was needed.

Chief Engineer Mahon, if he had been called, could have verified his captain's attitude, and whether he had expressed any such remark. We know Mahon, like all the other crew, gave a deposition at Liverpool. And he was not called, despite his further ability to prove from his engine log the simple fact of the *Californian* being stopped all night. In fact, Captain Lord brought that engine log to the Inquiry – but it wasn't examined either, at least not in evidence.

So Lord would have responded had Evans stayed up and at his key, regardless of whether Cottam and Rostron went to bed on another vessel. Meanwhile Rostron in his memoirs was scrupulously fair in recounting his dramatic role in the *Titanic* rescue, expressing no opinion on what he could not know about, namely the identity of the latter vessel's Mystery Ship.

Yet he did recall, naturally, what had been his own evidence in 1912: that when it was daylight enough to see all around the horizon, at 5 a.m. that morning of 15 April, Rostron had noticed two ships some way off, and 'neither was the *Californian*.'

He said the same in his autobiography: 'Except for the boats beside the ship [*Carpathia*] and the icebergs, the sea was strangely empty.' It was about 8 a.m., he wrote, when they saw another ship coming up. It would prove to be the *Californian*, responding late, but getting there all the same – when other vessels did not.

The next person to recall the *Titanic* disaster in print, and the last of its significant players, was her senior surviving officer, Charles Herbert Lightoller. He penned his work, Titanic *and Other Ships*, in 1935. It was published in the middle of a worldwide depression that had lain up shipping by the million tons, although Lightoller had long since quit the White Star Line:

At this time [he wrote of the sinking], we were firing rocket distress signals, which explode with a loud report a couple of hundred feet in the air. Every minute or two one of these went up, bursting overhead with a cascade of stars.

'Why were we firing these signals, if there was no danger?' was the question, to which I replied that we were trying to call the attention of the ship nearby, as we could not get her with wireless. *That ship was the* Californian.

Here again we see exemplified what has become almost proverbial at sea, that in cases of disaster, one ship, the first on the scene, will be in a position to rescue, and yet, through some circumstance or combination of circumstances, fails to make that rescue.

The distress signals we fired were seen by the Officer of the Watch on board the *Californian*, also by several [sic – incorrect] members of her crew. Even the flashes of our Morse lamp were seen but finally judged to be 'just the masthead light flickering.' Though at one time the thought evidently did arise that we were trying to call them.

To let pass the possibility of a ship calling by Morse, in the existing circumstances then surrounding her, was bad enough; but to mistake distress signals was inexcusable, and to ignore them, criminal.

In point of fact the O.O.W. alone saw, and counted, five distress signals (or, as he reported them to Captain Lord, 'five white rockets'). Evidently the captain's curiosity was more than a little aroused for him to ask 'Are they company's signals?' To which the O.O.W. replied that he did not know, but they 'Appear to me to be white rockets.' Captain Lord merely told him to 'go on Morsing,' and if he received any further information to send it down to him.

It is an unqualified fact that every single one of our distress signals – unmistakable and urgent calls for help, were clearly seen by the *Californian*. These signals are never made, except in cases of dire necessity.

The italics are Lightoller's own, and twenty-three years on he was following Gracie's assumption that the Inquiries were right and that the ship seen was the *Californian*. Yet Officer Lightoller had sent this letter of support to Captain Lord in 1912:

12 October, 1912 (on board RMS *Majestic*)

Dear Capt Lord,

I can truly assure you that you have my sincerest sympathy, and I would have written to you before to that effect had I known your address. I sincerely hope that your efforts may be successful in clearing up the mystery of which you speak.

That another ship or ships might have been in the vicinity is quite possible and it seems a strange attitude for the B of T [Board of Trade] to take. I quite see how horribly hard it is for you – in fact that has been my feeling all along – and it must be doubly so with this other ship in your mind. I certainly wish you every success in clearing the matter up. Believe me, yours very sincerely,

C.H. Lightoller

Two months later, Lightoller was again writing to Captain Lord:

With regard to the steamer seen – I saw a light about two points on the port bow and could not say whether it was one or two masthead lights or a stern light – but it seemed there about 5 or 6 miles away. I did not pay much attention to it beyond calling the passengers' attention to it for their assurance.

I really do hope you will be able to clear the matter up. As to the B.T., their attitude towards you is as inexplicable as in many other things — I don't hold any brief for them.

Wishing you success.
Believe me, sincerely yours,
C.H. Lightoller

Now, nearly a quarter of a century later, the *Titanic's* most senior survivor was accepting the proposition that a Boston-bound steamer had been close to his ship on the New York track... although he notably didn't mention Captain Lord's destination in his book. Instead he wrote of the Officer of the Watch:

A great sea tragedy had been consummated before his very eyes.

Lightoller's claim that the officer, Stone, had reported five rockets to Lord is unsupported; Lord testified that he was told about only one rocket by Stone, who himself never specified how many he mentioned to Lord. The apprentice was eventually sent down to report eight altogether fired, after 2 a.m. by the *Californian* clock, by which time the *Titanic* was beyond help.

Captain Lord, although the apprentice said that he had responded during that visit, had no recollection of the encounter two-and-a-half hours later when roused. Fifth Officer Harold Lowe of the *Titanic*, interestingly, had similarly no recollection of being visited in his room and told that his ship had collided with an iceberg – 'When we sleep, we die', was his explanation.

Elsewhere in his memoir Lightoller described how the ship to which they had looked for immediate help had turned out tragically to be a false hope:

Time and again I had used her lights as a means to buoy up the hopes of the many that I now knew, only too well, were soon to find themselves struggling in that icy water.

Why couldn't she hear our wireless calls? Why couldn't her Officer of the Watch, or some of her crew, see our distress signals with their showers of stars, visible for miles and miles around? – A signal that is never used except when a ship is in dire need of assistance. What wouldn't I have given for a six-inch gun and a couple of shells to wake them up?

I had assured and reassured the passengers throughout these anxious hours 'She cannot help but see these signals, and must soon steam over and pick everyone up.' And what an absolutely unique opportunity Captain Lord, of the *Californian*, had that night of rendering aid and saving close on 1,500 lives.

Nothing could have been easier than to have laid his ship actually alongside the *Titanic* and taken every soul on board. Yet not a thing was done, not even was their wireless operator aroused to see if there *were* any distress calls.

There are no police, fire brigades or lifeboats out at sea, therefore it becomes nothing less than a fetish – the tenet above all tenets in the religion among sailors, that absolutely no effort should be spared in an endeavour to save life at sea. A man must even be prepared to hazard his ship and his life.

Lightoller's 'loud reports' account of the rockets was echoed by fellow surviving officers Lowe and Herbert Pitman, who respectively said that the reverberations were 'nearly deafening me' and 'like the report of a gun', meaning artillery.

The only other surviving officer, Boxhall, made no comment on the loudness of the rockets, but did remark in America: 'Of course, sound travels quite a long way on the water… and it being such a calm night…'

Thus the Mystery Ship hardly needed to be woken up and certainly heard the bangs, although why she ignored them is a part of her name. If Lightoller and the captain had thought of it, meanwhile, it might have been a good idea to send a single lifeboat, manned only by sturdy crew, equipped with plenty of rockets, to pull alone for the nearby source of hope.

Unencumbered by passengers and dedicated to closing the gap as quickly as possible, they might have made a difference. It is another 'what if' of the entire disaster, highlighted by the installation on the mighty *Aquitania* just two years later of the first motorised lifeboat aboard a major British passenger liner. Such a craft could have changed history in April 1912. It could have revealed everything and become the instrument of saving all.

Nothing could have been easier than to have come to the rescue, says Lightoller, and if indeed the *Californian* had actually been the Mystery Ship, a scant few miles away, the prize would have been beyond the dreams of riches. In other words, even if the Mystery Ship had been occupied by homicidal cut-throats and evil pirates (as so many fulminating writers would almost have us believe), then naked self-interest would haven taken them towards the *Titanic*, and certainly not away from her:

It was the height of every shipmaster's ambition in those days – and officers and crew too – to pick up a ship in distress [says Lord in his 1961 recording]. That means [a ship] losing a propeller, losing a rudder, and getting a tow. The wages were so small in those days that a man getting a few hundred pounds salvage money, it was a godsend. And if we'd had a sign of anything like that, we'd have been after it like a shot. Everyone on the ship would have been.

A rowboat approaching the *William Cliff*, with men standing in a lighter at her port bow. Captain Lord, who once commanded this vessel, had experience of picking up soldiers in small craft. He was not aboard her when she performed a prolonged rescue of the *Cambrian*, but said salvage was uppermost in sailors' minds in that period because of the riches it could bring. *Author collection.*

Captain Lord was paid £20 a month salary and a £50 a year bonus for avoiding accidents. He recalled on tape a case involving the small Leyland liner *William Cliff* – of which he took command in November 1909, staying her skipper for nearly fourteen months before assuming the captaincy of the *Californian* in March 1911.

Lord's taped recollections of a successful salvage operation by the *William Cliff* are hazy, but the facts are these. In the early morning of 16 December, 1907, when on a voyage from New Orleans to Liverpool, she came up with the *Cambrian*, operated by Wilson Furness & Co., which was wallowing helplessly with her propeller shaft carried away.

The *Cambrian*, of 5,625 tons and 450ft long, was on a voyage from London to Boston with a general cargo and a crew of fifty. She had broken down the previous lunchtime and was rolling heavily in a northwesterly swell.

The chief officer and a volunteer crew from the smaller vessel [*William Cliff* was 3,352 tons] entered a lifeboat, were lowered, and brought a hawser to the stricken ship. Several attempts at towing ended with the connection parting, and the vessels also had to stand by each other for a day or two on occasion because bad weather, including gales, made a resumption of operations impossible.

Nonetheless, after twelve days, the *William Cliff* towed the *Cambrian* into Crookhaven harbour in Co. Cork, Ireland, after a journey of 1,031 miles. Mr Justice Bargrave Deane later awarded a salvage prize of £5,300 to the *William Cliff*, to be divided into £3,750 for the owners (Leyland Line), £1,250 for her crew, and £300 for the captain.

If Captain Lord had been inherently selfish and inhumane, then any conscious choice he made that night, knowing a ship to be in difficulty, would have impelled him to rush to the scene as quickly as possible – even if that ship lay far over the horizon.

And strange to relate, salvage had been a huge topic of conversation between wireless operators and ships' crews during the long day before the *Titanic* collided on the evening of 14 April. An oil tanker named the *Deutschland*, bound from Stettin to Philadelphia, had reported herself not under control and short of coal, appealing urgently for assistance from other steamers.

At least a few undertook the race, including the *Parisian* of the Allan Line, and the *Asian*, of the Leyland Line, which eventually won the dash by taking the *Deutschland* in tow. Four days later, the pair arrived safely in Halifax, Nova Scotia – but what would otherwise have been a dramatic news story had by then been somewhat surpassed. Halifax was sending out ships to search for the *Titanic's* dead.

This is just a small part of what destroyed the story told by Ernest Gill of seeing rockets and a 'too large' ship surging past the stopped *Californian*. Gill was an engineer donkeyman who had fortunately come up for a smoke on deck, thereby 'seeing' things that he later translated into a $500 newspaper payment in the wake of the *Titanic* going down.

But while Gill claimed to see rockets, promptly saying to himself 'that must be a vessel in distress,' he added immediately, 'It was not my business to notify the bridge or the lookouts, but they could not have helped but see them.' Nor did he tell his bunkmate or any other crew of anything at all when he finished his smoke and went back below.

Gill was asked at the British Inquiry: 'I suppose, like all seamen, you are on the outlook to get a bit out of a salvage service, if you can render assistance to a vessel in distress?' He replied: 'In the first place, we have to render that assistance and what is coming to us afterwards, well, we get it.'

But Gill took no steps to render assistance, or to 'get what is coming to us', and his credibility thus evaporates. Indeed, his later action in obtaining personal monetary reward clearly establishes what he would have done had his story been true in the first place. Left undone on the night, those in/actions show him to be most deceitful.

A year after Lightoller's book, another passenger told her *Titanic* account. Lady Lucile Duff Gordon was a famous couturier, saved in Lifeboat 1, 'the millionaires' boat', which held only twelve occupants. Her husband, Sir Cosmo Duff Gordon, at one stage offered to replace the kit of all the seamen in the boat, since their dunnage bags were about to go down with the ship they had abandoned. Later, on the *Carpathia*, Sir Cosmo wrote out cheques for £5 a time, drawn on Coutts, the bank which also held an account for His Majesty the King.

This sheaf of promissory generosity was looked at askance, in light of the low occupancy of the boat, in case it was designed to deter the men from going back towards the piteous cries of those in the water. Sir Cosmo and Lucile had to endure some society gossip, but no more than that. They both asked if they could testify, (the only passengers to do so, along with Bruce Ismay – all first class) and were rewarded for their fortitude when Lord Mersey dismissed, 'the very gross charge that he [Sir Cosmo] bribed the men to row away from drowning people'.

A kind of 'anti-salvage' money perhaps – yet the suggestion was officially deemed unfounded, and Lord Mersey observed on the subject that it was no part of the business of his Inquiry to enquire into matters of moral conduct. This might have been news to Captain Lord.

Sir Cosmo himself had a certain moral outlook, recovering on the rescue vessel to lecture the beneficiaries of his largesse: 'I am sorry I cannot give you money [actual cash], but if you had it, you would probably spend it all in New York, so it is just as well it should be in a cheque which will enable you to start your kit again.'

Lucile Duff Gordon, in her work *Discretions and Indiscretions*, had nothing at all to say about the Mystery Ship, but did mention the 'ear-splitting noise' of the rockets and the *Titanic's* 'dark hull towering like a giant hotel', which suggests the White Star vessel would have been difficult to mistake for a small tramp steamer, as Lord, Stone and Gibson perceived their own nearby visitor.

Another year clicked by, and in October 1937, the vilified Bruce Ismay passed quietly from this life. He had never committed to paper his thoughts about the disaster in the quarter-century that had elapsed since, and the name of the maiden voyager had in fact been banned from mention in his house.

Ismay himself had written a £5 cheque, two years earlier, for his valet Angus Thwaite. It was to buy a pram for Angus and his wife Agnes, who also worked below stairs as an Ismay maid. Ismay's former valet, John Richard Fry, had been drowned on the *Titanic*, his body never recovered. (Number 239 taken from the sea was that of Ernest Freeman, secretary to Ismay, who paid for a grave marker in Halifax 'to commemorate a long and faithful service'.)

The maid remembers:

From the day I started, Mr Ismay had a sore on his leg, which he used to bandage up himself. He'd had it for years and wouldn't see a doctor. He used to rip up his underclothes and use them to bandage his leg. It went gangrenous in the end, and he had to have it off. I think both legs were bad.

I don't think he ever discussed the *Titanic* with Angus. Mr Ismay would just go and sit in Hyde Park, or go to the cinema and sit in the cheapest seats. Everyone else stayed home. It was more than a little sad.

Ismay's obituary in the *Times*, for its part, scrupulously avoided any mention of the *Titanic*. It was respectful in tone, which was rather different from one it had carried eight years earlier, in 1929, on the death of Lord Mersey. In an unusually negative note, Mersey was assessed in death as having been: 'too apt to take short cuts; and by no means free from the judicial fault of premature expression of opinion or bias, nor always patient with counsel whose minds did not work on the same lines as his own.'

The Second World War arrived and with it ended the lives of Captain Arthur Rostron and *Titanic* helmsman Robert Hichens (both of natural causes), along with former *Californian* chief officer George Stewart (killed when a German aircraft bombed the freighter *Barn Hill* off Eastbourne). The disaster of 1912 paled in the light of many more sinkings, although Officer Lightoller came out of retirement in 1940 to make several risk-laden runs to Dunkirk, rescuing troops from the beaches in his pleasure boat *Sundowner*.

Also active in that war was an American named Walter Lord, who served in the Office of Strategic Services (OSS), the forerunner of the Central Intelligence Agency. A decade after the end of the war, Lord authored the landmark work that was to hugely re-ignite interest in the tale of the *Titanic*.

Walter Lord was a supreme stylist and a peerless storyteller, even if his grasp of facts was often as slippery as his supple prose. His book remains a tremendous read – its primary purpose – but he was certainly not going to allow himself to be accused of over-indulgence towards his namesake, the captain of the *Californian*, who was no relation.

Nor might the captain himself have borne any resemblance to his portrayal in *A Night to Remember*, a book which would soon become an engrossing movie starring Kenneth More as Officer Lightoller. In its pages Walter Lord weaved a dazzling narrative, perfectly paced, and largely knitted of the testimonies given in both the American and British Inquiries. He also unquestioningly accepted their findings in relation to the *Californian*.

It was all one might expect. The author hadn't been there, and no-one alive knew where the *Titanic* actually sank or where the *Californian* might have been. There were few particular physical problems to get in the way of the telling.

The late Lord Mersey had angrily interrupted in 1912 on this very point, when counsel for the Leyland Line was questioning the *Californian's* third officer. Charles

Victor Groves was the man who belatedly considered it might have been *Titanic* that he saw before going off watch – although if it had been, then the White Star wonder-ship would have been horribly off course.

Groves had just told how he trusted implicitly in the stop position given by Captain Lord. Indeed, as the Officer of the Watch himself (up to the time *Californian* stopped), it was Groves who checked regularly that they were still on course to Boston. But the concept of a Boston ship having a neighbouring New Yorker drew this interference from the bench: 'If his judgment on the matter is true, it shows that those figures, latitudes and longitudes that you are referring to, are not accurate. That is all it shows.'

Mersey was telling effectively counsel that it need not be a case of Boston-plus-one, but rather a matter of New York-plus-one. There was ample testimony that the New York-bound *Titanic* had a ship near her on that track; and on the other hand, there was solely the *Californian's* word about a vessel also being within a few miles of her, much further to the north.

The President of the British Inquiry obviously chose to believe the *Californian* was part of New York-plus-one, rather than Boston-plus-one. It meant Captain Lord's ship would have been massively misguided as to her actual position, but the finding was good enough for author Walter Lord. He could overlook the verified three icebergs *Californian* saw on the Boston course...

Of course the evidence today, especially since the discovery of the wreck site, thirty years after Walter Lord's book came out, shows that Mersey's dilemma did not have to be a case of either/or. Finding the shattered *Titanic* hull on the seabed has realistically meant a co-existence of Boston-plus-one *and* New York-plus-one. Both pairs were over the curvature of the earth from each other, hull down and unseen, with many miles in the distance.

Four times in his book (and once on the dustjacket) Walter Lord opens an extract relating to the *Californian* with the bald statement that she was '10 miles away'. The entire testimony of *Titanic* witnesses coalesced around the central point that the Mystery Ship was much closer than that, half the distance, but the British Inquiry dismissed eyewitness accounts on the basis that the *Titanic* simply could not have looked like a tramp or small steamer at that remove. The distance was thus arbitrarily doubled.

Perhaps this one decision alone sums up the Mersey Inquiry and its desire to fit the evidence to the preferred outcome. Surviving *Titanic* officers, on the other hand never wavered. At a court case in 1913, Boxhall reiterated that the Mystery Ship was approximately 5 miles away, while Lowe, judging the distance in evidence for the first time, judged her at 4 miles. Pitman, doing likewise, suggested a separation of just 2 miles.

At the end of the first chapter of Walter Lord's book appear the words: 'About 10 miles away, Third Officer Charles Victor Groves stood on the bridge of the Leyland Liner *Californian*, bound from London to Boston. A plodding 6,000-tonner…'

No explanation is made of how she wouldn't have been on her course for Boston if she were 10 miles from *Titanic*. But Captain Stanley Lord would later tell how: 'We got to Boston no bother, picked up the Boston pilot and went in. Navigation was quite correct. Coming back, we arrived in Liverpool without any bother, without any zigzagging or anything.'

Walter Lord says she was a *plodding* vessel, an adjective with immediate overtones of dullness of intellect aboard. Meanwhile the author would duly write of *Titanic* wireless operators sending their urgent appeals for assistance into the ether, adding that: '10 miles away, Third Officer Groves of the *Californian* sat on the bunk of Wireless Operator Cyril F. Evans…'

Groves was interested in any news the wireless man might have picked up, and this was fine by Evans. 'There weren't many officers on third-rate liners interested in the outside world…'

Look again at this use of language, which serves to condition the reader once more. The *Californian* was *third-rate*. The majority of her officers were not interested in the outside world — not interested in anyone but themselves, is the implication. And once more they are baldly stated to be '10 miles away'.

A Night to Remember concedes that the *Californian* 'had been stopped since 10.30 p.m.' (actually 10.21 p.m.) but declares that at about 11.10 p.m. Groves 'noticed the lights of another ship, racing up from the east on the starboard side'.

Racing, indeed? Groves stated in evidence that he saw her first at 11.10 p.m. when the light was '10 to 12 miles away' (Q. 8160). He never described her speed at all. Instead he told how she stopped half an hour later at 11.40 p.m., by which time she was 'about 5 to 7 miles off' (Q. 8385).

This is a declination of 5 miles in half an hour. The steamer seen, therefore, was moving at a speed of 10 knots. The *Titanic* at this time was doing more than double that, verifiably 'racing', wherever she was.

Nor was this light coming from the east, in the view of Groves. He makes it clear in his testimony that she was approaching from the south — heading towards Greenland in other words. The *Titanic* was bound west, and therefore coming from the east, and it should be pointed out that Captain Lord — who said he saw the light as early as 10.30 p.m. (further proof of her slow speed) thought that it was coming from the east. But Groves certainly never said that. He said something that totally contradicted it.

'As the newcomer rapidly overhauled the motionless *Californian*,' wrote Walter Lord, without basis for either 'rapidly' or 'overhauled', 'a blaze of deck lights showed she was a large passenger liner.'

What was actually said in *Californian* testimony does not support this. While Groves told the British Inquiry that he had remarked to Captain Lord that she was a passenger steamer, Captain Lord denied he was told any such thing. Nor did Groves say it to the wireless operator, or to Officer Stone, who took over the watch and was told by Groves only of a stopped 'steamer'. Groves, in his evidence, never mentioned her size at all. There is thus no basis for the author's use of the word 'large'.

Captain Lord, Stone and apprentice officer James Gibson all saw a steamer that was 'something like ourselves' [6,200 tons], a small steamer, or one of medium size at best. Gibson repeatedly testified that she was a tramp steamer, adding that, 'she had no appearance at all of a passenger boat', and that he knew this as soon as he looked at her. The *Titanic*, on the other hand, was over 46,000 tons:

> Q. 7728: [The Commissioner] What was it made you think it was a tramp steamer? You saw nothing but the lights?
> Gibson: Well, I have seen nearly all the large passenger boats out at sea, and there was nothing at all about it to resemble a passenger boat.
> Q. 7729: What is it you expected to see?
> Gibson: A passenger boat is generally lit up from the water's edge.

Gibson, the twenty-year-old singled out for special pressure on the point, insisted he could tell the difference from the quantity of lights. He had seen all kinds of passenger steamers at night in his three-and-a-half years at sea, he declared.

Stone, for his part, said there was 'very little' glow round the lights, and in his first account, written at sea for Captain Lord, said that he observed the other steamer: 'showing one masthead light, her red sidelight and one or two small indistinct lights around the deck, which looked like portholes or open doors. I judged her to be a small tramp steamer and about 5 miles distant.'

Captain Lord echoed in evidence that when she stopped nearby, the vessel had 'a few deck lights'. He testified a little later: 'They might have been anything – lights from the portholes, doorways, or anything.'

Never mind that Groves only spoke about 'a lot of light' (but later testified that she had 'a few indistinct lights') and was unable to help with questions about the height of the ship he saw, or indeed her length. The point is that Walter Lord in *A Night to Remember* selected certain pieces of evidence, ignoring whole reams of testimony in contradiction, and worked backwards from the conclusion that *Californian* was the Mystery Ship. But as an ever-elegant writer, he did it very well.

Walter Lord obviously had to make choices to tell his story, which is a succinct and gripping summation. He hadn't space to detail all the disputes in testimony (any more than this book needs to tire the reader out), but he must have known that some of the statements he was making were unlikely.

He has the light seen by the *Californian* coming from the east, and being the *Titanic*, turning to port in a desperate bid to avoid the iceberg. This would have displayed *Titanic's* green light (starboard side) to any vessel to the north, even if that stranger had approached from the *south*, as Groves said, before making her turn.

Coming from either the south or the east, a turn to port would shut out the red light on the port side on any vessel. But Walter Lord must deal with the startling fact of a red light alone being seen on the *Californian's* visitor, after she has stopped, by all of her witnesses (including Groves, whom the author describes as 'young, alert and always interested'). The author avoids this obvious anomaly by banishing any mention of the red light to another part of his book, deftly divorcing it from the *Titanic's* port turn.

The book also has the first rocket tearing up from the *Titanic* deck with a blinding flash, only for it to detonate with a 'distant, muffled report.' This is the very opposite of what *Titanic* witnesses described. The socket signals, as we have seen, were 'in lieu of guns' and used a powerful new explosive named Tonite, deemed the loudest yet created. No-one said the reports were muffled. And nothing whatever was heard on the *Californian*. The author would appear to be over-earnestly attempting to split the difference.

On page seventy-six, Walter Lord wrote that the Mystery Ship 'seemed agonizingly near. So near that Captain Smith told the people in Boat 8 to go over, land its passengers and come back for more.'

It is exceptionally well attested that Captain Smith indeed gave precisely these instructions. But in mentioning such specific orders, the author now discreetly drops his otherwise prolific mention of this vessel, which he always identifies as the *Californian*, as being '10 miles away.' One can immediately see the problem of including that recurring reference at this point.

Is this all sleight of hand? Nor does the author mention his preferred distance when Captain Smith instructs Quartermaster Rowe to call up the Mystery Ship on the Morse light and to give her a detailed message, which the author renders as: 'We are the *Titanic* sinking; please have all your boats ready.' Yet he would have us believe that it was to be sent over 10 miles…

A Night to Remember granted itself 'a right to re-model'. While memorialising the disaster, very laudably, it should perhaps be noted that memory itself was done at least a partial disservice. Impartial it was not.

PERCEPTIONS

———•·•———

PHANTASMS AND PHOTOGENICS

It is worth spending a little time on *A Night to Remember*, because its undoubted narrative power made it the grounding document for the modern cult of the *Titanic*. Sometimes referred to as the 'Bible' of *Titanic* enthusiasts, it certainly became the received truth. Heroes were created anew, and villains recast.

In his Acknowledgements, Walter Lord noted that: 'Charles Victor Groves has aided me greatly in piecing together the story of the *Californian...*'

He did not make contact with Captain Lord. His book, however, did make use of a photograph originally given to the *Daily Sketch* by Captain Lord's wife, Mabel, more than forty years earlier when journalists had hurried to the address to relate the news that her husband's ship had rushed to the scene of a great disaster. They begged for a picture.

In the *Daily Sketch* on 26 April, 1912, the caption had been: 'Captain Stanley Lord (with telescope) who has reported that on the night the *Titanic* foundered the *Californian* was only 17 miles distant. Beside him is Mr Stewart, chief officer, and standing behind are the second and third officers. Their Marconi apparatus was not working until dawn.'

But in *A Night to Remember*, the caption became: 'Officers of the Leyland Liner *Californian*. The spyglass in Captain Lord's lap is somewhat ironical, considering she lay within 10 miles of the *Titanic* all during the sinking.'

Six years after the publication of *A Night to Remember* (which he did not read), Captain Lord is heard on audiotape expressing wonderment at the placing of every reliance on Groves, the latter only mentioning on his return to Britain that he thought the steamer they saw might have been the mightily heralded maiden voyager:

Why should the junior officer's evidence be taken in preference to the three senior officers – myself, the chief officer and the second officer? And they take the third officer's evidence, the junior man of all, as being the infallible man, to make their statement out, their judgement.

No reason why Groves shouldn't have an opinion of his own, I am not saying anything about that. Groves was a very nice young fellow, nothing wrong with his abilities. I think he was inclined to exaggerate a little… he wanted publicity. He went to the *Boston Herald* on the next voyage, when I wasn't there, but they refused to see him…

But Walter Lord was certainly listening, getting his acknowledged one side of the story, although he may not have realised that Captain Lord was still alive. Nor had Captain Lord realised it when, in early 1925, he met Groves again. By now the former third officer of the *Californian* was Master of the *Sheaf Mount*, descending a rope ladder to a tender alongside that already had Captain Lord in it:

I saw Groves that day in Sydney, going ashore. It's strange I didn't remember him. Wasn't it funny, a fellow like that – well of course [he] was the last man in the world I was thinking of, coming down captain of an old tramp. I'd heard he went back in the P&O, and we never talked – we just chatted on the way ashore.

In Sydney they had a small motorboat picking up the skippers to take them ashore to see their agents. And we went alongside this ship, and I saw his letters all dropped down. He was coming down. He had a packet of letters which all fell. I picked them up for him out of the water.

He came and sat down with me and we talked and chatted – nice weather; where are you going; how long are you in, or something. It never struck me it was Groves. Strange wasn't it? We might have gone further into it, if I'd noticed, although I was rather sore about it, I must admit, at the time.

Captain Lord 'picked them up for him out of the water', these letters belonging to Captain Groves – a minor kindness by a man who allegedly wouldn't have bothered plucking human beings from the same element.

Back to that night of infamy. When the *Californian* sent her last warning to the *Titanic*, the transmission itself justified the angry reaction of that ship's wireless operator Jack Phillips, at least according to Walter Lord. He wrote: 'She was so close she almost blew his ears off. No wonder he snapped back: "Shut up, shut up! I am busy. I am working Cape Race."'

Note the phrase, 'so close'. In fact the *Californian* call was only interfering because it was closer than the land station at Cape Race lighthouse, jamming the latter's signals. Jack Phillips was drowned, and never said anything about his ears being blown off – although one can imagine that those of Evans must have burned at the *Titanic's* reaction.

After the accident, and speaking of wireless, the book adds: 'None of the ships contacted seemed as promising as the light that winked 10 miles off the *Titanic's* port bow.' The White Star witnesses of course put her much closer than that, and the author offers no explanation of how the light came to be winking at that distance when it hadn't been seen by either of the *Titanic* lookouts.

They had been on duty since 10 p.m., and remained aloft for forty minutes after the impact. They reported nothing about another vessel in all that time. The Mystery Ship approached just after they had descended.

Meanwhile the book talks of *Californian* Second Officer Stone and apprentice Gibson and the 'strange ship' they saw, always preferring the grander word 'ship' to the prosaic word 'steamer' in terms of what was seen from the *Californian*. And still no mention of the two men's unimpressive, dull and downbeat description of the vessel they watched.

Walter Lord puts into Gibson's mouth a remark that he didn't think the 'rockets were being sent up for fun', but in fact this was a phrase not said by Gibson, but by an aggressive legal counsel in questioning Gibson's shipmate, Stone.

Stone conceded that he 'may possibly have passed the expression' that a vessel was 'not going to fire rockets at sea for nothing'. He did not think the vessel in view was in distress at any time, and may have been musing aloud. This was Gibson's reaction:

Q. 7537: Didn't that convey to you that the ship was, in his opinion, in distress?
Gibson: Not exactly in distress, Sir.
Q. 7538: What then?
Gibson: That everything was not all right with her.

If there was a misgiving, there was only one such quote – but Walter Lord gives 'for nothing' to Stone, and 'for fun' to Gibson, although the latter comment was uttered only by Butler Aspinall, counsel for the Board of Trade at the British Inquiry.

Stone's evidence indicates that any slight doubt he may have been entertaining evaporated when the saw the steamer change her bearings – which meant to visibly move away. Gibson confirms that Stone told him the vessel was steaming away at 1.20 a.m., and Stone tracked her personally across points of the compass. Such a method of discerning movement is unmistakable.

But Walter Lord says: 'the two men felt she must be steaming away'. These are weasel words which suck the meaning out of what the pair did see – a vessel moving from the SSE to the SW – replacing it with a doubt about what they 'felt'. As if the observed steamer was declining in the same part of the ocean, whereas she had moved to an entirely different sector of the seascape. [Stone and Lord's estimates for the amount of water traversed in this time vary between 5 and 8 miles.]

This ship had supposedly 'fascinated' the men, the 'way she kept firing rockets', according to the book, but Gibson only saw three rockets during his entire time on the bridge, while Stone denied they were consumed by curiosity about her:

Q. 7986: And were you talking about the ship all the time until she disappeared?
Stone: No.
Q. 7987: Are you sure?
Stone: Yes.

This is understandable; they saw a tramp steamer they linked to puzzling rockets, but she later glided off. As Captain Lord said later: 'We weren't suspecting any *Titanic* being sunk.' The fascination came afterwards. And now *A Night to Remember* carries the line that: 'At 2.20 a.m. Stone decided that the other ship was definitely gone.'

This is a crude attempt to link the near steamer with the *Titanic*, which sank at 2.20 a.m. Stone did not mention 2.20 a.m. in evidence, and instead spoke of relating at 2.40 a.m. that the ship had disappeared. In any case, *Titanic* and *Californian* clocks were not the same. And after this, by way of emphasis, the book tendentiously has Stone resume studying 'the empty night'.

Daybreak arrived. Walter Lord's book implies that *Californian* Chief Officer Stewart eventually woke up his ship's wireless operator that morning on his own initiative. But in fact it was Captain Lord who ordered that it be done – the chief officer carrying it out – after realising that there had been a series of rockets. He had been told this by the apprentice at 2.05 a.m., but evidently it hadn't registered.

When himself woken by Stewart, Captain Lord is said in *A Night to Remember* to have 'pulled on some clothes', whereas in fact he had been fully dressed throughout. The overtones of his having been in bed are of a piece with an earlier claim that he had 'rolled over' after Gibson's visit.

We next meet the *Californian* in the narrative when she has arrived at the scene of the rescue of the last *Titanic* survivors: 'Captain Lord uneasily examining the *Carpathia*'s house-flag flying at half-mast.' The word 'uneasily' clearly imputes guilt and self-recrimination. The *Carpathia* then turns for New York, leaving the *Californian* to 'go through the motions' of looking for others alive – the suggestion being that she has merely gone through the motions to arrive as late as she did.

This book cemented the public perception of Captain Lord as an ogre. It topped the bestseller charts, and was followed by a copycat account the following year by one Richard O'Connor, entitled *Down to Eternity*. This followed Walter's well-worn rut, right down to the two watchstanders 'taking it for granted' that the steamer they saw 'was moving off to the southwest'.

'All unconscious of the tragedy being played out before their eyes, Stone and Gibson had watched the *Titanic* send up rockets as a last hope, watched her sink and die, even as men aboard the *Titanic* puzzled over the inert lights of the ship to their south,' O'Connor penned. So now Boston was to the south of New York!

It was well established that the *Californian* was in easy rescue range of the *Titanic*, pronounced this latter author (although 'testimony was at some variance'). And O'Connor followed that with this beauty:

> Captain Lord estimated the other ship was 19 miles away, and continued to maintain that it was an unknown freighter he saw, although how he could be certain at a distance of 19 miles he did not say and was not asked to explain.

The Earth is not flat. Its curvature, and *Californian's* relatively low height, meant her visible horizon was only of the order of 8 miles.

It is safe to assume Captain Lord did not read this poppycock either. But the *Titanic* next came to his attention when the movie was released of *A Night to Remember*. He went to his professional body, the Mercantile Marine Services Association, of which he had been a continuous member for sixty years, and it undertook to research the matter on his behalf. The MMSA would thereafter begin a long campaign to clear Stanley Lord.

The motion picture showed the *Californian* and *Titanic* within sight of each other. The rockets seen by the *Californian* were not shown to be low-lying, as Stone had described. Captain Lord was portrayed as asleep in bed, pushing back the bedclothes and sitting up in pyjamas when called on the voicepipe; switching on the light, and switching it off after a perfunctory conversation. There had only been a settee in real life, and the light had been on throughout.

The celluloid treatment was a great success, with the Mystery Ship incident playing only a small cameo role in the course of the whole, but the caricature of Captain Lord had been confirmed – even if some of the more libellous references in the book were removed on subsequent printings, of which there were many. The square peg had been well and truly forced into a round hole.

Captain Lord died in January 1962, at the age of eighty-four. A press release from the MMSA stated that he had always 'emphatically rejected' the Inquiry findings, but his requests for the case to be reopened were refused. 'His closing years were overshadowed by a revival of public interest in the disaster, particularly the publicity afforded to the book *A Night to Remember* and the widely-shown film of that name.' The statement added that he was a most capable shipmaster and a man of absolute integrity.

The MMSA had never wavered in its support. As far back as January 1913, its *Reporter* magazine published an article entitled *Pushed under the Wheels of the Juggernaut*, written by nautical adviser Captain John d'Arcy Morton. He postulated that the ship seen from the *Californian* lay on the line of rockets appearing over the horizon from the unseen *Titanic*, whose own Mystery Ship could be anywhere within a five mile radius, being also 'hull down' to the *Californian* in nautical parlance.

The piece ended: 'The details we have given in this article represent absolute facts and show that the blame and obloquy which have been cast upon the unfortunate shipmaster were entirely undeserved.'

Half a century and more later, there was suddenly some new support for Captain Lord. In 1964, the naval and maritime chronicler Peter Padfield wrote a book entitled *The Titanic and the Californian*, and proceeded to knock huge holes in the received wisdom.

In his Introduction, Padfield told how he had been initially researching a book about collisions at sea (later published as *An Agony of Collisions*) when he became angered reading the transcripts of the British *Titanic* Inquiry with its 'crazy deductions, distortions, prejudice... [and] occasional boneheaded obstinacy... refusing to accept facts which are obvious outside and fifty years away from the court room'.

Padfield told how, with each day of reading, his astonishment grew 'that Captain Lord was censured on the half-cock evidence'. It helped that he fully understood the complex testimony about bearings, drift, headings, compass readings, longitude and latitude, ship lights, dead reckoning, horizons, curvature of the earth, and the myriad nautical and navigational terms with which the Inquiry had to grapple. But there were points that were plain, as he made sure to stress.

Indeed, to paraphrase the Duke of Wellington about he who is born in a stable not necessarily being a horse, it ought to be obvious that just because a ship sees rockets does not make it the Mystery Ship – the vessel that *Titanic* crew had sought to rouse to further action after she had initially approached them, albeit that *Titanic* rockets were summoning help from anywhere and rising over the visible horizon to reach out in all directions.

Furthermore, just because one person among four eyewitnesses aboard the *Californian* should see two masthead lights (rather than one) upon their own nearby stranger, should patently not the *Titanic* make. But in official terms, it did.

The 1985 discovery of the wreck co-ordinates effectively means the argument today is over. Authors before this time had the comfort blanket of there being no 'body' in the 'murder investigation'. The forensics now tell a very different story – the *Titanic* always having been on the New York track, although far short of the transmitted SOS position. The *Californian*, which endangered herself in 1912 by claiming to see rockets in the 'wrong' direction from her stopping place on the Boston track, now sees them in the right location, the *Titanic* always sinking in line with where the wreck was found.

Geoffrey Marcus did not know any of this when he produced a new treatment entitled *The Maiden Voyage* in 1969, thereby becoming another would-be *Poirot* in the case of the missing ship.

Marcus spoke about a 'series of fatal blunders perpetrated that night by someone or other aboard the *Californian*', which is rather rich, since he grudgingly admits that the same ship had taken the basic precaution against fatal blunder by stopping as soon as she encountered ice.

He also archly claimed that the *Californian*'s wireless operator, on duty for seventeen hours, should have remained on duty through the night, since ice was a peril. To whom? And where was Captain Smith when such attention to duty called on a racing liner?

The hindsight of Marcus seems to go rather further than the prescription of two operators for every tub, however humble, that was later enacted. His stance is a ridiculous double-standard in favour of surging passenger liners against nondescript freighters, whom he would have as their betters' keepers. However few lifeboats the aristocrats might have, the tradesmen must watch for them day and night – keeping out when told, of course.

Marcus, most tellingly, was unable to resist commenting on Captain Lord's physical appearance, calling him 'a tall, well-built man with a high forehead and distinctly autocratic features'.

It is naturally the 'distinctly autocratic' comment that is of interest, although Captain Lord was patently not 'well-built'. The adjective 'autocratic' characterises Lord as, 'a ruler who has absolute power, a domineering person' (Concise Oxford English dictionary) and does so purely on his physiognomy. If Marcus had been able to feel the bumps on his head, as in the wretched pseudo-science of phrenology, he might also have felt able to expound on Lord's propensity to criminality.

Judging a man on his photograph is one thing, and a very poor thing indeed, but author Marcus shamelessly attempted to justify doing so. In a chapter entitled, 'The Row about the *Californian*' he writes: 'There is always a natural inclination to keep on the right side of an autocratic and overbearing Master; and if the Master in question were not both autocratic and overbearing, it is to be surmised that his photographs, as well as the evidence, do him a grave injustice.' Let this be called what it is: arrogant tosh. The arrogance resides in assessing another on the basis of a one-dimensional image, and offering that to readers – being a veritable portrait in black and white. The man is traduced, the public short-changed.

The real Captain Lord and his character can best be judged by the reader from the verbatim excerpts of his tape recording, in which he is totally at ease and under no pressure – unlike at the British Inquiry. Officer Groves was the man who belatedly 'sank' Captain Lord with his notions of seeing the *Titanic*, but Captain Lord's comments about him at the head of this chapter hardly speak to contempt of his fellow man.

We remember the tributes at the time – Captain MacNab of the Board of Trade said in 1912 that: 'I have ever heard him spoken of as a humane and clever officer and commander,' and the MMSA had gathered many tributes from men who served under him in the years since, men regarded by their Master as shipmates, not as slaves.

The real Captain Lord was not *over*bearing, but *fore*bearing. The true autocrat despises his underlings. The man who could 'roll over' and let 1,500 people die would not be inclined to roll over easily when the Inquiries came a-hunting. The autocrat, cornered, would blame his crew.

Lord did not do that. He said of Stone: 'I had a responsible officer on the bridge,' and when asked whether he had any reason to doubt that Stone was speaking the truth, replied: 'I do not see why he should not tell me the truth.'

Lord Mersey interrupted (Q. 7305) to ask: 'Is he a reliable, trustworthy man?' and received the reply: 'As far as I know of him, he is.' And the captain retained his confidence in Stone years later, saying in 1961: 'He was a quiet young fellow, and he wouldn't tell me lies. I'm quite sure of that.'

The Inquiry, rather transparently, wanted Lord to blame his crew. Lord Mersey later pushed him on the evidence of the apprentice, James Gibson:

Lord Mersey: Is he telling the truth?
Captain Lord: Is the boy telling the truth?
Mersey: [Q. 7285]: Yes.
Lord: I do not know. I do not doubt it for a moment.

In his voice recording, Lord says of Gibson: 'I don't know what became of him. Nice boy. He called me all right; I'm not denying that. He called me and I told him 'Alright, tell the second officer to let me know if he wants anything', or something like that, and I dozed off again.'

But Marcus maintains: 'It is possible that Captain Lord had never encouraged his subordinates to speak their minds openly and freely.' He has now read a lot of possibility into the photograph of the weathered, lined face with its rather unlovely lips that Marcus would like to contort into a sneer.

To the contrary, Lord said in evidence that he was surprised the next day at Stone not getting him out of the chartroom, considering rockets had been fired:

He said if they had been distress rockets he would most certainly have come down and called me himself, but he was not a little bit worried about it at all. If they had been distress rockets he would have 'come down and insisted upon my getting up'.

Marcus declares of the *Californian* officers' relationship with their captain that 'in fact, they were unmistakably afraid of him'. He does not offer a single source for this alleged 'fact', but is giving voice to the always latent suspicion (in the mind of officialdom and the penny press) of a 'fear factor' in the apparent failure to rouse Captain Lord.

But, unfortunately for Marcus, there is complete proof that Stone was not afraid of Captain Lord. The second officer shows steeliness in one of his replies to Lord Mersey:

Q. 7978: But why could not have you told him in the morning? Why wake up the poor man?
Stone: Because it was my duty to do so, and it was his duty to listen to it.

This completely supports Lord's account of how Stone told him he would he have 'pulled you out' if he had really discerned distress. Stone was the Officer of the Watch and he plainly knew where his duty, and the captain's duty, lay. Although perhaps Herbert Stone *looked* cowardly in his photograph – in the eyes of an author writing fifty-seven years after the event.

Secondly, and what totally destroys the Marcus 'possibility' which the author also turned into an 'unmistakable fact', is the truth that Stone had total responsibility and every power as the designated man on watch.

If he was afraid of his captain (a state of affairs that would make normal navigation practically impossible in the long run), then it was open to him to say nothing to Lord but to wake the chief officer, or indeed the wireless operator, or both, on his own initiative.

Marcus would have us believe that Stone secretly knew. But if he quaked in terror of his captain (which the evidence disproves), was he also in trembling trepidation of the bespectacled, twenty-year-old wireless lad?

Third Officer Groves had barged in on operator Evans after midnight for a chat, when the latter was in bed. But the second officer, senior in rank to Groves, apparently turned to jelly at the prospect of confronting the Sparks in his lair. Was Evans autocratic and overbearing too?

Evans had been qualified just six months. He cheerfully referred to Captain Lord in his American evidence as 'the Skipper'. And he himself had no difficulties going down to the Master: 'We were stopped, and I went to the captain and I asked him if there was anything the matter. The captain told me he was going to stop because of the ice…'

None of this makes for an unapproachable Captain Lord. Even the apprentice had no difficulty disturbing his sleep after 2 a.m., when, if he had been 'unmistakably afraid,' he might rather have stood up to jelly-man Stone and told him to do it instead. But Stone was dutifully complying with orders: 'Let me know by Gibson'. Gibson was willing – and the duty of visiting the captain as he slept was ordinary enough, even for him.

And here is where Gibson, in evidence, himself explodes the idea that Stone was afraid of Captain Lord:

> Q. 7752: Did he [Second Officer Stone] make any remarks to you as to the captain taking no action? Did he say anything to you at the time?
> Gibson: No.
> Q. 7753: Are you sure?
> Gibson: Yes.

It is surely not credible that a man who had actually detected an emergency at sea would not make any comment at all to Gibson – like Evans, another twenty-year-old – if the Master had decided to wilfully ignore it.

Please, Mr Marcus, don't let us say that Stone feared the apprentice might later let any adverse comments slip! No, the evidence shows clearly where the truth lies, and demonstrates Stone's certainty of his duty, even in the case of telling Captain Lord that the steamer they were looking at had journeyed off.

Marcus' verdict of Lord as a seagoing Frankenstein is the Coronation March of a lazy and poorly-informed opinion – a guess, merely – based on divining personality traits from a photograph. Not that he included in his book a photograph of Captain Lord, or even of the author himself, so that people could judge for themselves. Lord is presented as a sourpuss, based on the scantiest of impressions, and that idle representation suits certain purposes very well.

If only Captain Lord had grown facial hair, to disguise the unappealing line of his mouth, in order to more resemble Captain Smith, why, he may have better satisfied Geoffrey Marcus. He may even have thereby become 'fatherly' and 'benevolent'. But we can imagine that if the respective Masters had been switched, then the whiskery features of Captain Smith of the *Californian* would only have 'cruelly belied the true nature of the man beneath'. Marcus was always going to offer pat answers.

Of course all captains were literally autocrats in the strict sense of the word. Their word was law on all ships; literally the law, because land courts recognised and endorsed the absolute authority of Masters on ships at sea, and did so time and

Right: Captain Lord and his wife on a vessel in the late 1920s. Mabel's husband had been finally forced to quit the sea because of failing eyesight, and is seen here wearing glasses. The couple thereafter shared a life of quiet domesticity.

time again. But the Marcus book has done the debate a favour in at least flushing out the fox of common-or-garden prejudice.

We do draw impressions of people based on their image. And it is true that Captain Lord 'doesn't look very nice'. Instead he looks every inch the available villain in a cocktail of social values that includes the 'need' for blame as much as for heroes, and which contains within its mix all manner of conditioning, including the subtleties of power versus non-power. (See the picture section of this book for some of the photographs of Captain Lord discussed below.)

Another author, Leslie Reade, couldn't resist either. In one of his original captions to a photograph, he called Captain Lord: 'A Roman Emperor in a sailor suit.' Intending both to demean Lord and to mock his implied vanity and cruelty, it actually neatly captions the naked animus of the man who could offer such a summation.

Captain Lord became a phantasm over time, a bogeyman, a brute. Never mind that family photographs show him nattily attired on a night out with his wife, enjoying the countryside or driving a car with pals; or that images from his time at sea show smiling officers relaxed in a line-up with their captain, or easygoing passengers grinning broadly in his company.

In one such, featuring a group of jolly American passengers, he has been prevailed on to swap hats – and is wearing a straw boater, while a paying customer proudly sports the peaked cap of Leyland captaincy.

And the picture most often used, the one willingly handed over by his wife in 1912, was actually taken by a passenger family – who then sent copies of their snaps to the captain who had looked after them so well. Apparently they had asked him to hold a telescope (Walter Lord's 'spyglass') because it would make him look more Skipper-like.

This photograph, originally passed to the *Daily Sketch* by Mabel Lord, shows Stone, Groves, Lord and Stewart. One writer gave the prop a picaresque twist, saying that the 'spyglass' of the *Californian* was 'ironical considering she lay within 10 miles of the *Titanic* during the sinking'. *Daily Mirror.*

Opposite below: The size of the RMS *Titanic*, then the largest moving object ever built, can perhaps be gauged in theis photograph taken in 1911 as she nears completion in Belfast. Yet Officer Stone and apprentice Gibson of the *Californian* were sure they had seen a small- to medium-sized steamer, while Captain Lord described her as being 'something like ourselves'. *Author collection.*

Below right: A detail portrait of Captain Lord (from cover photo) in which shadows appear to invest him with a sinister mien. *Author collection.*

This picture, and a similar one of Lord and his chief officer posing with two girl passengers, shows the captain and his team frowning in the sun. The frowning will do very well to some people, the shadow under their peaked caps better again. Lord in this picture has a shadow falling away under his nose onto the edge of his mouth, such that it might appear down-turned into that desired sneer of the villain…

It is a photograph that has undoubtedly played its own role in what might literally be called snap judgements.

But the child in his lap has the captain's glasses in her hands, the same glasses Lord allowed his son to hold in a photo taken before this voyage (to New Orleans) began. How many other Transatlantic captains, even the non-autocratic or non-domineering ones, would have posed for pictures with passengers' children on their knee? How many swap hats with adult travellers?

Is Captain Lord to blame for the glaring sunshine that makes him look, to modern viewers, eerily reminiscent of Lee Harvey Oswald posing in the Texan sun with his Mannlicher-Carcano rifle, or a dozen war crime suspects under Death's Head caps somewhere in Nazi-conquered territory?

The story is told in *A Titanic Myth*, one of the rare books defending Lord (written by former MMSA general secretary Leslie Harrison, who recorded his voice), that the child seen in the captain's lap was reported to him by her mother during the voyage as suffering from constipation.

Not having a doctor aboard, Lord 'prescribed the standard shipborne remedy, black draught'. The child flatly refused to swallow it. 'Eventually, however, she compromised, agreeing to do so on one condition – that the captain also took a dose.'

Lord, the Master of the *Californian*, but more importantly the father of a child of similar age, answered the dictates of commonplace humanity in such a case – and would suffer the grim rumblings of 'the runs' for hours afterwards. So much for the 'austere' and 'aloof' man of misguided prejudice.

Thus it gradually emerges that it is not Lord who is a brute, but that it is the very *stereotype* of him as a brute that is unyielding, inflexible, cold and utterly colourless.

This book shows the other pictures in a series of images, all taken within a few minutes of each other on Saturday, February 10, 1912 (one of the numbered pictures has that date on the reverse, together with the legend 'SS *Californian*' in Captain Lord's handwriting). The much prouder *Titanic* was still being readied on this day, far away in a distant Belfast dry dock.

The kiddies have their props, but in a corner of the officers' photograph, commonly cropped, is a discarded sunhat. Other pictures show the captain smiling as he almost disappears in a sea of eight family members, not counting the dog, the photograph presumably taken by one of the crew, or perhaps another passenger.

There is another photo like this one, followed by one of the gingham-clad sisters, now wearing their sun hats again, guiding their little brother on a walk at the stern. In the background an officer grins at the happy scene, and from the dickie-bow (all the other officers are wearing straight ties in the sequence and have entirely dark caps) the smiling figure would appear to be none other than Captain Lord. The autocrat.

So he had humanity after all – while in others of his pictures, from different voyages, adults are shown posing with telescopes, looking out to sea, or poking their heads out of a line of portholes. Whatever about the latter, Geoffrey Marcus might lecture us that it is criminally irresponsible to allow passengers to play with the ship's equipment, particularly an item as essential as a telescope, when at any moment a sudden emergency might befall some other vessel…

Captain Lord may not have needed to dine with passengers to demonstrate his avuncular 'niceness', and while Captain Smith did so on the night the *Titanic* went down, the captains of the Transatlantic liners made it a habit in their memoirs to complain about the dreary folk they carried and had to endure, while reserving the right to also retail anecdotes about those who were really famous.

Masters seemed to have complained so much in private about the 'social side' (stressed by the companies for the public relations value of the captain's table, and still marketed today) that many of the Lines later conceded the point and introduced 'Staff Captains' on ships, specifically to engage the paying customer. Now there would be two captains and two wireless operators on every Leviathan of the seas…

Captain Lord (centre) in a picture taken at the stern housing of the *Californian* (see photo p111). He attended as a witness at the British Inquiry and was not specifically legally represented. If he thought himself in an avalanche when this picture was taken, he had no idea what was coming next.

The best that Marcus can do, meanwhile, is to observe: 'It would appear that, following the *Titanic* affair, Lord's disposition suffered something of a sea-change. He was no longer the self-assured, autocratic, overbearing character that he had been; he went softly, so to speak, throughout the rest of his time afloat.' As if he had not 'gone softly' before.

Is it unfair to point out a blemish on this nauseating front? Because the Marcus assessment is quite simply horribly wrong when he argues strongly in favour of the accuracy of the *Titanic*'s SOS position, the better to cast doubt on Captain Lord's opinion of its *inaccuracy*.

> Amongst other things, it has been argued by Captain Lord's apologists [not 'support-ers,' or even 'defenders,' mark you] that the *Titanic*'s position that night was incorrect [Marcus writes].
>
> Yet the Hydrographer to the [US] Navy Department, the British Naval Attaché, and other Naval experts attending the American Inquiry in Washington were quite unconvinced as to a possible error in the *Titanic*'s position.

But Marcus owes an apology to whatever apologists he is talking about. The SOS position was wrong by over 13 nautical miles, which is practically three Mystery-Ship-distances tacked onto one another.

'Everyone, it would appear, is out of step but the Master of the *Californian*...' Yet the truth, revealed in the latter half of the 1980s, is that the Master in question was absolutely right in his expressed doubts and everyone else indeed wrong, including many authors. Nor does the 'everyone' cited by the author in fact include the British Naval Attaché or 'other Naval experts' that he mentions – Marcus has misused a report that the Attaché filed to His Majesty's Ambassador in Washington, James Bryce, on 22 April, 1912.

Nowhere does the Attaché, Captain Charles F.G. Sowerby, make mention in his report of the *Titanic's* SOS co-ordinates or any discussion about them. Instead he talks of how impressed he was at Fourth Officer Boxhall's testimony about a *moving* Mystery Ship – the very opposite of what Geoffrey Marcus would have his readers believe.

Sowerby [in Foreign Office document 115/1710 in the British National Archives] states as follows:

Sir – In accordance with your instructions, I attended the inquiry by the Senate Committee into the sinking of the *Titanic* this afternoon. Mr Franklin was the first witness, but his evidence was mainly on the connection of the White Star Line with the International Mercantile Marine Company.

The fourth officer of the *Titanic* was the next witness, who was on watch under the first officer at the time of the disaster. Perhaps his most interesting testimony was that he distinctly saw the Steaming and Port side light of a ship steaming across the *Titanic's* course, at an estimated distance of 5 miles. Rockets were fired and attempts made to communicate by flashing light, but without success. After hearing the evidence of this officer I formed a high opinion of his straightforwardness, which was also shared by American naval officers seated near me, although the attitude of the Chairman of the Committee was not conducive to his saying any more than he could help…

Marcus does not quote the Attaché's report, or its file number, and he clearly misrepresents its contents. There was no discussion of where the sinking had occurred on this day of evidence, and certainly the precise location was hardly likely to matter a whit to any 'naval expert', who might only care to know that a merchant vessel has gone under the waves.

Incidentally, since mention is made of the US Navy Hydrographer, it might be mentioned that this gentleman, John J. Knapp, expressed an opinion to the New York *Sun* (Thursday 18 April, 1912, p2) and separately in a report for President Taft, that 'the ship [*Titanic*] must have struck at latitude 41° 16' N, instead of at 41° 46' N, as reported in despatches'.

The wreck is in latitude 41° 43' N, a few miles south of the New York track. The US Hydrographer's opinion was out by only 27 nautical miles. But Geoffrey Marcus wrote in *The Maiden Voyage* that: 'to clear Captain Lord of the heavy charges brought against him a good many people would have to be proved wrong.' Indeed.

Another author to argue passionately, and wrongly, in favour of the reliability of the SOS position – as if it were sinister of Captain Lord to attempt to muddy the waters – was the aforementioned Leslie Reade, whose book, *The Ship That Stood Still*, was published posthumously in 1993, four years after his death, having been 'edited and updated' by a friend. Reade had originally finished the manuscript in 1975.

Bear in mind that the *Titanic* wreck was discovered ten years later, in September 1985, although the exact co-ordinates [41° 43' N; 49° 56' W, as against the SOS position of 41° 46' N; 50° 14' W] did not begin to leak out for another two years. The difference, as the crow flies, is over 13 nautical miles.

The Ship That Stood Still spends several pages and much of Chapter 9 in arguing the accuracy of the transmitted distress position. It pours scorn on the idea that the *Carpathia* met the lifeboats short of the SOS position, but given the wreck site, that is exactly what happened – indeed the SOS position was to the west of a dense icefield deemed 'impassable' by Hydrographer Knapp, and of which Captain Moore of the *Mount Temple* testified: 'She [*Titanic*] could not have been through this pack of ice.'

'Captain Lord's supporters made much of the allegation that the *Titanic* got her reckoning wrong, and sent out the wrong position', declares Reade. But it wasn't an allegation. It is an absolute truth, established by tens of thousands of tons of steel in two pieces of shattered, rust-riveleted hull piled on the seabed.

Despite being 'updated' and including references to the finding of the wreck, this book at no time considers the reality of what the location of the rediscovered *Titanic* means – that the *Californian*, stopped at the top of a triangle grounded (left and right) on the 1912 SOS site and 1985 discovery site, is now seeing rockets in the right place. And that stop position is over 20 miles distant from where the *Titanic* likely collided before drifting to her grave.

'Lord claimed the *Titanic* gave the wrong position...' But the *Californian* captain judged the situation, and he was right. And this literally *anchoring* evidence of the location of the wreck site today must throw out all other ideas about a Boston-bound steamer having been close to any New York-bound ship.

Reade, helpfully, accepts that the *Californian* was on the Boston track when she sent a wireless message about three bergs whose location is known. On p117, he writes: 'This was, of course, hours before the disaster, and, as Lord said, there could be no question of preparing an alibi.'

How can he then get a Boston-bound steamer down to a Manhattan-motivated maiden voyager?

Interestingly, because the *Californian* was undeniably stopped since 10.21 p.m., Reade is found to be arguing the contradiction that the Mystery Ship was *also* stopped – because he wants her to be the *Californian*!

If she's stopped, the Mystery Ship can't have been on the Boston track as Reade admits the *Californian* had been earlier in the evening. But he keeps saying it: 'Carefully considering all the relevant evidence, and not only part of it, the conclusion must be that Boxhall mistook a stationary, but swinging, steamer for a moving one.' (p57; similarly pps 315/6)

'It is in fact only Boxhall who speaks in detail of a moving ship...' – a carefully worded sentence on p55 that sweeps away a number of witnesses, including Officer Lightoller, by requiring them to speak not only of a moving ship, as they assuredly do, but to speak of her *in detail.*

Boxhall was indeed the only one to speak in detail – because he had been specifically tasked by Captain Smith with making contact with the potential rescuer. This is why his evidence as to that vessel's clear approach should be given special weight. And if Boxhall doesn't impress Reade, decades later, we have just seen how he impressed the specialists who actually heard him speak in person in 1912.

Stone didn't impress Reade either, who decided that he must have had 'a feeling of such inferiority as amounted to actual fear' of his captain (p326), despite Stone's evident firmness about sending down Gibson because it was Lord's duty to hear his message.

Instead Stone, a married man, is burlesqued as an 'obedient child' under the influence of 'Papa told me'. Lord is then a 'dominating father figure' (rather than the father who sent postcards to his toddler son from every port of call, signed 'Daddy') and the book ludicrously suggests that Stone then perjured himself because he would otherwise be 'betraying and incriminating his own father'.

But Stone never wavered in the witness box when faced by the Attorney General and Solicitor General of the United Kingdom. There was no inferiority complex on display in the sailorman's replies to 'superior' intellects. He was not some troubled teenager in any 'actual fear' of those august gentlemen either!

Tellingly, Reade succumbs to the usual cheap shots, referring to 'Captain Lord's characteristic arrogance', and how 'Nature itself had handicapped Captain Lord' with a 'countenance of stone' that 'seemed neither to invoke, nor to welcome, sympathy'. He was 'not a figure to arouse public compassion'.

'He seems the very reverse of a jolly and companionable Skipper.' A lot of surmise, but the pictures published here, rather than the stock one available from a newspaper agency, would 'seem' to suggest the opposite.

Whether Lord was jolly or arrogant, ugly or an Adonis, kind or cruel, really has little to do with the crucial issues of where the *Californian* and the *Titanic* could have been that night. But the severed *Titanic* 'body' has now been found, and in the case of the Mystery Ship, the *Californian* – however reluctantly for some – must simply be eliminated from further enquiries.

DISTANCE AND DISCERNMENT

---•◆•---

INFAMY AND INFALLIBILITY

Interesting stories about icebergs were told by Sir Clement Markham in a recent lecture:

> Once I was on the bridge of a discovery ship on a bright moonlit night with a youthful and inexperienced officer of the watch.
>
> I told him that to the man who touched ice first, the mess gave a champagne dinner. So, in the innocence of his heart, he steered direct for a lump of ice and went stem on it, going 4 knots. It was a deceitful piece of ice, for instead of being small it had a great mass under water, and the ship was brought up 'all standing'.
>
> If we had been going 22 knots I would not have been here tonight and my young friend would not have been a Lord of the Admiralty. There was not much harm done, but disapprobation was expressed – and there was no champagne.

(*Saturday Post*, 18 May, 1912)

Newspapers in 1912 were full of this vaunted, vainglorious talk, even when the enormous risk of such extravagant deeds was from time to time demonstrated. It was Sir Clement Markham who also happened to select Robert Falcon Scott as leader of the British Polar Expedition that ended in disastrous circumstances in 1912, although the bodies of Scott and his companions were not discovered until a year later.

Boasting about encouraging a ship's officer to strike ice in the month after a ship's sinking with dumbfounding loss of life through such a collision, would today be seen as monumentally crass, or a rank lapse in taste. But in 1912 it demonstrated how Edwardian optimism (to put it at its mildest) could bounce back from almost any setback.

That a man who impelled his ship towards an icefield, and then impaled her at great speed upon a jagged spur, should be regarded as 'fatherly', while a man who prudently stopped his vessel in ice is denounced as arrogant, seems one of the stranger legacies of that Atlantic episode when the British-built largest ship in the world went under, and asunder, taking with her a staggering population of victims.

The British Inquiry was keen to stress how the *Titanic* sank intact, grasping the last fig leaves of pride rather than admitting to a ghastly and chastening lesson. 'The ship did not break in two', pronounced Lord Mersey in his final report, although there was much testimony that she did. 'There can be no question of that', intoned the Attorney General soothingly on the thirty-fifth day, and yet the two halves now lie separated by some considerable distance on the seabed.

But in a real sense she was never intact; she had been pierced fatally by a mound of frozen water, and whether in one piece, or several, or a hundred, the shattering should have led to a fracturing of the Empire-building conceit she embodied. Yet that was the very thing – overconfidence, reckoned heavily in lives lost, could never be allowed to erode national confidence, the basic building block of achievement. The fractures simply had to be papered over, and papered over they were.

If fiction was the glue, then it served for a time. Britannia ruled the waves and continued to do so, even when the haemorrhage of sacrifice on Flanders fields, by its sheer scale, would drain almost the last drop of hauteur from a finally shaken Establishment.

And even thereafter, the talk was of forging 'a land fit for heroes', ignoring the likelihood that Mr Thomas Atkins (by the hundred thousand) no more wanted to be regarded as a hero than Mr Thomas Andrews ever did. What is heroism, in such a case, if it is to be regarded as but another jewel, a further encrustation, in the crown of the Old Order?

The poet Wilfred Owen summed up perfectly the hypocrisy of patriotic nonsense in considering what those at home would make of prattle about pink on a map and suchlike, were they to actually trudge behind a wagon containing the expiring frame of a man who had just been gassed, 'and hear, at every jolt, the blood come gargling from the froth-corrupted lungs':

> My friend, you would not tell with such high zest,
> To children ardent for some desperate glory,
> The old Lie: *Dulce et decorum est*
> *Pro patria mori.*

A lie with a capital L, says Owen of the ode by Horace that extols how sweet and fitting it is to die for one's country. For the poet, a man whose very stock-in-trade is contemplation of the ideal, the injunction to 'Be British!' has become an empty slogan. Being British, on a placidly continuing basis, stripped of intimations of sacrifice, will do much better.

But was it ever really so, or have human beings always behaved much like each other from generation to generation, down the ages and from century to century? Does the self-satisfaction of one era lift it supremely above the epochs?

The Edwardians may have insisted there were no flies in their ointment – and they were an ointment-obsessed society, as any cursory turning of the pages of newspapers and magazines of the period will demonstrate – but half a century later, one small voice emerged to suggest what being British had really been like on the *Titanic*.

Charles Judd, a humble fireman who gave deposition to investigators from the Board of Trade on his arrival back in England at Plymouth in 1912, was never selected for the witness box.

But he told the *Belfast Weekly Telegraph* in a 1962 interview, printed to mark the half-century since the disaster, how he was 'swept into a collapsible boat which never properly opened' [Collapsible A]. He added: 'Six people died in my boat from exposure, two of them in my own arms':

> The first one I'll never forget. She was a young lady, a bride perhaps, who was swimming very pluckily through the water. 'Take care of me,' she said to me as she came up to our boat, and as soon as I could get a good position I took her under the arms and pulled her in. Only then I saw that she had nothing on, only a nightdress and a long black cloak.
>
> She had rings on her fingers, enough to keep her for the rest of her life, but they were no good to her then. It must have been half an hour we sat on the edge of the boat, I steadying her up with my arm, chafing her limbs and cheering her up.
>
> Suddenly I noticed her head had dropped forward, and she was still. I tried the tests every man on shipboard knows, and found she was dead. So the next time the boat listed, I let her slip gently overboard. We only had room for the living.
>
> A trimmer was next, puffing and exhausted. I pulled him in too, but he died in a few minutes. The cold was awful. All the time I was sitting myself with icy water above my knees. They took me aboard the *Carpathia* in blankets.

What Judd had to say next, fifty years after the alleged event, is not what would have been reported by any British newspaper of the time. He declared:

> I learned from other members of the crew why more third-class passengers were not saved.

It is because somebody among the officers started the cry 'British First!' This, of course, did not discriminate against Americans, but it encouraged forcing back into the water Portuguese, even the women, Italians, and other foreigners, to save people who cried for help in English.

'A British life above all others,' was the word passed round, said a seaman to me. There was no command so far as I know to get the steerage people up onto the decks ready for the boats.

There were lots of babies on deck during the last moments. One Portuguese woman had three. God knows where they all went to, but we're pledged to tell all we know no matter who suffers.

Judd, who was aged thirty-two on the *Titanic*, was by then eighty-two, but his extraordinary claims drew precisely no letters from readers, and no interest from the authorities. He may have been pledged to tell all he knew, with one or two others (the article also innocuously quoted a fellow Belfast crew survivor), but he would not get the chance. Three years later he was dead.

This was a man who had been summoned to attend the British Inquiry (and paid £12 13s in witness expenses, twice the average) yet he never testified or could thereby be cross-examined. Thus his newspaper tale is pure hearsay… and has no status.

Yet much sub-hearsay rubbish was pushed, and published, in 1912. It was both sweet and fitting to die on that ship, according to the tone and tenor of swathes of newsprint. In that climate, anyone who tended to 'rock the boat' was not wanted

A total of 212 witnesses from the crew of the *Titanic*, including four officers, had their depositions taken for the British Inquiry. But only forty-seven, including the officers, were called to give evidence – less than a quarter of the total. Another twenty-two men gave evidence in America, leaving a large majority of individuals whose accounts are still unknown, for the depositions are lost. We think we know everything about the *Titanic* disaster, but in fact we still know very little – and much of what we 'know' must, like the British Inquiry conclusions, inevitably be wrong.

It might be hard to imagine today, but there were many who regarded the *Titanic* Inquiry's thirty-nine days and ninety-eight witnesses as ridiculously prolonged. The whole business was denounced in the House of Commons as a 'monstrous pie', into which many lawyers had eagerly plunged their fingers.

Political jibes were made at how they could listen for so very long to the 'interesting explanation' of how a ship might not float through having the bottom torn out of it. By this yardstick (*Hansard*, February 1914; on a supplementary vote for the costs of the Court) we are fortunate indeed that so much evidence was adduced.

Few realise that the Wreck Commissioner's Court was originally intended to sit for a perfunctory day or two in Southampton.

At the same time, however, the Board of Trade controlled absolutely the calling of witnesses. And the selection of witnesses is always crucial to what is likely to emerge. Witnesses who are called are likely to confirm what is already in their depositions. And those who are not called perforce stay silent in the wider scheme of things.

The persons who selected the crew witnesses from the mass of depositions were those who led the presentation of evidence in the Wreck Commissioner's Court. This primarily meant the Attorney General, Sir Rufus Isaacs, and the Solicitor General, Sir John Simon, both of whom appeared (with others) for the Board of Trade.

These two august men were nothing less than the Government's highest-ranking legal advisers. Not mere officeholders of the judiciary, note well, but of the executive branch. The Attorney General even sat at Cabinet – the first holder of that office ever to do so.

A demonstration of this conflict of interest lies in the amendment moved in the House of Commons by the Opposition in 1913 to have both men denied their substantial legal fees for the *Titanic* Inquiry – awarded by Lord Mersey – because they were already amply-salaried Law Officers of the State.

In appearing nominally for the Board of Trade before the Board's own Inquiry they can thus also be said to have had the wishes and sensitivities of the Asquith administration close at heart. In short, they were highly political as well as legal entities.

These men could, and did, pick and choose the material. The Attorney General was allowed the widest latitude by Lord Mersey in leading the evidence through calling witnesses, even though he occasionally offered the bench another source of corroboration for a point already led.

Only three passengers were called, the Duff Gordons and Bruce Ismay, as we have seen – yet the Inquiry was supposed to be for the reassurance of the paying public, rather than a wholesale inquiry into the duties of crew or technical matters to do with how a ship might be prevented from foundering.

A short exchange on Tuesday, 11 June, 1912, the twenty-first day of evidence, shows how the thirty-seven-year-old counsel for third class passengers, William Dawson Harbinson, was utterly frustrated by a deliberately straitjacketed Inquiry – and betrays to a nicety the class prejudice and defensiveness of that investigation.

It is worth quoting it in full:

Mr Harbinson: My Lord, there is at this stage a subject I should like to mention to the court, which I conceive it my duty to bring forward. Up to the present, representatives of the owners, the officers, and crew of the *Titanic* have been called, and have been allowed to present that aspect of the case, and I think this would not be an inopportune time when some indication might be given by those who represent the Board of Trade as to what time we might expect the representatives of the passengers, and especially the passengers in whom I am more deeply interested, to be called? I think it is only fair as one side of the case has been presented, in the interests of justice and public confidence, that the other side of the story should also be presented.

Attorney General: I find some difficulty in understanding what it is my friend wants.

Lord Mersey: What is it you do want?

Mr Harbinson: I want some indication from the representatives of the Board of Trade as to when representatives of the different classes of passengers will be called.

Lord Mersey: You cannot have untimely intimations of that kind. They will conduct their case as they think right. That is all.

Attorney General: I should like to say this, so that at any rate, if my friend has any witnesses whom he likes to call, he should not let them go under any misapprehension. So far as I am aware, and from the material before us, there is no useful light which can be shed upon the facts into which we are enquiring by any passengers whose evidence is available to us.

Lord Mersey: Can you suggest any passenger, Mr Harbinson?

Mr Harbinson: I dare say, my Lord, that my solicitor may be able to.

Lord Mersey: Do not say your solicitor. Can you suggest any person who can help in this Inquiry that you know of?

Mr Harbinson: Yes, my Lord, I have the names of several survivors in America who, I think, would shed a useful light upon the subject.

Lord Mersey: Survivors are not necessarily of the least value.

Mr Harbinsom: I submit to your Lordship that under the circumstances it would be desirable that the evidence of survivors should be produced in order that we may know exactly what took place at the time of the collision, and more especially to throw some light on the great disparity that exists in the number of deaths in the different classes of passengers.

Lord Mersey: Have you any proofs [depositions, or sworn affidavits] from anybody?

Mr Harbinson: It is because I have not proofs that I –

Lord Mersey: Do answer my question. Have you any proofs from anybody?

Mr Harbinson: I have not.

Lord Mersey: Then I cannot form any opinion. If you have any proofs of witnesses that you desire to call, you may let me see them.

Mr Harbinson: Statements have been made in the public press, and it is because that has been done –

Lord Mersey: What public press?

Mr Harbinson: In the papers.

Lord Mersey: Will you tell me the name?

Mr Harbinson: The *Freeman's Journal*, of Dublin, and the *Irish Independent*, of Dublin.

Lord Mersey: Will you hand up to me the *Freeman's Journal* and the *Irish Independent*?

Mr Harbinson: If I have the extracts here your Lordship shall have them.

Attorney General: May I point this out to my friend. Of course, a number of state-ments have appeared; some statements have been before us, and we have enquired into them, and I see no use whatever in calling the witnesses.

Lord Mersey: Never mind, let me see those two papers.

Attorney General: I am ready to call any witnesses –

Lord Mersey: To found a case upon statements found in newspapers seems to me most extraordinary.

Attorney General: All I am anxious to make plain is that I will call any witnesses who can give us any more light than we have at present. I do not intend to call witnesses who will only repeat evidence that we already have.

Lord Mersey [reading aloud]: 'A terrible story of women and children locked in the steerage of the *Titanic* is told by Miss Margaret J. Murphy, of Fostragh, County Longford, who, with her sister, Miss Katherine Murphy, were saved from the wreck.' That lady does not appear to have been locked in the steerage. 'Interviewed by a representative of the *New York American*' – that is another paper.

Mr Harbinson: No, my Lord.

Lord Mersey: Is the *New York American* the same paper?

Mr Harbinson: No, it is an extract.

Lord Mersey [resumes reading]: 'Interviewed by a representative of the *New York American* at the residence of their sister, Mrs J. Toomey, No. 3,649 Olinville Avenue, the Bronx, Miss Murphy stated: "Before all the steerage passengers had even a chance for their lives, the *Titanic's* sailors fastened the doors and companion-ways leading up from the third class section. That meant certain death to all who remained below."' You have never asked any man who has been in the box any question directed to this.

Mr Harbinson: Oh, yes, my Lord, with great respect, I have.

Lord Mersey: Tell me where you asked whether the sailors didn't fasten the doors and companion-ways?

Mr Harbinson: I have asked them were they opened.

Lord Mersey: That is not a fair way of asking such a question. The fair and proper way is to say: 'Were they fastened by you or by any of the men working with you?'

Mr Harbinson: That question, I believe, has been asked too.

Lord Mersey: Well, then, tell me where it is – [reading] 'And while the sailors were beating back the steerage passengers, lifeboats were putting away, some of them not half filled.' Then do you want me to read about 'A brave Irish youth'?

Mr Harbinson: No; your Lordship asked me for the paper, and I gave it to you.

Lord Mersey: It is much longer than the part I have read. Do you want me to read the passage headed 'A brave Irish youth'?'

Mr Harbinson: I should hope, my Lord, that it is not a solitary example of Irish bravery.

Lord Mersey: I dare say not; but has it any bearing upon this Inquiry, because, if so, I will read it?

Mr Harbinson: No, my Lord.

Lord Mersey: Very well, what is the other extract from a newspaper? Is this the only foundation you have?

Sir Robert Finlay [for the White Star Line]: May I make this suggestion to Mr Harbinson? If he would supply the Attorney General with a proof taken of any witness he thinks it would be desirable to call, the Attorney General will consider that.

Lord Mersey: I have suggested that. Apparently no proofs of anybody have been taken, and I really cannot prolong this Inquiry while we seek to verify statements which come apparently from the *New York American*, whatever paper that is; I do not know what paper it is. I cannot do that, Mr Harbinson.

Mr Harbinson: My object was that the Board of Trade should –

Attorney General: We will call any witness who really can help.

Mr Harbinson: I will submit to the Attorney-General a list of names.

Attorney General: That will not do.

Lord Mersey: Oh, no, you must give the names, and you must show that a statement has been taken from them, and you must show that that statement contains material evidence, and then, you know, either my discretion will be exercised, or the discretion of the gentlemen at the Bar will be exercised, as to whether they ought to be called. But I cannot adjourn the Inquiry on the speculation that some witnesses may be found to bear out the statements of the *New York American*.

Much earlier, on the fourth day, Harbinson had applied for the evidence of other steerage witnesses to be taken on commission in the United States, since they were unlikely to voluntarily return from the land to which they had emigrated, especially in view of what they had been through. 'I think I am very unlikely to do that', replied Mersey curtly.

Harbinson cited the names of Bernard McCoy and Thomas McCormack, saying that the latter 'alleges that when swimming in the sea he endeavoured to board two boats and was struck on the head and the hands and shoved back into the sea, and endeavoured to be drowned. That is one charge.'

Alice McCoy helps her younger brother Bernard into a lifeboat, as her sister Agnes holds off a crewman. Lawyers were not permitted to take a deposition from McCoy for the purposes of consideration by the British Inquiry. *New York Herald.*

'The gentleman who did it may be guilty of an attempt to commit manslaughter,' observed Lord Mersey, introducing an entirely new concept to the law since 'attempted manslaughter' must be premeditated and therefore cannot be manslaughter, which of its nature lacks malice aforethought.

'I cannot try that,' Lord Mersey added, replying to a query as to whether it was not a question for investigation by the Court with the words: 'I do not think so... That, I do not think, comes within my jurisdiction at all. If any crime has been committed by some individual in connection with this unfortunate matter, that has to be tried by somebody else.'

Mr J.P. Farrell, a Member of Parliament, whose brother was a solicitor acting for some Irish families, interrupted plaintively: 'But my Lord, we also appear for others. We have gone to a great deal of expense...'

Mersey was unmoved. And so it is that much of the information that has come down to us about the *Titanic* belongs to a grey area, or to no area at all.

For instance, the passenger cited above, Thomas McCormack, told a New Jersey newspaper that:

> After being beaten severely by sailors with oars [while he was in the sea] I managed to get into one of the lifeboats, and my cousins, Alice and Kate McCoy sat on me, and tried to cover me up.
>
> After a while one of the sailors saw my legs protruding, and seizing them, asked me, 'What in hell' I was doing in the boat. He dragged me out and tried to throw me into the water. I grabbed him by the throat and said if I went overboard I would take him with me. When he saw that he could not throw me over he finally desisted and I was allowed to remain.
>
> When we got aboard the *Carpathia*, we did not get the best of rations. That ship had not sailed with the intention of taking on seven hundred survivors from a wrecked boat. One of my cousins had some money in a purse, which she wore with a chain around her neck, and with this money some brandy was bought which came in very handy.

There are a myriad such stories, reported and mediated in the press, frequently with obvious errors and impossibilities; stories about suicides, about being locked in or held back, about shots and shootings on the Boat Deck, and mention of the many brutish and bestial things that are likely to occur when desperation and then panic sets in.

But the nobility of the disaster is what we have been steadily served up in the decades since. The playwright George Bernard Shaw detected it at the very earliest, asking:

> What is the use of all this ghastly, blasphemous, inhuman, braggartly lying? Here is a calamity which might well make the proudest man humble, and the wildest joker serious. It makes us vainglorious, insolent, and mendacious... the effect on me was one of profound disgust, almost of national dishonour. Am I mad?

Not when the President of the Court of Inquiry can actually opine that: '*Survivors are not necessarily of the least value.*' Mersey may have meant it in a peculiar, probative, sense – but it was almost an encapsulation of official and 'right-thinking' thought at the time. The dead died well and salvaged their State some sacrifice to sell – for the greater good, of course.

And the official story was true, because officialdom was in possession of 'the full facts' – as the doubters patently were not. The fact that officialdom decided what were the facts, and did not disclose anything like their full extent to public view, was just an incidental advantage of power that happened to go effectively unquestioned.

Any living witnesses to a different truth were to be drowned out (if they had not been physically drowned), submerged in a blaring cacophony about the bravery of their less fortunate, yet more fortunate, shipmates. All was well, and all always would be well. Hurrah! A statue for Captain Smith!

Captain Lord – the name of an infuriating, rattling skeleton that just *will not* lie down and take its allotted place – commented about the Master of the *Titanic*:

He was certainly not on the bridge, which is very particular in the White Star Line. If there were any risky waters that they were in, doubtful conditions, they [captains] were usually supposed to be on the bridge. He may have had some reason, I don't know, but he wasn't on the bridge.

The Master of an old tramp *was* on the bridge. He was on deck from six o'clock that morning, fooling around and looking around, and getting a bit anxious. And when dark came, he went on the bridge and stopped her [*Californian*].

We had no instructions about staying on the bridge in ice. I did everything I was supposed to do. There wasn't a thing they could point a finger at me to say I did wrong [Lord had doubled lookouts, while Smith, travelling at twice the speed, had not].

My navigation was correct. I reached Boston without the slightest difficulty. We found the position of this ice and broadcast it to everybody.

No, I've always thought they wanted to shut up the *Titanic* Inquiry as quickly as possible. They'd had enough of it...

They wanted a [scape]goat, that was my opinion. That's what Strachan said: 'They wanted a bloody goat, Lord, and they got you...'

SPEED IN THICK WEATHER
To the Editor of *The Times*

Sir – Now that public interest is being aroused on the question of official regulations providing for the safety of ships and their passengers, may I be permitted to draw attention to that obsolete Article 17 of the Regulations for Preventing Collisions at Sea?

It runs: 'Every vessel shall, in a fog, mist, falling snow, or heavy rainstorms, go at a moderate speed, having careful regard to the existing conditions.'

But what is a moderate speed?

In November 1907, I wrote to the President of the Board of Trade, calling his attention to the high speed at which Transatlantic steamers are navigated through fog. I instanced the Marconigrams published in the Press the previous September of a giant liner 'emerging from the dense fog which had enveloped her for the past sixteen hours in which speed had frequently to be reduced to 19 knots.'

I contended that it would be 'very doubtful that those on board such a vessel, going at 19 knots, would even know should they run down a small craft, and the course of any vessel going at such a speed in thick weather may well be termed murderous.'

As showing it was more than suspected these high speeds were maintained in thick weather in opposition to the Commander's judgement, I quoted these words taken from Admiral de Horsey's letter to the *Daily Mail*: 'I recall to mind,' he wrote, 'many years ago, when giving evidence at the Society of the Arts before a committee on the subject of speed in a fog, that certain captains of liners, on being assured that their names would be kept secret, stated that it was their practice to maintain high speed in a fog as being safer for their own ship, and because compliance with the rule of moderate speed would cause such delay of mails and passengers as would lead to their company dispensing with their services and appointing less conscientious commanders.'

In concluding I suggested that a maximum speed allowed (say 8 knots, to be decided by nautical experts) be inserted, the article to read thus – 'go at a moderate speed, in no case exceeding (say) 8 knots.'

Mr Lloyd George, in replying, referred me to an answer given in the House of Commons by his predecessor at the Board of Trade in 1900, who said the rule was adopted after: 'very full discussion and consideration at the Washington Maritime Conference in 1889. It is now International, and, as I am not aware that any sufficient reasons have been adduced for altering it, I do not propose to take any steps in that direction.'

It is an incontrovertible fact that ships have increased four-fold in size and nearly doubled in speed since 1889, and the numerous casualties resulting from high speed in thick weather is surely 'sufficient reason' why international action should be taken.

Within a few months of my correspondence with the Board of Trade, the HMS *Gladiator* and SS *St Paul* collision occurred in a snowstorm off the Isle of Wight, when the *Gladiator* sank with a loss of twenty-seven officers and men.

Your obedient servant,

James J. Page, Bengal Pilot Service (retired)
3, West Cliff Mansions, Eastbourne, April 19.

(*The Times*, 20 April, 1912, p12)

CASUALTIES DUE TO EXCESSIVE SPEED

Answering Sir Clement Kinloch-Cooke in yesterday's parliamentary papers, Mr Buxton writes: 'The number of cases in the last eleven years in which courts of inquiry into shipping casualties in the United Kingdom have found that the vessels concerned were navigated at too high a rate of speed in thick weather is ninety, of which sixty-one casualties occurred in fog, nineteen in mist, six in snow, and four in rain.

The suggestion of the Right Hon. member that some amendment should be made to the Article of the regulations for preventing collisions at sea, so as to ensure careful navigation in the presence of icebergs, would receive very careful consideration, but international consent is required for any alteration in the collision regulations.'

(*Northern Whig*, 17 May, 1912, p9)

The *Titanic* was supposed to be 'her own lifeboat', availing of heavy discounts in the number of lifesaving craft she need carry through certain credits for construction precautions within the hull. But she might, at least, have been *navigated* as if she were her own lifeboat.

Pointing the finger of blame often points it away from somewhere else. *Titanic* witnesses saw a Mystery Ship, which behaved in a way that was not heroic, but not necessarily inhuman. The vessel and her conduct are unexplained – as uncertain as any winking light at sea, and as unknowable as such a light – but the Inquiries claimed to know. They could not have known.

'The [*Californian*] position was given, the correct position,' insisted her Master, decades later. 'Mersey seemed to think the position was wrong. It was not. There was no fooling or falsifying of any position at all.'

'No, I think I've had a dirty deal,' Stanley Lord added. 'It all turned out, as it happened, very well. But there's always that stigma: Was Lord to blame, or was he not to blame?'

Authors of the *Titanic* story, or half-story, have sometimes used subtleties of language to confirm the black-and-white sketches of the disaster that history has so far had foisted upon it. And sometimes it is simply startling what we will choose to believe.

'What will happen when the 100,000-ton liner comes along?' wondered the *Cork Constitution* on the day before the *Titanic* impacted her iceberg at fatal speed. 'She will come. It is only five years since the *Lusitania*'s 32,000 tons seemed the limit; and already we have the *Titanic* with 46,000. And each monster, bigger than the last, brings new problems with it. Titanic, indeed, are the times.'

Before that paper's next edition (a non-publishing Sunday intervening) there came about a colossal disaster, much of which has stayed at sea. The human condition means that we often cannot know all of any story, that loose ends frequently do not tie up but dangle aimlessly as the empty lifeboat falls, that puzzles remain maddeningly puzzles, and mystery ships have no name. If there is any lesson to the wanton loss of the *Titanic* at all, it is that we should doubt our very confidence, just as we see the super-confidence that was theirs.

We can trust, perhaps, in the essential goodness of human nature, never overlooking the deeds done in desperation, or summoned for the struggle by base survival instinct. This being so, allowing that emergencies are unusual, we can, as Senator Smith would have it, see again a wonderful vessel in the day of her brightest colour.

We can see her when she was a stupendous stronghold upon the sea, a four-funnelled fastness, the radiant reality of her time, with great walls of iron and masts of majesty – and not as what she has become, a tawdry coin in the shabby and debased currency of gobbledygook culture:

A SALOON PASSENGER'S IMPRESSIONS
Interesting Notes

'Look how that ship is rolling, I never thought it was so rough.' The voice was a lady's, and the place was the sun deck of the *Titanic*. We had just got well clear of the eastern end of the Isle of Wight, and were shaping our course down the English Channel towards Cherbourg.

The ship that had elicited the remark was a large three-masted sailing vessel, which rolled and pitched so heavily that over her bows the seas were constantly breaking. But up where we were – some 60ft above the water line – there was no indication of the strength of the tossing swell below. This indeed, is the one great impression I received from my first trip in the *Titanic* – and everyone with whom I spoke shared it – her wonderful steadiness. Were it not for the brisk breeze blowing along the decks, one would have scarcely imagined that every hour found us some 20 knots further upon our course. And then this morning, when the full Atlantic swell came upon our port side, so stately and measured was the roll of the mighty ship that one needed to compare the movement of the side with the steady line of the clear horizon.

After a windy night on the Irish Sea, when the sturdy packet boat tossed and tumbled to her heart's content – by the way, have ships a heart? – the lordly contempt of the *Titanic* for anything less than a hurricane seemed most marvellous and comforting.

But other things besides her steadiness filled us with wonder. Deck over deck and apartment after apartment lent their deceitful aid to persuade us that instead of being on the sea we were still on terra firma. It is useless for me to attempt a description of the wonders of the saloon – the smoking room with its inlaid mother-of-pearl, the lounge with its green velvet and dull polished oak, the reading room with its marble fireplace and deep soft chairs and rich carpet of old rose hue – all these things have been told over and over again and only lose in the telling.

So vast was it all that after several hours on board some of us were still uncertain of our way about, though we must state that, with commendable alacrity and accuracy, some 325 found their way to the great dining room at 7.32 p.m., when the bugle sounded the call to dinner. After dinner, as we sat in the beautiful lounge listening to the White Star orchestra playing the *Tales of Hoffman* and [a] *Cavalleria Rusticana* selection, more than once we heard the remark, 'You would never imagine you were on a ship'.

Still harder was it to believe that up on the top deck it was blowing a gale, but we had to go to bed, and this reminds me that on the *Titanic* the expression is literally accurate. Nowhere were the berths of other days seen, and everywhere comfortable oaken bedsteads gave place to furniture in the famous suites beloved by millionaires.

Then the morning plunge in the great swimming bath, where the ceaseless ripple of the tepid sea water was almost the only indication that somewhere in the distance 72,000 horses in the guise of steam engines fretted and strained under the skilful guidance of the engineers, and after the plunge a half-hour in the gymnasium helped to send one's blood coursing freely, and created a big appetite for the morning meal.

But if the saloon of the *Titanic* is wonderful, no less so is the second class, and in its degree the third class. A word from the genial purser acted as the 'Open Sesame' of the Arabian Nights, and secured us an English officer and his son, whose acquaintance I had made at lunch, and a free passage through all the floating wonder. Lifts and lounges and libraries are not generally associated in the public mind with second-class accommodation, yet in the *Titanic* all are found. It needed the assurance of our guide that we had left the saloon and were really in second class.

On the crowded third class deck were hundreds of English, Dutch, Italian and French mingling in happy fellowship, and when we wandered down among them we found that for them too the *Titanic* was a wonder. No more general cabins, but hundreds of comfortable rooms, with two, four, or six berths, each beautifully covered in red and white coverlets. Here too are lounges and smoking rooms, less magnificent than those amidships to be sure, but none the less comfortable, and which, with the swivel chairs and separate tables in the dining rooms, struck me as not quite fitting in with my previous notion of steerage accommodation.

(*Cork Constitution*, Saturday 13 April, 1912, p4)
Written anonymously by Titanic *photographer Fr Francis Browne, who disembarked at Queenstown.*

THE *TITANIC*
GIANT LINER AT QUEENSTOWN
SHIP'S MAIDEN VOYAGE

Our Queenstown correspondent writes – Some hours before the *Titanic* arrived at Queenstown on Thursday, on her maiden voyage, many people assembled on the high headlands which guard the harbour at either side, to catch a glimpse of the latest triumph of ship construction ere she rested to her anchors in our waters for the first time.

Those observers were rewarded with a unique spectacle, for shortly before noon-time a great object appeared on the horizon to southward, and all eyes were eagerly turned to the towering vessel, which made herself more apparent as she steamed due north towards the two tenders, *America* and *Ireland*, which were waiting with mails and passengers for the *Titanic*.

To look at the giant proportions of the *Titanic* as she steamed to her anchorage ground, and to see the immense water space she filled, the conclusion was forced on one's mind that surely whatever ship may come in the years that are to be, the *Titanic* and her sister ship the *Olympic* would stand out as unparalleled in all that pertained to ship construction, for whether viewed from the outside or from within, the *Titanic* as she rode to her anchors looked a stupendous monument to all that science in ship construction could suggest.

But magnificent as her outward proportions are, it was when visitors got alongside in the tenders and glanced from the bridge to the towering mass overhead that one saw how the new liner dwarfed everything completely. The travellers who looked down from the upper decks seemed far away – and they were in a sense. Later when going up from alongside, the same feelings of amazement filled everyone, for on all sides there was evidence in the living rooms, the corridors, and the saloons of the *Titanic*, which clearly showed that the White Star people, in putting such a ship on the waters, meant to place at the disposal of the travelling public a ship which should not be eclipsed in our time.

Visitors should have been lost in the confines of the *Titanic* were they left to their own judgement to go from compartment to compartment, but by the courtesy of Messrs James Scott & Co., agents, a number of guides were provided, and they conducted visitors through the vast proportions of the *Titanic*. It was only a cursory glance, so to speak, that could be obtained of the incomparable saloon, in which over 500 persons can be seated at the one time. This also applies to her second cabin, and to her third class accommodation, which is of such a character as to make people realise to the full that the White Star Company's directors do nothing by halves, and that they are as anxious to elicit the approval of the humbler as the wealthier passengers.

Internationally the *Titanic* is verily the ship deluxe of the fleet. In her, the illusion of a great hotel is complete. One of the upper decks is completely enclosed to serve as a ballroom, which can also be used as a skating rink, or theatre. The regular ball on the last night out is usually held on deck, with partitions of canvas hastily contrived to keep out wind or rain.

A ballroom completely enclosed with glass and heated will obviously lend all the comforts of the land to the high seas. By day this enclosure, the windows of which are constructed on the railway carriage principle, fitted with jalousie shutters, may be used as a sun parlour and promenade. It is large enough to accommodate several hundred passengers.

In planning the cabins of the new liners, the luxuries of the most up-to-date hotels have been kept in sight, and even improved upon. These boats offer not only extended suites of rooms, but complete flats, which make it possible to cross the Atlantic while enjoying all the privacy of one's own home.

The ocean-going 'flats' comprise bedrooms, sitting room and parlours, private baths, and even a private library, all en suite. The parlours are furnished with tables suitable for serving meals, however elaborate. It will not be necessary for the occupants of these private flats, so to speak, to enter the dining rooms in crossing, while enjoying the best the ship affords.

The *Titanic* is the first steamer to offer cabins with private shower baths attached. In addition there is a great swimming bath aboard large enough to enjoy all the pleasures of sea bathing while at sea. A gymnasium, the largest and most completely equipped afloat, is a feature.

THE KITCHEN ARRANGEMENTS

The main dining saloon will seat more than 600 passengers, is the largest single apartment on the ship, and in its furnishing and decoration the most elaborate. Should a guest tire of this apartment in the week he is at sea, he can wander from one café to another, enjoying practically as much variety as he might ashore.

Not only will the utmost variety in the form and decoration of these dining rooms be found, but there will be considerable variety in cooking as well, the kitchen arrangements for such being probably the most elaborate yet seen on board a ship. Needless to say a vast amount of care and forethought has been bestowed on the general arrangements in this important detail, with the result that the kitchens represent the last word.

The most striking departure in dining saloons on the new ship is the verandah café. It is built on one of the upper decks, far astern, looking out over the sea, and about 50ft above water. The decorations and general management carry out the idea of the open-air cafés of southern Europe. The meals are served at small tables with movable chairs. The café is erected with the exposed rafters entwined with vines, while the sides are latticed, the effect being to make the illusion of a café at the seaside as complete as possible.

Flower and palm gardens and conservatories containing seasonable flowers and plants the whole year round and a fish pond are also among the liner's equipment, while a carefully selected orchestra on a grand concert scale will at intervals discourse the latest operatic and other music, and a grand organ, presided at by a skilled organist, will lend variety and charm to the entertainments on board.

Other features are children's nurseries, a high-class tailor's shop, modiste's parlour, and a jewellery store for the convenience of the first and second class passengers.

PRACTICALLY UNSINKABLE

The *Titanic* is as complete in her safety devices as in her luxurious outfit. She is divided into upwards of thirty steel compartments separated by heavy bulkheads. An automatic device on the bridge controls all these heavy steel doors, making it possible for a single hand to close them all in case of danger. The priceless time conserved in closing them in case of accident may thus be saved.

Each of these doors in turn is electrically connected with a chart on the bridge, where each floor is represented by a small electric light. When one of these doors closes the light will burn red; while it remains open it will remain dark. The officer on the bridge will thus be able to see at a glance if all the compartments are closed.

Still another set of safety devices guards against fire in every part of the ship. A series of thermostats is scattered throughout the great framework, which will indicate a rise in the temperature above a certain point. Should the temperature reach the danger point, the fact is at once communicated to the officer on the bridge by the ringing of a bell, while an electric light on a great chart displayed on the wall will burn red. In other words, the *Titanic* is practically unsinkable and absolutely fireproof.

Time is always of immense importance in the despatch of the White Star ships, which are never unnecessarily delayed at Queenstown. Scarcely had the last hundred sacks of mail been in process of transfer from tender to liner, when the siren of the liner and the whistle of the tender indicated to all shore visitors that the time was up.

A few moments more and the ship was ready – in fact, was moving westward; but ere she did so, passengers and visitors joined on board in wishing the superb ship a life of prosperity on the great highway she was entering for the first time.

The *Titanic* has on board in all 350 saloon, 300 second cabin, and 800 third class passengers, together with a crew of 903. At Queenstown she embarked over 120 passengers, 1,344 sacks of mail and forty-one parcel hampers. Her entire mail on board numbers 3,416 sacks.

Her time of departure from Queenstown was 1.20, which, considering the heavy embarkation, was a rapid despatch, and was in keeping with the excellent arrangements always made at Queenstown by Messrs James Scott and Co.

(*Cork Constitution*, Saturday 13 April, 1912, p4)

'A ship which should not be eclipsed in our time' – and yet she was; and just over a day later.

She never came back. But in another, still larger sense, the sentiment stays true. The *Titanic*, misdirected, has never been eclipsed.

A Pathetic Picture.
(The last Photo of the *Titanic*, taken by Mr John Morrogh at Red Bay, Crosshaven, after the vessel had left Queenstown.)

The last-ever photograph of the *Titanic* before her rediscovery in 1985. *Castleknock Chronicle. Author collection.*

POSTSCRIPT

Andrew Hume, of 42 George Street, Dumfries, thought that he had been through all a man could bear. His son had perished in the *Titanic* disaster.

Jock, the band's violinist, was twenty-eight when he faded away in freezing seawater. His father, an accomplished musician who had tutored the boy from an early age, was understandably distraught at his searing loss. But he was comforted by the constant assurances of others that his son had died a hero.

Two years later Jock Hume's father was dealt another indescribable blow. He received news that his daughter Grace, twenty-two, had been tortured to death by German soldiers on the Western Front.

John 'Jock' Hume, violinist in the *Titanic* orchestra. Buried under a simple headstone in Halifax, Nova Scotia, a granite obelisk to his honour and that of another Dumfries victim was unveiled in a town park, a little way from the bandstand, later that year. *The Sphere.*

A NURSE'S TRAGEDY
DUMFRIES GIRL THE VICTIM OF SHOCKING BARBARITY

News has reached Dumfries of the shocking death of a Dumfries young woman, Nurse Grace Hume, who went out to Belgium at the outbreak of war.

Nurse Hume was engaged at the camp hospital at Vilvorde, and she was the victim of horrible cruelty at the hands of German soldiers. Her breasts were cut off and she died in great agony. Nurse Hume's family received a note written shortly before she died. It was dated September 6th, and ran:

'Dear Kate, this is to say goodbye. Have not long to live. Hospital has been set on fire. Germans cruel. A man here had his head cut off. My right breast has been taken away. Give my love to ----. Goodbye, Grace.'

Nurse Hume's left breast was cut away after she had written the note. She was a young woman of twenty-three and was formerly a nurse in Huddersfield Hospital. Nurse Mullard, of Inverness, delivered the note personally to Nurse Hume's sister at Dumfries. She was also at Vilvorde, and she states that Nurse Hume acted the part of a heroine. A German attacked a wounded soldier whom Nurse Hume was taking to hospital. The nurse took his gun and shot the German dead.

(*The Star*, 16 September, 1914)

Andrew Hume had been told by another daughter, Kate, of Grace's horrible killing – days before the shocking details were reported in the Press.

He lost no time, immediately writing to the War Office seeking full details of what had taken place in Vilvorde, Belgium. The news meanwhile raced around Dumfries. How could such appalling agonies visit a local family twice in two years?

The *Dumfries Standard* was the first to break what would be a major story across the newspapers of the nation. The paper published a facsimile of the dying girl's note to her loved ones.

An account of the scandalous killing swiftly appeared in the London *Evening Standard* with the note: 'This message has been submitted to the Press Bureau, which does not object to the publication.'

The story – a vindication of Britain's decision to wage war on Germany in defence of 'little Belgium' a month earlier – was said to be particularly well authenticated. It was further published by a number of London papers, including the *Pall Mall Gazette*, *Globe* and *Westminster Gazette*.

NURSE THE GERMANS DID NOT KILL.

Girl's Trial on Charge of Forging Letters from Belgium.

'DEAD' SISTER'S EVIDENCE

Above: How the story panned out. A *Daily Mirror* headline reporting the strange twists and turns in a tale of alleged German barbarity that had gripped a gullible public.

Right: Kate Hume, the *Titanic* violinist's sister, pictured in the dock of a Scottish courthouse by the *Daily Mirror* on 29 December, 1914. *Author collection.*

The deeply disturbing incident would eventually lead to a full criminal trial – held in Dumfries itself. This time a third family member would be swept up in the horror. Because it was Kate Hume who was indicted:

Kate Hume, seventeen, was charged at Dumfries yesterday, before Sheriff Substitute Primrose, with having uttered a forged letter purporting to have been written by her sister, Nurse Grace Hume in Huddersfield. She declined to make any statement, on the advice of her agent, and was committed to prison to await trial.

(*The Times*, 30 September, 1914)

The Times had called for an immediate inquiry, having earlier learned that the story was false – an alive-and-kicking Grace Hume having raised a hue and cry in Huddersfield as soon as the reports were published. This newspaper, the voice of official Britain, also suggested, somewhat extravagantly, that the story may have been invented by 'German agents, in order to discredit all atrocity stories'.

The case eventually came to trial three months later, Kate Hume having been arrested and detained in custody from the moment her sister discredited the story by proving she was still among the living:

THE DUMFRIES ATROCITY HOAX
Trial of Nurse Hume's Sister
Girl's Remarkable Evidence

Edinburgh, 28 December

In September last it was published in Dumfries a story of German atrocities, the alleged victim being a young Dumfries nurse. The authorities investigated the story and as a result a young girl of prepossessing appearance named Kate Hume was tried here today in the High Court before the Lord Justice General, Lord Strathclyde, and a jury on a charge of fabricating and forging the two letters which embodied the story of the atrocities.

The accused, who was aged seventeen, pleaded not guilty and entered an alternative plea to the effect that she was not at the time responsible for what she did. Wearing a fur hat and stole and long blue serge jacket, she was for the most part quite cool and collected.

When, however, reference was made to the loss of her brother in the *Titanic*, she broke down. The hearing of evidence took up an entire day, and the case was adjourned 'til tomorrow for the hearing of counsel on the evidence.

The most dramatic moment was when the accused entered the witness box and admitted to her own counsel that she wrote the letters. She had no object in view, and did not know why she wrote them, but the doings of the Germans had got on her nerves, and she was so worked up that she believed what she wrote.

Distinguished mental experts testified that the accused at the time was suffering from a species of hysteria.

Kate Hume, who was a clerk employed at Dumfries, was indicted for having concocted and fabricated letters declaring that her sister Grace Hume had been subjected to brutalities in Vilvorde, near Brussels, which resulted in her death.

The indictment stated that 'this the prisoner did with the intention of alarming and annoying… her father, Andrew Hume, and stepmother Alice Mary Hume, of George Street, Dumfries'. At the time of the alleged outrage, Miss Grace Hume was engaged as a nurse at Huddersfield. Early in September a letter purporting to come from Grace Hume from Belgium was received by the accused, saying she had been mutilated, and another letter from a nurse at the Front named J.M. Mullard, recounting the death of Grace.

The prisoner, who has been in custody for thirteen weeks, pleaded not guilty and further pleaded specially and as an alternative that when the alleged offence was said to have been committed her mind was so unbalanced that she could not and did not understand what she was doing, or the effect thereof, and was not responsible.

Mr Andrew Hume was at once called. He is a teacher of music at Dumfries. He stated that he had married a second time and that before his first wife died he had several children. His son John was lost in the *Titanic*.

His daughter Grace was formerly engaged as a nurse at Huddersfield, and the accused left his house in August last and went into lodgings in Dumfries. He heard in September last of the supposed death of his daughter Grace at the Front. It came to his knowledge by letters which contained an account of what was supposed to have befallen her.

One, addressed to the prisoner, was as follows:

Dear Kate,
This is to say goodbye. I have not long to live. The hospital has been set on fire. Germans cruel. A man here had his head cut off. My breast taken away. Give my love to ----. Goodbye – Grace.

The witness said a second letter was handed to him which purported to be written at Vilvorde on 7 September. It was as follows:

To Miss Hume –
I have been asked by your sister, Miss Grace Hume, to hand the enclosed letter to you. My name is nurse Mullard, and I was with your sister when she died. Our camp hospital at Vilvorde was burnt to the ground and out of 1,517 men and twenty-three nurses only nineteen nurses were saved, but 149 men managed to get away.

Grace requested me to tell you that her last thoughts were of ---- and you, and that you are not to worry over her. She would be going to meet her Jock. These were her last words. She endured great agony in her last hours.

One of the soldiers (our men) caught two German soldiers in the act of cutting off her left breast, her right one having already been cut off. They were killed instantly by our soldiers. Grace managed to scrawl this enclosed note before I found her, but we all say that your sister was a heroine.

She was out on the fields looking for wounded soldiers and on one occasion when bringing in a wounded soldier a German attacked her. She threw the soldier's gun at him and shot him with her rifle. Of course all nurses here are armed.

I have just received word this moment to pack for Scotland. Will try to get this handed to you as there is no post from here, and we are making the best of a broken-down wagon truck for a shelter.

Will give you fuller details when I see you. We are all quite safe now as there have been reinforcements.

Andrew Hume testified that on 17 September he received a telegram from Grace stating: 'Reports untrue. Safe in Huddersfield.'

He also had a letter from her saying she was sorry he had been made miserable over false reports, adding: 'It is an absolute mystery to me. I never heard of such a person as Nurse Mullard. I hope the police will take it up. The person who concocted the tale evidently knew all about us.'

In reply to Mr Wilson, Mr Hume agreed that his first wife was an invalid for about eight years and for some time before her death she was subject to fits of depression:

> Wilson: About two years ago was there a very sad blow to your family in relation to the death of one of its members?
>
> Andrew Hume: Yes, my son John, who was 21 years of age [28 years by ship's manifest], went down in the *Titanic*. Particular attention was called to my son as he was the leader of the band which played, as the ship went down, *Nearer my God to Thee*.
>
> Wilson: Is it the case that your son John and daughter Kate were very much bound up in each other?
>
> Hume: Yes, very much.
>
> Wilson: And did she take the death of her mother very much to heart?
>
> Hume: Yes.
>
> Wilson: Looking back upon the last two years, do you say she has ever been the same girl since?
>
> Hume: She has not.

'The thing that hits me hardest,' said Louis Cross, bass viola of the *Celtic* in 1912, 'is the loss of Happy Jack Hume, who was one of the violinists. Hume was the life of every ship he ever played on and was beloved by everyone from cabin boys to captain on the White Star Line.

Over in Dumfries, Scotland, I happen to know there's a sweet young girl hoping against hope. Jock was to have been married the next time that he made the trip across the ocean. He was a young man of exceptional musical ability. If he had lived I believe he would not long have remained a member of the ship's orchestra. He studied a great deal, although he could pick up without trouble difficult composition which would have taken others long to learn.

He was on the sister ship, *Olympic*, a few months ago when on her maiden voyage [sic] she collided with the warship *Hawke*. There was a rent torn in the side of the *Olympic* at that time and she had to be towed back to Belfast.

Young Hume went back to his home in Dumfries to spend the time until she should be repaired. Jock had his eye on going in for concert music sooner or later.

He was known on many ships, and has friends in New York. Last winter he got to know Americans who had been staying at the Springs Hotel in Kingston, Jamaica. He had been on the *Carmania*, of the Cunard Line, and also the *Majestic*, the *Californian* of the Anchor Line, and the *Megantic*, of White Star, which plies between Liverpool and Montreal.

Hume was a light hearted, fine tempered young fellow, with curly blond hair, a light complexion and a pleasant smile. He was the life of every ship he ever sailed on and was full of fun. He is mourned by every man who knew him.'

———•·•———

In answer to further questions, Mr Hume said the accused had displayed marked musical talent, and the only trouble with her stepmother was that his daughter wanted to get more and more liberty.

He did not think Kate was capable of doing anything of this sort for the purposes of injuring him. There was nothing to cause her to act in such a way towards her stepmother. But Mrs Hume, the stepmother, testified that Kate was 'rather a headstrong girl, who resented any interference'. She left and took lodgings, their relations having become a little strained. She was 'rather excitable and childish for her years'.

A Mrs McMinn, of Dumfries, said the accused came to lodge with her. The reason she gave for this was because she was unhappy at home. She always seemed a bright and intelligent girl. Miss McMinn, daughter of Mrs McMinn, also stated that the girl was intelligent, and did not seem to be mentally affected.

Several witnesses were called, among them Mrs Irving, an aunt of the accused, who said that when she saw her, Kate said that one of the letters had been 'crumpled in the dying grasp of Grace'.

The sister, Grace Hume, aged twenty-two, then went into the witness box to explain that she was engaged for a time in nursing at Huddersfield and had not written to her sister. She was rather startled to hear of her own death. (Laughter). Her sister was very fond of her brother John, but the witness did not know that his death brought about any change in her. The witness did not consider her emotional or excitable – or particularly clever.

The Lord Advocate: Not so clever as you are – that is impossible. [Laughter.]
Witness: I never saw any mental weakness about her.

The case for the Crown having concluded, Kate Hume created an immediate stir by being asked into the witness box and gave evidence in her own defence. She told how, after her sister Grace went away, she did not hear from her and came to the conclusion that she was gone to the front.

She was in a depressed state, could not sleep at night, and suffered from headaches. She had 'read a great deal of German cruelties to women' and she got into her head that her sister had been killed at the front:

> I had no intention of causing any sensation or alarming my father, stepmother or anybody else. I do not know now why I wrote it, but I fancied what I said would be the way Grace would have written of herself in her last minutes. I could fancy the whole thing as it was written, but I had no idea that anyone would see the letters.
>
> I cannot say what made me do it, except the cruelties the Germans were committing. I was seeing and imagining the things I wrote. I cannot think why I wrote the name of Mullard, except that I believed a man of that name went down on the *Titanic* [a steward named Thomas Mullin, also from Dumfries, had drowned in the disaster], and perhaps it got into my head, which at the time seemed to be turning around.
>
> I firmly believed what was in the letters was true and that Grace had been killed. I had worked myself into that belief. I did not think I was doing anything improper.

Evidence was then given as to the mental condition of the accused. Sir Thomas Clouston, an expert in mental and nervous disease, expressed the opinion that the prisoner at the time was in a state of adolescent hysteria, and such conditions might have made her quite abnormal in fancy and in actions.

The letters were stupid, inconsistent, illogical and absurd, and such as might have been written by a person in the condition he described. There was no suggestion that she was definitely insane or that she was wanting in ordinary intelligence, but she might conjure up in her mind vivid pictures which could not be distinguished from the real.

In cross-examination, the witness said he could not certify her to be insane, but she was suffering at the time from a species of hysteria.

Dr G.M. Robertson of the Royal Edinburgh Asylum, said the girl was intelligently alert, but the death of her brother might have reduced her to a condition of emotional excitement.

THE ATROCITY HOAX
Verdict and Recommendation of the Jury
Accused Girl Released

The trial of Kate Hume, aged seventeen, of Dumfries, was concluded today. The jury returned a verdict of Guilty with a recommendation to leniency. The Lord Justice General (Lord Strathclyde) said that seeing the accused had been in prison for three months, he would order her immediate release.

His Lordship indicated that he would welcome a recommendation as to leniency. When after seventeen minutes the jury returned their verdict it was couched in such ambiguous terms that counsel for the accused claimed it as a verdict of Not Guilty, but the foreman, on being appealed to by the judge, explained that it was a verdict of Guilty, with a strong recommendation to leniency.

The accused, who had borne up remarkably well, collapsed on hearing that she was to be released, and was led sobbing from the dock. The verdict was received with applause.

The judge in his summing–up occupied nearly fifty minutes. During his remarks the accused several times burst into tears. His Lordship said this was a peculiar and painful case. What had been proved was that the letters were both fabrications, that they had been fabricated by the accused, and that she deliberately authorised the handing–over of them to the newspaper reporter for publication. That constituted the crime:

> It seems to me, that if she did fabricate the letters, there could be one motive and one motive only – to create a sensation, to alarm and horrify people by allegations of atrocities of an unspeakable and savage character. You can scarcely imagine any more inhuman treatment to which a human being could be subjected than that described in these letters. It is palpable that it was done with the motive of horrifying her father and stepmother.

If the jury found that she was hysterical at the time, it would not affect the crime, but it would affect seriously the degree of guilt, and might even lead to no further punishment being imposed. They will have noted her appearance in the witness box. She was composed, entirely free from excitement, and gave her answers clearly and distinctly:

> It is not easy to believe that a girl who was labouring under such violent hysteria as has been suggested when she wrote the letters could speak so rationally about them only a few days later.

In all the statements she made afterwards she was perfectly rational and intelligent, but she did not speak the truth. Under these circumstances it is difficult to believe that she was in the hysterical condition which has been spoken of, but you are the judges of that. If you think she was, then in that case it would not warrant you finding her Not Guilty. It would warrant you, however, in offering a strong recommendation to leniency.

The foreman read the finding of the jury as follows: 'We, the jury, unanimously find the accused Guilty of writing the letters as charged, but that at the time she did not realise she was committing a crime, and we earnestly recommend her to the leniency of the court.'

The accused then stood up and His Lordship said:

Kate Hume, I am very willing to accede to the recommendation of the jury, who have given the most careful and anxious consideration of your case. In consideration of the fact that you have already been three months in prison, and having regard to your previous good character and to your age, I consider that you may be released now on probation.

There is much that might be commented upon here in relation to the nature of myth and propaganda. The press had clearly feasted on the story when it first appeared, rather reminiscent of a time two years earlier. The official censor, no less, had given it an imprimatur. And only the day before the verdict, the *Daily Mirror* had headlined its extensive court report: *Nurse The Germans Did Not Kill* – as if this ministering angel was, after all, an exception.

The incident came at the beginning of the war. As that conflict dragged on disastrously, the entrenched carnage came to be increasingly described by politicians and the press as 'the titanic struggle' in which the nation was engaged.

They thus explained the awfulness of the war's impasse by a subtle appeal – through use of the very word *titanic* – to the nature of absolute Good and Evil.

Whatever motivated Kate Hume to invent her story, it must be that the sensational newspaper coverage of the death of her brother in the RMS *Titanic* two years earlier had lodged in her mind. It might have generated a subconscious need for a renewal of the mass sympathy and thrilling attention then lavished on the family, a recognised psychological condition now known as Munchhausen syndrome by proxy.

Here was a single *Titanic* family that embodied both heroism and villainy within its tiny membership… and yet deserved neither praise nor blame, but only unending sympathy.

Jock Hume's body – No. 193 – was recovered and buried in Halifax, Nova Scotia, still clad in its green uniform of the ship's orchestra. Before April 1912 was out, his father Andrew had received a bill from Jock's employer agency asking for the five shillings and fourpence outstanding for the purchase of elements of that uniform, including the lapel badges of silver lyres. Heroism evidently buttered no parsnips.

The celebrated case of the 'Mutilated Nurse' made a chapter in the 1928 book *Falsehood in Wartime* written by Arthur Ponsonby, a Member of Parliament. But there is much that is also false in peacetime, when the only front is the one erected for purposes of pretence, and it certainly occurs with preening Powers.

Heroism, if displayed, is wonderful; but the loss of human life is never anything but an unutterable tragedy in every case. The portrayal of villainy, on the other hand, is often pure charade. An instrument towards another end.

Both heroism and villainy might be thought of as 'little absolutes', designed as scale models of Good and Evil for application to individuals. Yet it was Rudyard Kipling, the ultimate hero-poet of that audacious age, the Edwardian era, who branded success and failure 'two impostors' – and urged that both be treated just the same.

The *Titanic* herself has become heroic to the modern age, but like all earthly affairs and inhabitants, she was inherently flawed. Nor were many of those aboard her particular paragons of virtue, despite the patina of piety applied through succeeding generations.

From the 1992 Reappraisal of Evidence relating to the SS *Californian* as it bore on the vast *Titanic* tragedy:

There are no villains in this story: just human beings with human characteristics.

The sea claimed her forfeit in April 1912. But, as ever, there were larger forces at play on land – and they came together to successfully suppress the grim reality of the *Titanic* disaster in the public mind.

Even if it were partially a willing self-delusion, the message manufactured then has continued to shape perceptions since. A new century should bring new sensibility.

INDEX

FURTHER READING

Senan Molony's earlier Tempus book, *Titanic and the Mystery Ship* (2006), deals at length with the evidence bearing on this aspect of the tragedy.

It contains full evidence, information and assessment of all matters relating to the vessel seen off the port bow of the *Titanic* and the subsequent embroilment of the *Californian*, the Leyland liner which saw both rockets and a nearby 'tramp' steamer. ISBN 0 7524 3743 7

Other books by Senan Molony include *The Irish Aboard* Titanic (Wolfhound) and Lusitania, *an Irish Tragedy* (Mercier).

The author is always interested in hearing from individuals with a personal link to the tragedy or to the vessels involved that night, such as the *Titanic, Californian, Birma, Virginian*, and *Mount Temple*. Please email sennbrig@indigo.ie or kindly write in care of the publishers.